THE SCIENCE AND HUMANISM
OF STEPHEN JAY GOULD

THE SCIENCE AND HUMANISM
of STEPHEN JAY GOULD

by Richard York and Brett Clark

MONTHLY REVIEW PRESS
New York

Library of Congress Cataloging-in-Publication Data

York, Richard, 1971–

  The science and humanism of Stephen Jay Gould / by Richard York and Brett Clark.

    p. cm.

  Includes bibliographical references and index.

  ISBN 978-1-58367-216-7 (pbk.) — ISBN 978-1-58367-217-4 (cloth) 1. Gould, Stephen Jay. 2. Evolution (Biology) 3. Natural history. 4. Science—Philosophy. I. Clark, Brett. II. Title.

  QH366.2.Y67 2010

  501—dc22

                    2010046271

Monthly Review Press

146 West 29th Street, Suite 6W

New York, NY 10001

www.monthlyreview.org

5 4 3 2 1

Contents

PREFACE 7

INTRODUCTION: Stephen Jay Gould's View of Life 11

PART ONE
Evolutionary Theory and the History of Life / 31

1. Natural History and the Nature of History 33
2. The Structure of Nature and the Nature of Structure 43
3. Contingency and Convergence 67
4. Emergence, Hierarchy,
   and the Limits of Reductionism 93

PART TWO
Science and Humanity / 109

5. Debunking as Positive Science 111
6. The Critique of Biological Determinism 127
7. *Homo Floresiensis* and Human Equality 153
8. Art, Science, and Humanism 161

CONCLUSION: Nonmoral Nature and the
   Human Condition 177

NOTES 189

INDEX 215

Preface

As materialists from antiquity to the present have known, all of us are born into a world without higher meaning, where nature is indifferent to our desires and aspirations, our dreams and our hopes. It is in this context that we struggle to make our lives and understand the world and our place in it. The great traditions of both science and humanism are central to this struggle. We must strive to know the ways of nature, the project of science, no more or less than we must endeavor to understand the ways humans throughout history have made meaning in a world that was not made for us nor cares about our existence, the project of humanism. Understanding what it is to be human lies at the intersection of science and humanism, since even though we are uniquely conscious we are products of nature. Stephen Jay Gould was one of the great intellectuals of his time, who had a deep appreciation for both science and humanism, and who sought to use both to understand the human condition. The central contention of this book is that Gould had powerful insights about nature and humanity and an engagement with his work can enrich both science and humanism.

Gould had a great influence on both authors of this book. We each came to Gould's work in his own way, but both of us took from it an appreciation of Gould's enthusiasm for learning, fascination with and love of nature, and concern for humanity. Gould is inspiring in many ways, and different readers will take different things from his work. In this book, we engage many of the ideas we learned from him that have been particularly valuable to us as professional sociologists with wide-ranging interests in the natural sciences, philosophy, and history. With the sharp divisions among academic disciplines, there has been a tendency within the social sciences to succumb to human exemptionalism, a position that either denies or disregards human interdependence with nature.[1] The folly of this narrowness is apparent when attempting to address some of our most pressing questions—including those pertaining to the ecological crisis, evolution, and human history—which demand a sophisticated approach that combines the natural and social sciences. Insofar as environmental sociology, our own particular specialization, is concerned, an understanding of how nature works is absolutely necessary for examining the intersections between nature and society. Beyond this, Gould's work provides powerful insights into a wide range of fields. We aim to explore Gould's worldview, emphasizing key scientific and philosophical contributions.

Over the past several years, we have together and apart drawn on Gould's work in our writing and research. Our initial joint foray into an assessment of Gould's work was a review essay of two of his final books, which we published in the journal *Critical Sociology*.[2] We have drawn on various passages of that essay throughout this book. Sections of chapters 1, 2, and 3 draw on parts of two short articles we published in *Monthly Review*.[3] Additionally, chapter 5 is a revised version of an article we published in *Monthly Review*, and chapter 7 is a revised version of an article Richard published in the same magazine.[4] The substantial majority of the contents of this book has never been published before, and the parts that have been are in modified and updated form.

All intellectual work happens in a context, and we are grateful to the many people—family, friends, and colleagues—who have inspired us over the years. To be a teacher is one of the most honorable roles one can perform, and numerous individuals have served in this role and influenced us over the course of our lives. We especially appreciate the importance of each of our own mentors, Eugene Rosa and John Bellamy Foster, in nurturing our intellectual development. We also thank everyone at *Monthly Review* and Monthly Review Press for their support and encouragement through the years.

We are particularly grateful to our beloved wives, Theresa Koford and Kris Shields, who are surely two of the finest people in the world. Theresa introduced Richard to Gould's work at a time when he was uncertain about his future, something for which he will always be indebted. It is quite likely that had he not read Gould and imbibed the latter's love of scholarship, he would not have gone on to pursue a graduate education. In this sense, Gould's work was to Richard's intellectual life what the early Cambrian era was to multi-cellular animal life: the crucible in which the building blocks of the future were formed. Kris gave Brett his first book by Karl Marx when he was an undergraduate, sparking his interest in graduate school. On countless hikes, marveling at the natural world, she encouraged the journey from Marx to Gould, asking questions that facilitated such an interaction and synthesis. The engagement with Gould's work served as a punctuated moment for Brett, allowing for the emergence of new intellectual and personal possibilities.

Central to the evolutionary view of life is that we all descend from others. We each love, respect, and value our mothers, who are intelligent, generous, kind, and nurturing. Without their love, we would not be the people we are. We dedicate this book to our fathers, neither of whom survived to see it. They were both men who adapted to worlds now gone, whose lives were shaped by contingency.

INTRODUCTION

Stephen Jay Gould's View of Life

Stephen Jay Gould, the acclaimed Harvard professor, paleontologist, evolutionary theorist, historian of science, and prolific writer, died on May 20, 2002, leaving an intellectual legacy that will take many years to properly assess. His long-running column (from 1974 to 2001) in the popular magazine *Natural History* and his many books (two dozen) made him well known not only to professional scholars, but to a large share of the literate public. His remarkable success as a scholar and public intellectual was due not only to his lucid thought and keen insights about nature, but also to his masterful prose and unmatched erudition. Although, by his own identification, he was a tradesman, focusing on his specialization, paleontology and evolutionary biology, his knowledge and writing stretched well beyond the natural sciences, covering some of the most exciting intellectual ground in the social sciences and humanities. A survey of his body of work points to the conclusion that he contributed to evolutionary theory and our understanding of a great many particulars of the natural world, and he developed a wide-ranging and intellectually rich worldview and philosophy, marking him as one of the great thinkers of the latter half of the twentieth century.

Countless books could be written examining various aspects of the rich and diverse body of work Gould produced. There is no simple statement that can summarize Gould's intellectual contribution. Rather, an ongoing engagement with his work is a worthy enterprise, which will likely yield insights for a long time to come. In the context of this great potential, we aim to make a modest contribution to understanding the value of his work. As both of us are practicing sociologists with a keen interest in the philosophy of science, we are primarily concerned with the broader intellectual issues that underlie Gould's work, rather than debating any single particular claim about natural history. It is our contention that Gould's worldview and intellectual philosophy are in themselves of great importance and worthy of serious assessment. Therefore, we examine some of the major issues that Gould focused on in his assessment of natural history and evolutionary theory. In particular, the first half of this book (chapters 1 to 4) examines four major themes that ran throughout Gould's work: the tempo of historical change, the structural underpinnings of order in nature, the contingent character of history, and the multilevel character of natural processes. We explain these in the context of Gould's science and his research and theorization about evolution. Taken together these themes are part of his lifelong critique of the prevailing assumptions in science and society, namely those that favor reductionism and functionalism and view history as unfolding in a progressive manner, inevitably leading to the present.

Then, in the second half of this book (chapters 5 to 8), utilizing these themes, we examine Gould's assessment of the human condition, exploring his critique of biological determinism and his appreciation for humanism in all its richness. His approach to understanding biological evolution is useful to social scientists because both the social and natural worlds are products of history and, therefore, require historical methods for a comprehensive analysis. Embedded in all of these chapters is an assessment of Gould's particular philosophy of science: his specific way of understanding the scientific project and how humans struggle to gain understanding of the world and our own place in it. Thus, in the end, we hope to highlight some of

Gould's most important intellectual and philosophical contributions in natural science and show how they can inform the social sciences and the humanities.

Before we outline these issues, it is important to follow Gould's own approach to understanding intellectuals by placing them in their historical context. Although a strikingly original and distinctive thinker, Gould, like all people, existed in a social context and was influenced by his contemporaries and the thinkers that came before him. Gould knew as well as anyone that to see further, one inevitably stands on the shoulders of giants. Although Gould had many influences on his thinking, he was particularly influenced by the Marxian tradition and scholars who aimed to open science to the public and build an informed citizenry that could actively engage in intellectual matters, rather than let science remain exclusively in the hands of a social elite. He was committed to progressive values of human equality and social justice, and he fits in the tradition of other scholars with similar values.

GOULD AND THE RADICAL TRADITION
IN THE NATURAL SCIENCES

Gould was committed to leftist politics. Although not explicitly a Marxist, he was part of the Marxian tradition in the natural sciences. He contributed to the development of a "dialectical biology" (a tradition more commonly associated with his close colleagues Richard Levins and Richard Lewontin) and debunked theories of biological determinism and assaults on the notion of human equality.[1] He worked to enhance public understanding of science, stressing both its power to help humanity and its potential to be abused, believing that this was essential for an enlightened society.

Gould's position as both an "evolutionary biologist and historian of science," his role as a public essayist of science, and his political activism "in support of socialism and in opposition to all forms of colonialism and oppression" was reminiscent of J. B. S. Haldane, the radical British biologist who helped reorient scientific studies in the

1930s.[2] Haldane was part of a group of British scientists who were influenced by the work of a Soviet delegation of Marxist theorists and scientists who attended the International Congress of the History of Science and Technology conference in London in 1931.

At this Congress, Boris Hessen, a Soviet physicist and historian of science, presented a paper titled "The Social and Economic Roots of Newton's 'Principia'" that revolutionized studies of science, making the history of science a major subject. He clearly recognized Newton's genuine discoveries about nature and the empirical validity of Newtonian models. However, Hessen broke with the idealist conception of science, which presented science as simply the accumulation of knowledge and saw the theories of Newton and other scientists as springing purely from nature.[3] Hessen contended that a more accurate depiction of science required an understanding of the material conditions—social, economic, and natural—in which such ideas evolved. Hessen took as his case Newton's *Principia*—the most prestigious work in pre-twentieth-century physics and the symbol of a pure scientific viewpoint. He demonstrated how practical problems and considerations regarding technology contributed to Newton's mechanistic worldview and how class perspective influenced this process. The necessities of economic production and military development under merchant capitalism generated an array of specific material-technological concerns that influenced scientific questions and objectives. Applied science was directed to matters such as improving water transportation and navigation, mining, and processing of minerals for further transformation into marketable goods. Hessen made a powerful case with regard to how external material influences—both sociological and natural—contributed to the development of a mechanistic worldview and the scientific revolution in the seventeenth century.[4] It was firmly established that science was a social process embedded within and constrained by the changing conditions of nature and society.

The British "Baconian Marxist" scientists—J. D. Bernal, J. B. S. Haldane, Hyman Levy, Lancelot Hogben, Joseph Needham, and Benjamin Farrington—were among the conference participants. They took Hessen's paper as a central text for their research, which helped further develop a dialectical, historical-materialist view of both nature and society. Together they came to represent a formative influence in the history and sociology of science, as they contextualized science within social history, studied nature and its processes, and examined the interchange between society and nature.[5] While diverse as a group, these scholars carried forward the radical tradition in the natural sciences.

Hogben, a biologist who briefly lived in South Africa, opposed the racist policies of the state as well as the racism that was present within the ecological science associated with Jan Christian Smuts's concept of holism.[6] He also contested the eugenics movement in the early twentieth century, which asserted that there was a strict separation between nature and nurture. He proposed that due to the interaction between genes and environment, it was not possible to statistically partition the contribution of each realm. Instead, there is an interdependence between "nature and nurture" within living forms.[7]

Levy, a mathematician, contributed to the philosophical development of a dialectical conception of science and nature. He described the interactions within ecosystems, whereby plants transform the immediate environment, altering the conditions for other species. He illuminated how human actions, often tied to short-term interests such as profit, have ecological consequences, such as how the destruction of natural habitat threatens the survival of many species. He stressed that the exact consequences of human actions were tied to specific historical conditions. Levy pointed to how the introduction of invasive species, such as rabbits in Australia, contributed to erosion problems, as the vegetation that held the soil in place was eaten. Over time, rabbits undermined the natural conditions for other plants and animals.[8]

The Baconian Marxists helped illuminate emergent relationships within organisms and the universe. Both Haldane and Alexander I. Oparin—a Soviet biochemist—proposed, separately, the origin of life theory, whereby living matter emerges from non-living molecules, changing the conditions that made such a transformation possible in the first place. This position reinforces the conception that contingent moments are an important part of history.[9] In addition to his scientific research, Haldane wrote essays for the general public to increase scientific knowledge. Joseph Needham, a biochemist, embraced Hessen's historical-materialist approach to studying science. He devoted much of his adult life to conducting an exhaustive study of Chinese science, technology, and civilization. For these scientists, the history of science was a necessary component of pursuing good science. They determined that science should provide the public with an understanding of the world, in all of its complexity. Furthermore, they believed that scientists should question established doctrine and challenge the social relations that influence society as a whole.[10]

Gould is part of this radical tradition within the natural sciences. As Lewontin and Levins point out, he was a radical in the sense that he sought to get to the root of any argument, a relationship, or process within nature. Gould's "radical rule for explanation" was "always go back to basic biological processes and see where that takes you."[11] It was his commitment to materialism that served as the radical foundation of his science and worldview. Gould noted his own "intellectual ontogeny" included an openness to Hegelian dialectics and a Marxian conception of "revolutionary social change in human history." This mooring is part of what "predisposed" him to considering the potential for abrupt historical change in nature.

Both Gould's science and his commitment to leftist politics demanded that he assess the social relations of society and challenge cultural biases in an attempt to increase social equality and enhance public understanding of science. His three hundred essays in *Natural History* carry on "an old tradition . . . in scientific writing from Galileo to Darwin" of writing for both professionals and the public.[12] He refused to simplify his discussion of nature's complexity, insisting that to do otherwise would trivialize the subject. So he attempted to write with great clarity, defining scientific concepts, while revealing details of the scientific process, findings, and debates. In both his popular essays and his academic articles, he introduced "genuine discoveries, or at least distinctive interpretations."[13] Through these essays, he shared the thrill of scientific knowledge and the learning process, believing that this work was necessary to enhance public comprehension of science.

Gould participated in public campaigns to defend science and to promote a more just world. As a young man, he was active in the civil rights movement, both in the United States and while as a visiting undergraduate student in England. He participated in the anti–Vietnam War movement and was part of the Science for the People organization, which formed in the 1970s as part of the antiwar campaign and often served as a basis to address the misuse of science.[14] In 1981, he went to Little Rock, Arkansas, to be an expert witness in a trial about the teaching of creationism in public schools. He explained that scientific evidence contradicted the claims of creationism, which is rooted in religious doctrine. The state law requiring the teaching of creationism was overturned.

He actively defended human equality, which was "a contingent fact of history."[15] His critique of biological determinism included an extensive historical study of science in order to unmask the cultural biases that were used—whether intentionally or not—to naturalize the ranking and ordering of humanity. He fervently believed in expanding the opportunities and possibilities for all people and ending inequality. As part of this task, both a critique and defense of science was necessary. Scientists, Gould indicated, had a social obligation on this matter:

> We must never forget the human meaning of lives diminished by these false arguments [justifying social inequalities based on biological determinism]—and we must, primarily for this reason, never flag in our resolve to expose the fallacies of science misused for alien social purposes. . . . We pass through this world but once. Few tragedies can be more extensive than the stunting of life, few injustices deeper than the denial of an opportunity to strive or even to hope, by a limit imposed from without, but falsely identified as lying within.[16]

Gould remains an important part of the radical tradition within natural science, given his commitment to both science and humanism. He was part of the long struggle to improve the human condition. Science serves to increase knowledge about the world, but as Gould stressed, knowledge alone does not guarantee social change. Action is needed to "beat all those swords . . . into plowshares, or whatever corresponding item of the new technology might best speed the gospel of peace and prosperity through better knowledge allied with wise application rooted in basic moral decency."[17] This is the challenge and task of any humane social program.

TEMPO, STRUCTURE, CONTINGENCY, AND HIERARCHY: GOULD'S CASE FOR PLURALISTIC THEORY

Gould admired Darwin more than he did any other scientist. He often stressed that Darwin was a meticulous and subtle thinker, who struggled with the numerous issues that the evolutionary perspective and his theory of natural selection raised. Darwin was neither narrow-minded nor dogmatic, but rather sought to understand the complexity of the natural world. Nonetheless, Gould did not believe in being a blind follower of any one person, even if it be the greatest of all scientists, and he continually interrogated Darwin's understanding of evolution. Although Gould never doubted that Darwin got the big things right, he criticized some of the assumptions and conclusions of Darwin's work and, more vigorously, the suppositions that underlay the neo-Darwinian orthodoxy of the latter half of the twentieth century. In particular, Gould challenged the "modern synthesis" (sometimes written imposingly as the Modern Synthesis), the neo-Darwinian theory based on the merger of Darwinian natural selection and Mendelian genetics that began to take shape in the early 1930s and solidified by the 1950s. This scientific tradition sees all of evolution as merely changing gene frequencies in populations regulated by natural selection, neglecting the structure of organisms, processes occurring at levels other than selection among genes or individuals, and processes that operate on timescales other than the day-to-day interaction in ecological time. Gould's major goal in challenging the orthodoxy of the modern synthesis was to expand evolutionary theory, so that it incorporated a plurality of explanative principles, instead of focusing on a narrow selectionism.[18] In this, as Gould himself often noted, he was not in a broad sense that much different from Darwin himself, who had a more pluralistic view of evolutionary forces than modern neo-Darwinians, recognizing that natural selection was one among several forces shaping the history of life. In his critique of the modern synthesis, Gould was prescient. In the past few years, it has become increasingly common among evolutionary theorists to acknowledge the limitations of the modern synthesis and to call for its revision, much in line with the issues that Gould began raising several decades ago.[19]

In his magnum opus, *The Structure of Evolutionary Theory*, published in the last year of his life, Gould presented his vision for how the neo-Darwinian orthodoxy needed to be revised and expanded in light of the discoveries and reconceptualizations that had occurred over the latter half of the twentieth century. He presented three main themes—*agency*, *efficacy*, and *scope*—all of which are interconnected, which organized his assessment of where the modern synthesis needed revision.[20] Since this is how Gould organized his own thinking on evolutionary theory and these themes cover the major issues that intellectually engaged Gould, we explain this structure briefly here. However, our book is structured using a somewhat different thematic organization, because we have different purposes, although we focus on basically these same themes, if parsed and organized somewhat differently. Gould's first theme in *The Structure of Evolutionary Theory*, agency, is concerned with the level of causality in evolutionary change. Gould challenges Darwin's assertion that all of the "action" in evolution stems from selection among individual organisms, and, more strongly, he disputes the subsequent notion, argued by the renowned evolutionary biologist Richard Dawkins, that all evolutionary phenomena can be explained in terms of selection among individual genes.[21]

The second theme, efficacy, addresses the role non-adaptive structural constraint plays in evolution. Gould's concern was principally with recognizing that organisms are integrated wholes, not simply a collection of parts or genes. He emphasized that due to the structural nature of development, many parts of an organism cannot be modified by selection without having ripple effects throughout the whole organism. Variation, the material on which selection operates, is not equally likely in all directions, since inherited developmental structures limit the types of phenotypic variation that are possible. Thus the nature of development constrains and channels evolutionary options. Long before the rise of the modern synthesis, scientists were very interested in issues surrounding development. Subsequently, and thanks in part to Gould's work, a resurgence of research focusing on the role of development has taken place. Evolutionary developmental biology—informally known as "evo-devo"—is now well established as being of central importance to evolutionary theory.[22]

The third theme, scope, grows out of the first two and is concerned with a critique of Lyellian uniformitarianism and Darwinian gradualism—specifically, the explanation of evolutionary trends over the long duration of geologic time based on the extrapolation of micro-processes that are observed in ecological time. Gould's key argument here is that, just as different forces operate across various levels of aggregation (the first theme), distinct processes unfold at different temporal scales. A strict gradualist uniformitarianism—in the sense of viewing changes over long spans of time as simply the accumulation of small changes that we can observe at present—may miss other forces that only operate infrequently on social historical and sometimes even geologic timescales, such as the collision of large comets or asteroids with the earth, and, therefore may not have occurred in recorded human history.

One of the challenges in presenting Gould's ideas is that they are complexly integrated into a larger worldview, so that it is not easy to examine one idea or theme in isolation. This point will be apparent in this book: although we separate out certain themes into distinct chapters, our discussions inevitably engage the whole of Gould's worldview making the themes bleed together. In chapter 1, we start by examining Gould's assessment of the tempo of evolutionary change. Most broadly, this assesses the extent to which change happens in a slow and gradual manner or in rapid bursts of change followed by long periods of stasis—an important underpinning of

Gould's theme of scope. Central to this theme, and to much of Gould's work, is the theory of "punctuated equilibrium," which he developed early in his career, along with Niles Eldredge.[23] Punctuated equilibrium was based on a literal interpretation of the geological record and proposed that during most periods of time species do not change dramatically. Rather, they generally change rapidly (in geological, not socio-historical, time) but infrequently, typically at the point of speciation.[24] Thus the morphology of species when examined throughout time will change in short bursts (the punctuations), but then will be (dynamically) static for most stretches of time (the equilibrium). Punctuated equilibrium did not propose a new mechanism of change, but rather indicated that such a pattern is a reasonable expectation derived from the theoretical underpinnings of the modern synthesis. However, as we explain in chapter 1, the recognition of this pattern had major implications for how historical change is viewed and how it elevated the paleontological record from mere phenomenology, as it had become viewed under the modern synthesis, to data of theoretical importance.

In chapter 2, we address another one of Gould's major theoretical interests: the structural nature of development, fitting in his aforementioned theme of efficacy and its implications for the limitations of strictly adaptationist explanations of evolutionary change. Gould had a deep and long-standing interest in the formalist/structural biology tradition, which was a well-established perspective from before Darwin's time up to the present, particularly in Continental Europe. This tradition looked for laws of form, rules that governed the shape of organisms. Explanations of the "design" of organisms in this tradition were distinct from Darwinian explanations in that they emphasized non-adaptive structural constraints on form rather than seeing organisms as sculpted for functional reasons. Gould's approach was dialectical, advocating for the recognition of both external influences on organismal form, principally natural selection based on environmental context, and internal influences, the structural nature of development that limited the types of form that organisms could take. His first technical book, *Ontogeny and Phylogeny*, grappled with work in the formalist tradition, and Gould retained a deep respect for this body of work, even if he was also critical of it.

In chapter 3, we examine what was perhaps Gould's favorite theme: historical contingency, which is a central part of his aforementioned theme of scope. Gould stressed that geology, paleontology, and evolutionary biology, his fields of specialty, are historical sciences, and in this sense have as much or more in common with the social sciences as they do with particle physics, which deals with the timeless laws of nature. His fields of specialty aim to make sense of natural history and explain how the world became the way it is. In this, the particular quirks, chance events, and unpredictable twists and turns that shape history are of central importance to explanation, not just the laws of nature that limit the paths history can take. Gould's central argument is that history could have turned out other than it did. Evolution is not a deterministic process that yields certain results.

The critique of progress is a theme that runs throughout much of Gould's work, and it is closely intertwined with his views of historical contingency. This critique stems from his more general concern with understanding nature on its own terms rather than imposing our preferences on it. Gould frequently noted that humans often seek to find meaning in nature, but this reflects our own aspirations, not any property of the natural world. He argued that it is partly this desire to find meaning in nature that has led so many to see evolution as an inevitable march of progress, leading to "higher" and "better," rather than as an undirected wandering through the space of possibilities, where each turn is dictated more by chance and the particular circumstances of the moment than any higher-level order or drive. One of the central metaphors in evolution that Gould criticized was that of the ladder—the image of the evolutionary process as being a linear ascent to an ever-higher status. Counter to this image, Gould argued that we should see evolution as a bush, frequently branching, with some twigs dying, while others flourish—an image that suggests no overall direction or judgment of higher or lower, better or worse.[25] Another common image is that of the march of progress from ape to human, implying both the inevitability of our emergence and a continual improvement. (We address the general critique of progress in chapter 3, and we discuss how this relates to human evolution in chapter 7.) Gould frequently stressed how important images are for shaping our thinking, and he encouraged a conceptual shift away from ladders to bushes and undirected, twisted pathways.

Chapters 2 and 3 together address the respective importance of recurrent regularities throughout history that point to general organizing principles (structures) and the distinctiveness of each particular moment that makes each point in time unique (contingency). These themes relate to *Time's Arrow, Time's Cycle*, the title of one of Gould's books. "Time's arrow" focuses on the recognition that "history is an irreversible sequence of unrepeatable events. Each moment occupies its own distinct position in a temporal series, and all moments, considered in proper sequence, tell a story of linked events moving in a direction." In contrast, "time's cycle" reminds us that "fundamental states are immanent in time, always present and never changing. Apparent motions are parts of repeating cycles, and differences of the past will be realities of the future. Time has no direction."[26] Gould's recognition that both of these views of history are valid in their own ways shows his rich and nuanced understanding of the ways of nature. He succumbed to neither the crude view that history is free-form and unstructured nor the unreflective view that the particular events of history ultimately do not matter because of overarching forces that tightly constrain what is possible.

In chapter 4, we examine Gould's views on how different processes occur at different levels of aggregation, which goes to the heart of his theme of agency. Central to this is Gould's advocacy for the hierarchical theory of selection. The modern synthesis was a reductionist program that tried to reduce all causal explanations to the level of forces operating on individual organisms, a trend that was taken even further by Dawkins's focus on genes. Gould argued that there are emergent characteristics at different levels of aggregation, and thus evolution cannot be understood solely by examining processes occurring at the level of individual organisms or genes. For example, species may have characteristics (such as population size and geographical distribution) that are not reducible to the characteristics of the individual organisms that compose them. The long-term survival of a species may be affected by species-level characteristics, not just the characteristics of the individual organisms that compose that species. Punctuated equilibrium is of central importance to the hierarchical theory of selection, since it suggests that species legitimately can be seen as "individuals" throughout geologic time. Species typically have distinct "births," that is, they often originate in a punctual geologic moment, and distinct "deaths," that is, they frequently go extinct in a punctual moment as well. They usually remain roughly discrete and coherent during the equilibrium between origin and demise. Thus, as individuals, there can be selection among species as there is selection among organisms or genes, with some species being more likely than others to survive and/or produce descendants (via speciation), so that selection operates at multiple hierarchical levels. The hierarchical theory of selection has been highly controversial and is widely criticized. Our interest is not in defending it per se, but rather in pointing to the value of the conceptualizations that underpin it. In general, many of the social and natural sciences are based on recognition of emergent phenomena. For instance, social processes are not reducible to psychological ones, and need to be explained in their own terms. A model of hierarchical causation can help illuminate how distinct forces operate on different levels of aggregation.

SCIENCE AND THE HUMAN CONDITION

Gould maintained throughout his life a deep concern for the human condition. This position included a political commitment to seeking social justice and an end to inequality. But it also included a more general humanist interest in how humans interpret and understand the world and make meaning from a meaningless nature. Gould argued that it is pure human arrogance to believe that nature exists for any purpose or that humans are in any way central to it. The natural world operates on its own terms, without any higher meaning. However,

Gould saw this as liberating, not depressing, since it left us humans to make our own meaning, without expecting to find guidance in nature.

Although some of his detractors see Gould's criticism of sociobiology and biological determinism more generally as purely politically motivated, an assessment of his work shows that his critiques of crude applications of neo-Darwinian theory to social explanation were based on the same principles that underlay his efforts to refine and expand evolutionary theory. In chapters 5, 6, and 7 we present how Gould's critique of biological determinism points to the same flaws in the rigid modern synthesis that his larger body of work addresses, regardless of whether it is focused on humanity or not.

Of course, as noted above, Gould was explicit that his personal and political values favored social equality, but he was equally explicit that he did not believe it appropriate to impose his social preferences on nature. His argument on the connection between nature and culture, biology and society, is more subtle than his critics typically appreciate. Gould does not argue that humans are unconstrained by their biology, since they, like all organisms, surely are. Nor does he argue that socialism and democracy are more "natural" than other social systems. Rather, he contends that human nature does not preclude social systems based on justice and equality; that humans have the *potential* to form egalitarian societies. He does not argue that there are definitely no biological differences among human groups. Rather, he indicates that substantial differences across human groups have not been definitively established and that existing social inequalities are not convincingly explained by biological differences across humans. Once again, Gould's point is not that humans are unconstrained by their biology, nor is it that nature dictates social equality. Rather nature does not preclude social equality, and we humans are free to make our own world. Gould's critique of sociobiology and other biological justifications for the social status quo are thus not arguments for a different type of biological determinism that naturalizes equality, but rather an argument for biological *potentialism*, which recognizes the great flexibility of the human mind and societies. Gould's point with regard to human societies was much like Karl Marx's: even though we are constrained by the context in which we find ourselves, we can make our own future. It is an optimistic point that argues that rather than finding reasons not to work for social equality, we should use the capacities we have to bring about a more just world.

We complete this section of the book in chapter 8, where we examine most explicitly Gould's views on the humanities, particularly the connections between art and science. He was a great admirer of the arts. He wrote frequently on the humanities and sciences, expressing a more nuanced view than most commentators. He recognized that the humanities and sciences have different legitimate domains, where the sciences address factual questions about the empirical world and the humanities address issues of human meaning, aesthetics, and ethics. However, he also stressed the connections between the two domains, noting that rather than being opposed as they are popularly portrayed, both the humanities and sciences require creativity, accurate knowledge, attention to detail, and meticulous work. He also noted how artistic work can make scientific contributions by exploring human perception and expanding our thinking on the natural world. Gould was a thoughtful commentator, who worked to make connections between two worlds that are often, but inaccurately, seen as unbridgeable.

GOULD'S PHILOSOPHY OF SCIENCE

Gould's approach to scholarship was founded on a philosophy of science that recognized that the scientific project was embedded in society and carried out by men and women possessing the limitations, foibles, biases, and personal idiosyncrasies that characterize all of humanity. One remarkable aspect of Gould's science is that he incorporated an analysis of the history of scientific debate on evolutionary theory into his engagement with the substance of the theory. In fact, Gould saw the history of science as part of the scientific project, since it helps us to understand how society and nature interact to produce knowledge. In this sense, Gould is a reflexive scientist, thinking more like a sociologist than the typical physicist. He clearly and explicitly recognized that science is not simply a process of plucking pure unadulterated truth from nature's garden, but rather a socially situated institution influenced by politics, economics, culture, and psychology. Gould writes insightfully:

> Science, since people must do it, is a socially embedded activity. It progresses by hunch, vision, and intuition. Much of its change through time does not record a closer approach to absolute truth, but the alteration of cultural contexts that influence it so strongly. Facts are not pure and unsullied bits of information; culture also influences what we see and how we see it. Theories, moreover, are not inexorable inductions from facts. The most creative theories are often imaginative visions imposed upon facts; the source of imagination is also strongly cultural.
>
> This argument, although still anathema to many practicing scientists, would, I think, be accepted by nearly every historian of science. In advancing it, however, I do not ally myself with an overextension now popular in some historical circles: the purely relativistic claim that scientific change only reflects the modification of social contexts, that truth is a meaningless notion outside cultural assumptions, and that science can therefore provide no enduring answers. As a practicing scientist, I share the credo of my colleagues: I believe that a factual reality exists and that science, though often in an obtuse and erratic manner, can learn about it.[27]

Gould's approach to scientific analysis is well illustrated in *The Structure of Evolutionary Theory*, the first part of which is as much a historical and sociological analysis of the context-dependent development of evolutionary theory as it is a scientific evaluation of the logic of the theory and its major factual assertions.[28] Sociologists could learn a great deal from Gould's approach, since it is a model of reflexive science, one that does not fall prey to the anti-intellectualism inherent in the postmodernist denial of an objective external reality, while at the same time it maintains a central recognition of, and concern for, how social context influences the form of scientific theories.

His philosophy of science drew upon Charles Darwin, who wrote: "All observations must be for or against some view if it is to be of any service."[29] This comment points to the reality that theory cannot be developed by pure induction, and that our ideas influence how we interpret observations. As Gould indicated, "Scientific progress depends more upon replacing theories than adding observations." However, "cultural biases" generally augment existing theories, so "any process of replacement requires an unmasking of previous structures."[30] One point Gould makes frequently has to do with how preconceived notions not only distort how scientists interpret data and answer research questions but also how preconceptions influence what actually counts as data, and what questions are seen as acceptable and scientifically relevant. For example, Gould notes that before the development of punctuated equilibrium, paleontologists typically considered a fossil record for a species showing no change over substantial periods of time to be "no data" since, by the common preconception, evolution was about change. Punctuated equilibrium opened intellectual space for new inquiry by identifying evidence of stasis *as data*. Gould acknowledged that punctuational thinking has a connection with the Marxist tradition in that it identifies rapid (revolutionary) change as a key component of history.[31] However, Gould is careful to point out that the origin of an idea is separate from the validity of an idea.[32] The latter cannot rest on mere conjecture if it is to contribute to science; it must be tested against empirical evidence. Nonetheless, he makes the important point that a view such as punctionalism (or gradualism for that matter) is not "true" or "false" in some absolute sense, but rather helps organize our thoughts and directs us to (we hope) fruitful research questions.[33]

Gould's approach is distinct in that, counter to common perceptions among natural scientists, he sees work in the social studies of science tradition as potentially providing *constructive* critiques of scientific practice, rather than principally as irrational efforts to denigrate scientific knowledge. Although it is true that some scholars in the social studies of science have promoted an anti-intellectual, hyper-relativistic view of knowledge, many researchers are keen intellectuals who have gained important insights about the scientific process and how scientific practice can be improved by an understanding of sociology and history. Therefore, Gould, although a committed scientist, was not afraid of critiques of science—in fact, he often provided some of the most insightful critiques. He saw such critiques as an essential part of the scientific enterprise, since, like all fields of human inquiry, science is improved by thoughtful reflection on its practices. Gould, therefore, did not separate his interest in the history of science from the practice of science itself.

Gould recognized that many of the debates in natural history are about interpretation and characterization of diverse phenomena—such as, Do species progress over their evolutionary history? How smooth is the tempo of change in evolution?—and therefore do not have singularly correct answers, since in the vast array of nature's variety, examples supporting nearly any claim can be found somewhere. In this, theoretical claims are not typically deterministic and debates do not center on the mere existence of some particular but rather are over claims of *relative frequency*—that is, how common one type of phenomenon or pattern is relative to another. This recognition was central to Gould's assessment of punctuational versus gradualistic change. No one doubts that there are examples of gradual change or that there are examples of relatively rapid change. The question is which pattern is more common, which conceptualization better represents nature's ways, if only as a rough generalization. Gould helped open up intellectual territory within science, posing new questions as to how the world works. His analyses reveal that the world is a dynamic place filled with emergence and contingency. In the end, this is part of what makes learning the ways of nature so challenging, but also exciting.

PART ONE

Evolutionary Theory
and the History of Life

CHAPTER ONE

Natural History
and the Nature of History

Stephen Jay Gould was fundamentally concerned with the nature of history, particularly the tempo and mode (to use renowned evolutionary theorist George Gaylord Simpson's famous phrase) of historical change.[1] Does evolutionary and social history proceed in a steady, slow, and incremental manner, or does most historical change occur in occasional short bursts that lead to fundamental shifts from one era to another? Of course, there is no single answer here and no clear dichotomy: the tempo and mode of change have varied across history. It is important to understand the relative frequency of various types of change if we are to understand how the world came to be the way it is. However, as Gould often noted, how we conceptualize the nature of historical change affects our interpretation of the past, and our conceptualizations are influenced not only by evidence but by our social context.

In 1977, Gould and Niles Eldredge published an article in the scientific journal *Paleobiology* that explained how prevalent social views of the nineteenth century about the nature of history are embedded in the natural sciences, with Darwinian gradualism in biology providing a prime example.[2] In the midst of the Industrial Revolution, and the social upheavals that came in its wake, older notions of stasis, of an eternal order ordained by divine providence, had given way to conceptions of historical development, the view that history has a trajectory. However, the prevailing views generally favored slow incremental change, which did not threaten the status quo with the potential for revolution. Gould and Eldredge wrote that the preference for slow change in evolutionary theory represented in part "the translation into biology of the order, harmony and continuity that European rulers hoped to maintain in a society already assaulted by calls for fundamental social change." Charles Darwin reflected the zeitgeist in his strong preference for gradual change. In pointing to a social origin for Darwin's preference for gradualism, Gould and Eldredge clarify: "We mention this not to discredit Darwin in any way, but merely to point out that even the greatest scientific achievements are rooted in their cultural contexts—and to argue that gradualism was part of the cultural context, not of nature."

Gould and Eldredge presented an alternative view of historical change, one often associated with Karl Marx—a punctuational view that does not assume historical change occurs in a slow, smooth, and seamless manner. They argued that historical change occurred in many different ways, and there was no reason to assume that gradual change was more natural than rapid, even discontinuous change. They clearly noted that their theory of punctuated equilibrium,[3] which had already achieved widespread recognition and generated much controversy by the late 1970s, "is a model of discontinuous tempos of change at one biological level only: the process of speciation and the deployment of species in geological time." However, they also made clear their belief "that a general theory of punctuational change is broadly, though by no means exclusively, valid throughout biology." Gould and Eldredge were not arguing that gradualist or punctuationalist views are either "right" or "wrong" per se, but rather, different views may have various degrees of utility in helping us to understand the patterns of nature. Their case is that the Marxian tradition's conceptualization of the nature of historical change can open our eyes to possibilities that are not readily visible from other perspectives.

Gould was committed to understanding the context in which theories emerged, and was a dedicated intellectual historian. He not only studied Darwin and other key figures in the biological sciences with great care, he also was a student of the history of geology (which was not always entirely distinct from biology—note that Darwin primarily identified as a geologist). Indeed, Gould's first published paper examined the concept of uniformitarianism developed by the great geologist Charles Lyell.[4]

Lyell was the single most important influence on Darwin's thinking about nature, and it is from him most directly that Darwin gained his commitment to gradualism. In one of the most renowned scientific books ever written, *Principles of Geology* (published in three parts from 1830 to 1833), Lyell developed his case for a reform of the science of geology based on his methodological and substantive doctrine of uniformitarianism. This profoundly important work laid the foundations for modern geology and is rightly recognized as a towering intellectual achievement by virtually all modern geologists. However, although Lyell in his development of uniformitarianism surely did a great service to the science of geology, he also, perhaps more than anyone, impressed upon the natural sciences a preference for conceiving of change as a slow and incremental process. In his advocacy for uniformitarianism, he misrepresented other contemporary theories and mixed together under the banner of uniformity a variety of disparate claims, some of which remain widely accepted by scientists as fundamentally important and others that have quietly slipped out of favor.

Gould notes that Lyell's concept of uniformity has four distinct major components, but Lyell typically neglected to make explicit the differences among them.[5] First, Lyell argued for the spatiotemporal invariance of natural laws. This is one of the basic assumptions of modern science and was to a large extent as uncontroversial among Lyell's scientific contemporaries as it is among scientists today. In this, Lyell was merely affirming the materialist approach, which by necessity looks for natural causes of phenomena, rather than invoking sporadic intervention in the physical world by a capricious deity, in order to establish the independence of science from theology.

The second claim involves the uniformity of process, the assertion that only processes (such as erosion by wind or water) that can be observed to operate in the present should be used to explain events in the past. This is now, as it was then, a somewhat more controversial claim. Scientists generally agree on a preference for invoking presently observable processes to explain the past, but some scholars, particularly those in the catastrophist tradition during Lyell's time (more on this below), suggested "that some past events required the inference of causes no longer acting or acting now at markedly slower rates." Third, Lyell asserted the rate of geologic change was uniformly "slow, gradual, and steady, not cataclysmic or paroxysmal." In other words, it neither increases nor decreases dramatically in intensity, but remains roughly constant through time. This third claim is closely related to the second, and these two claims together provided the basis for Darwin's gradualism.

The fourth and final component is based on the assertion that the general configuration of the earth has remained basically the same since its formation, with only minor non-directional change— for example, while some mountains erode, others are built up so that the basic overall state of the world remains largely unchanged with time's passage. In other words, the earth is effectively in a dynamic, steady state. In this claim, Lyell was apparently assuming that terrestrial geologic processes mimicked the ahistorical characteristics of Newton's universe, as understood in Lyell's time, where the planets revolve around the sun in the same fashion they have done for eternity. Ironically, although this fourth component was part of a larger view that argued for the antiquity of the earth, in its insistence on enduring stasis it denied history in certain respects. This is the component of Lyell's uniformitarianism that is most typically ignored by modern geologists because a large body of evidence indicates that the character of the earth has changed dramatically over its history, such as the composition of the oceans and atmosphere and the location of the continents.

Counter to Lyell, catastrophists argued that a few cataclysmic events over the course of Earth's history were responsible for the major aspects of the geologic world of the present. Lyell, a master rhetorician, presented his uniformitarianism as the *scientific* alternative to catastrophism, which he characterized as a theologically motivated defense of the biblical timescale of Earth's history and of claims for God's direct intervention in worldly affairs. This characterization was highly misleading, since at the time of Lyell's writing most informed scholars, uniformitarians and catastrophists alike, accepted that the earth was ancient and sought to explain geologic history based on material causes (such as, volcanism, earthquakes). In fact, catastrophists arguably were in some respects *more* scientific than uniformitarians in that they advocated a literal interpretation of the empirical geologic record, which provided abundant evidence for catastrophic change (such as, mass extinctions). For them, the hand of God was not necessary to explain dramatic events in natural history. Instead, material forces operating during the history of Earth were enough.

Materialist explanation, then, was central to catastrophism and uniformitarianism alike. In spite of this, Lyell tried to explain away the evidence for catastrophic events by arguing for the imperfection of the geologic record, noting that geologic forces erased many pages of Earth's history as they wrote new ones. In effect, he argued that we should distrust empirical evidence, or at least temper it with a priori theoretical conceptualizations. This, of course, is not an unreasonable approach, since there is good cause to recognize the limits of empiricism. Nonetheless, however reasonable Lyell's rejection of a strict and narrow empiricism may have been, it does seem unfair of him to characterize his catastrophist opponents as *unscientific* when they often advocated a strong commitment to empiricism, which is often seen as the hallmark of science.

Properly understood, then, the uniformitarian-catastrophist debate primarily occurred *within* the scientific enterprise and was centered on contrasting materialist explanations of the tempo and mode of historical change; it was *not* principally a clash between scientists (uniformitarians) and theologians (catastrophists). It is indeed true that many theologians were wedded to a catastrophist approach, but that should not be taken to mean that catastrophists were in general more theologically motivated than uniformitarians. It is important to remember that Lyell himself retained a religious faith, as did most scientists of his time. He resisted Darwin's evolutionary theory for years, particularly as applied to humans, and never fully accepted it, due to concerns about its religious implications. Thus, although Lyell supported a methodological break with theologians when it came to natural history, he did not oppose religious faith nor completely shield his scientific judgment from his religious convictions. Understanding this context makes it clear that interpreting the uniformitarian/catastrophist divide as a science/religion divide is highly misleading. Lyell used the scientific/theological divide as a rhetorical device to align his uniformitarianism with the spirit of the Enlightenment and to make his catastrophist opponents appear medieval, but he could not claim to have adopted a fully materialist view himself. Regardless, Lyell won the day, and his interpretation was the one generally accepted by subsequent generations of geologists.

Darwin as a young man revered Lyell, taking the first volume of the *Principles of Geology* with him on the *Beagle* and having the subsequent volumes when they were published sent to him while he was away.[6] His intellectual commitment to gradualism was, arguably, second only to his commitment to natural selection. Darwin was an advocate of the claim generally attributed to Linnaeus: *Natura non facit saltum* (Nature does not make leaps). Like Lyell, Darwin invoked the imperfection of the fossil record to explain away apparent periods of dramatic change in geologic history, and sought to deny the reality of a handful of global mass extinctions that were followed by the "instantaneous" (in the geological sense) appearance of a suite of new species, which a literal reading of some parts of the fossil record suggested. Darwin consistently argued that extinctions and the emergence of new species were spread out in time, as organic history was the result of the accumulation of the imperceptibly small changes occurring all around us each day, where organisms struggle for their existence against one another and the physical environment.

Thus both geology (from Lyell) and biology (from Darwin) inherited a deep commitment to the view that historical change comes slowly and an explicit denial of the likelihood of occasional episodes of rapid and dramatic upheaval. As Gould and others have argued, there is substantial evidence that counters the two central claims for gradualism in Lyell's uniformitarian doctrine. First, it has become clear that there have been catastrophic events that differ *qualitatively* from presently observable forces shaping the earth. In the most striking example, over the past three decades it has become widely accepted that the impact of an asteroid (or other extraterrestrial object) on Earth was the cause of the End-Cretaceous extinction, which wiped out the dinosaurs and many other lineages. The key evidence for this conclusion (among several other important pieces of evidence) is a layer of iridium found all around the world at the Cretaceous-Tertiary boundary of the geologic record.[7] The fact that iridium is very rare on Earth but abundant in some extraterrestrial objects strongly suggests that the source of the iridium was extraterrestrial.[8] This is a key example of a catastrophic mechanism of change operating in the past that is distinct from forces in operation today. Counter to Lyell's assertion that only forces in operation today explain geologic history, and counter to Darwin's assertion that no mass extinctions occurred in Earth's history, it now appears nearly certain that at least one mass extinction was indeed abrupt, caused by forces not currently acting upon the earth, and not an illusion generated by an imperfect fossil record.

Second, there is also a substantially diverse body of evidence supporting the contention that forces in operation today have, at various times in the past, operated at different rates, occasionally leading to rapid change. Thus, as Marx asserted, it is necessary to understand the historical specificity of causes and events.[9] One of the best examples of this, which Gould presents in *The Panda's Thumb*, comes from the scablands of eastern Washington State. As Gould writes, "In the area between Spokane and the Snake and Columbia rivers to the south and west, many spectacular, elongate, subparallel channel-ways [which locals refer to as coulees] are gouged through the loess and deeply into the hard basalt itself." It was readily recognized by geologists that glacial meltwaters had run through the coulees, and it was generally assumed that the coulees had formed from the gradual process of erosion. Challenging this gradualist assumption, in 1923 J Harlen Bretz argued, based on several unusual features of the coulees, "that the channeled scablands had been formed all at once by a single, gigantic flood of glacial meltwater."[10] Due to the prevalent gradualist bias in geology, this catastrophic hypothesis was at first widely rejected, without being given serious consideration by most geologists. Eventually, Bretz proved to be in large part correct. Evidence was subsequently discovered indicating that Lake Missoula, an extensive, ice-dammed glacial lake in Montana, had emptied abruptly when the glacier's retreat caused the dam to burst. Furthermore, aerial photographs of the scablands showing huge ripples on the floors of some coulees, up to 22 feet high and 425 feet long, largely cinched Bretz's case. Bretz was wrong in his initial insistence on a *single* catastrophic event—Lake Missoula re-formed and emptied several times—but he was correct that the scablands did not assume their current form as the result of slow and constant erosion. Countering Lyell's third uniformitarian claim, Bretz helped establish that forces observed in operation today (such as erosion) have worked at dramatically different rates during certain times in the past.

The lesson to be learned here is that catastrophist claims about change in the material world are no less scientific than those of gradualism, and are widely supported by empirical evidence. The preference for gradualism common in the natural sciences, therefore, cannot be justified on scientific grounds, as Gould argued throughout his career. Rather, to some degree at least, the preference for gradualism reflects a social bias, likely stemming in part from the ideology of the social elite, for slow, predictable change and against the notion that dramatic historical change occasionally occurs in brief, revolutionary moments.

Eldredge and Gould allied themselves with the catastrophist/ punctuationalist perspective in developing their theory of punctuated equilibrium, the claim that the history of most species is best characterized as long periods of relative stasis, where there is only minor, non-directional change in organismal structure, punctuated by brief periods of rapid change where new species emerge from old in a geological "moment," which may be thousands or tens of thousands of years.[11] In proposing this theory, Eldredge and Gould were, like catastrophists before them, arguing for a more literal interpretation of the fossil record. They were not proposing a new mechanism of change, relying on natural selection as the primary force behind evolution, but were challenging widespread gradualist assumptions about the speed with which evolution can occur. However, they did suggest that most evolutionary change occurs around the point of speciation (the moment of punctuational change). Speciation often occurs when a small population becomes isolated from a larger population for an extended period of time. The isolated and initially small population is free to diverge from the parent population as it accumulates fortuitous mutations via natural selection. In large, geographically spread out populations, selection pressure differs across the range of a species so that genetic innovations that may be favorable in one part of the range are inhibited from spreading by different selection pressure in other parts of the range. Therefore, large populations tend to remain stable or change slowly. However, in a small population, a favored mutation can spread rapidly, becoming ubiquitous in subsequent generations. The initial isolation of a population may occur due to a variety of forces: rivers changing course, island formation, and so forth. The emergence of new species, then, is in part a consequence of historical events and changing environmental conditions and can happen rapidly (in the geologic sense).

In his magnum opus, *The Structure of Evolutionary Theory*, Gould provides an extended discussion of what punctuated equilibrium and punctuational views in general suggest about the nature of history.[12] If evolution unfolds in the manner suggested by the theory of punctuated equilibrium—and Gould presents an array of evidence that suggests punctuated equilibrium better characterizes evolutionary history than does gradualism—change over the geologic long haul cannot be properly understood as simply the steady accumulation of small changes happening during the typical period. This insight suggests that we cannot readily predict future conditions via the smooth extrapolation of current trends. In particular, if the world is shaped by occasional contingent events that have dramatic consequences—such as asteroid impacts, massive floods from glacial lakes—then history cannot be understood as a march of progress along a mandated path. Many paths exist, and the one that is actually trod upon is not inevitable, but rather determined by the often unpredictable events that actually occur and the historical-structural constraints that exist in tension. Every historical moment contains possibilities, and the future is not predetermined. (The recognition of the importance of contingency is a central aspect of Gould's thinking that we take up in greater depth in chapter 3.)

Throughout his career, Gould worked to show that the widespread assumption in the natural sciences that natural history unfolds in a predictable, progressive, and gradual manner is not necessarily a reflection of the factual processes of the natural world. Rather, it is in part the product of social history, and to some degree reflects the ruling elite's preference for the view that the present state of the world is the inevitable outcome of natural forces and that change is unlikely to come abruptly. Social biases often distort our view of the world, and scientists, even those as great as Darwin and Lyell, are not free from their sway. Gould, drawing on the Marxian tradition, helps us to open our eyes to the possibility that the world as it is did not have to be so and that the future remains open.

CHAPTER TWO

The Structure of Nature and the Nature of Structure

Raphael's fresco *The School of Athens*, completed in 1511, in the Stanza della Segnatura in the Vatican, depicts a scene containing many of the finest philosophers of classical antiquity, with Plato and Aristotle displayed in the center engaged in debate. The gestures of these two great scholars symbolize one of the fundamental differences in their philosophies. Plato holds the *Timaeus*, a work on abstract metaphysics, and points to the sky, suggesting, it appears, that the empirical world should not be the focus of our intellectual inquiry. Aristotle holds his *Ethics*, which is concerned with the practical aspects of living a good life, and lowers his opened hand to the ground in an apparent attempt to focus Plato on the world in which we live. The Platonic and Aristotelian paradigms have informed philosophical dialogues for over two millennia, and their distinct perspectives remain fundamental to many contemporary debates. According to the Platonic paradigm, true reality is an abstract ideal structure, while the physical world we perceive—the shadows on the cave wall—is only an imperfect representation of that fundamental reality. In contrast, physical reality in the Aristotelian paradigm is fundamental, and abstractions, though potentially useful for helping us to understand the world we experience, are merely approximations of reality.

As physicist Max Tegmark notes, "Modern theoretical physicists tend to be Platonists, suspecting that mathematics describes the universe so well because the universe is inherently mathematical."[1] In this paradigm "all of physics is ultimately a mathematics problem," and true reality is an abstract mathematical structure existing outside of space and time.[2] In other words, true reality *is* the mathematical structure that a hypothetical all-knowing physicist could use to describe the workings of the universe (or multiverse). Although explicitly acknowledged only rarely in biology, the distinction between Platonic and Aristotelian paradigms in the interpretation of mathematical models and statistical analyses of biological phenomena is important for understanding the assumptions of researchers about the nature of the biological world.

Stephen Jay Gould, as part of his support for a pluralistic theory of evolution, expended much energy defending structuralist biological theories (which were to some degree at least inspired by the Platonic tradition), while also being critical of extreme versions. He countered the tendency to apply physicists' preference for mathematical formulation as the definitive feature of scientific theories, noting that Charles Darwin's theory of selection was not reducible to a series of equations and emphasizing that organic evolution is about a messy world that is the product of contingent historical events.[3] However, he also argued that evolutionary theory, particularly following the "hardening" of the modern synthesis in the mid-twentieth century, had become too rigidly functionalist, excluding structuralist and other types of arguments from the biological sciences. Here we address the divide between structuralist and functionalist explanations in the biological sciences in a Gouldian fashion, by examining the tension between what we will refer to respectively as the "Platonic paradigm" (which favors structural explanations, typically rooted in the invocation of spatiotemporally invariant principles) and the "Aristotelian paradigm" (which remains grounded in the empirical world and seeks more immediate explanative principles). As we will explain, Gould fashioned a thoughtful synthesis of these that recognizes the importance of spatiotemporally invariant principles, while maintaining that most structural forces are the products of history.

PLATONIC AND ARISTOTELIAN
APPROACHES TO BIOLOGY

The Platonist assumes that mathematical analyses of natural phenomena are appropriate because on an ontological level the biological world is mathematical, or reflects timeless mathematical properties that exist independently of any particular material realization. As the historian of mathematics Morris Kline explains, in Plato's view

> relationships in the material world were subject to change and hence did not represent ultimate truth, but relationships in the ideal world were unchanging and absolute truths. . . . Plato . . . believed that the perfect ideals of physical objects are the reality. . . . The physical world is an imperfect realization of the ideal world.[4]

Likewise, one of the leading evolutionary biologists of the twentieth century, and Gould's colleague at Harvard, the late Ernst Mayr wrote:

> For Plato, the variable world of phenomena . . . was nothing but the reflection of a limited number of fixed and unchanging forms, *eide* (as Plato called them) or *essences*. . . . These essences are what is real and important in this world. As ideas they can exist independent of any objects. . . . Variation is attributed to the imperfect manifestation of the underlying essences.[5]

In fact, as Kline notes,

> Plato went further than the Pythagoreans in wishing not merely to understand nature through mathematics but to substitute mathematics

for nature itself. He believed that a few penetrating glances at the physical world would supply some basic truths with which reason could then carry on unaided. From that point there would be no nature, just mathematics, which would substitute for physical investigations as it does in geometry.[6]

The Aristotelian takes a quite different view from the Platonist, maintaining that mathematics is a useful epistemological tool, which can allow for an approximate description of the workings of the empirical world. It is not assumed that observed patterns that can be mathematically described reflect inherently mathematical phenomena. Kline explains:

> Whereas Plato believed that there was an independent, eternally existing world of ideas which constituted the reality of the universe and that mathematical concepts were part of this world, Aristotle favored concrete matter or substance. . . . [For Aristotle] numbers and geometrical forms . . . were properties of real objects; they were recognized by abstraction but belonged to the objects.[7]

Furthermore, Aristotle "criticized Plato's otherworldliness and his reduction of science to mathematics. Aristotle was a physicist; he believed in material things as the primary substance and source of reality."[8]

Whereas Plato took little interest in the particulars of natural history, Aristotle demonstrated a deep concern. Mayr points out that although Aristotle was generally, in classical Greek fashion, much like Plato, a rationalist, believing that philosophers "could solve scientific problems simply by sharp reasoning," in his zoological work he took a quite different approach.[9] He further explains: "In [*Historia animalium*] one has far more the impression of an empirical, almost pragmatic approach rather than that of deductive logic."[10] According to Mayr, Aristotle's system of taxonomy did not assume the existence of an abstract ideal type for each species, but rather categorized specimens pragmatically to facilitate comparisons among groups. In this,

Aristotle and Plato present two fundamentally different approaches to understanding the natural world.[11] While modern theoretical physicists tend to be Platonists, the biological sciences, since the rise of Darwinism, have to a large extent been dominated by Aristotelians, although Platonic positions persist.

DARWINISM AND THE DECLINE
OF THE PLATONIC PARADIGM

In the middle part of the twentieth century, historians of science and other scholars debated exactly when Darwin had his insight about the evolutionary origins of species by natural selection. One view held that Darwin had the key insight while visiting the Galápagos Islands, a position that fits well with the popular view of scientists as objective analysts who determine the workings of nature inductively by an unbiased examination of empirical evidence. This position had decisively fallen by the end of the century, as scholars examining Darwin's journals, notebooks, and collections from the voyage of the *Beagle* and afterward were able to locate his conversion to the evolutionary perspective to March 1837, several months after his return to England in October 1836, and his specific insight about natural selection as the mechanism driving evolutionary change to later still in the early fall of 1838.[12]

One particularly telling observation was that Darwin collected his specimens of finches and other species on the Galápagos Islands in the manner of a creationist, not an evolutionist.[13] In particular, Darwin collected very few specimens of each species, typically only a male and a female. As Gould noted, this is a collection strategy antithetical to what was to become the Darwinian evolutionary perspective, which sees intraspecific variation as fundamental, since it provides the raw material that is sorted by natural selection.[14] The creationist view is fundamentally Platonic, seeing intraspecific variation as mere superficial deviation from the ideal type of a species, which is believed to represent an idea in the mind of God. Platonists do not need a large sample, only a specimen that is closest to the ideal type, while Aristotelians need a diversity of specimens to represent the fundamental reality of the diversity that exists in the empirical world. Thus Darwin's collection strategy in the Galápagos Islands suggests that he was still a Platonist.

Darwin certainly struggled with the creationist conception while on the voyage. At the time, natural scientists, working from the Platonist position, accepted that species had a slight pliancy as they spread from the point of creation. Darwin pondered this, wondering "how far a species could be pushed" and noted that if the divergence from the original stock was sufficiently great, it "would undermine the stability of Species" argument.[15] On the voyage this issue gnawed at him, causing him to start a notebook on the relationships among species. In Australia, he observed the behaviors of birds that were similar to those in England, but were obviously of a different species, as well as miniature kangaroos that acted like rabbits and platypuses reminiscent of the European water rats. Darwin exclaimed in his diary that "the strange character of the animals of this country as compared to the rest of the World" would seem to the "unbeliever in everything beyond his own reason" that "two distinct Creators must have been at work" and "that the periods of Creation have been distinct & remote the one from the other."[16] The Platonist perspective remained in place while he was still away from England, but these observations stuck with Darwin as he grappled with the implications for natural history. His subsequent development of the theory of evolution by natural selection would fundamentally change the way scientists saw the natural world. The Darwinian revolution and its underlying materialism largely replaced the Platonic creationist view with an Aristotelian one, identifying the actual organisms that compose a species, not an abstract ideal type, as the fundamental reality of the natural world.

It is important to recognize that Darwinian evolutionary theory is strikingly different from Newtonian-style theories of the physical world, in that though it is based on certain postulates, concepts, and principles, it does not specify precise laws or a fundamental quantitative model of the natural world. As Gould notes, "Darwinism is not a mathematical formula or a set of statements, deductively arranged."[17] This is not to say that there is not an abundance of useful mathematical models of phenomena relevant to Darwinian evolutionary theory, such as those used in population genetics. However, Darwinian evolutionary theory cannot be reduced to a series of formulas, like Newton's laws of motion. After all, natural selection is not a force like gravity, but rather a dynamic process embedded in the interaction among organisms and their environments. Darwinism is very much about the messy and cluttered world of our perceptions, and does not posit the existence of a reality that is outside of space and time.

It is unsurprising that creationists tended to be Platonists, since early Christian scholars, most notably Saint Augustine, endeavored to fuse Platonism with their religious doctrines. However, it is not true that all those of a Platonic bent are necessarily hostile to scientific inquiry. In fact, as Gould has highlighted, a scientific Platonism regarding the essential characteristics of organisms, in the form of formalist (structuralist) theories about "unity of type," existed before Darwin's insight and continued well after the rise of Darwinism into the present (albeit with substantial conceptual modifications).[18] Theories in this vein were particularly common among Continental European morphologists, such as Étienne Geoffroy Saint-Hilaire, Johann Wolfgang von Goethe, and Louis Agassiz (who migrated to the United States in later life), in the eighteenth and nineteenth centuries. These formalists argued that species of a type were united by a shared underlying structural arrangement, or *bauplan* (body plan), and that differences within a type stemmed from modifications of superficial characteristics. This perspective also identified different parts of individual organisms as constructed based on the same underlying template. For example, Goethe, a poet with a keen interest in science, studied plants extensively and concluded, as Gould explains it, that "the leaf represented an archetypal form for all plant parts growing from the central stem—from cotyledons, to stem leaves, to sepals, petals, pistils and stamens, and fruit. . . . The 'leaf' represented an abstract generating principle, from which stem leaves depart least in actual expressions."[19]

As Gould has emphasized, one of the profound conceptual changes that Darwin wrought was a reinterpretation of an underlying ideal type shared by species in a particular group as a consequence of common ancestry—that is, shared body plans in Darwin's worldview did not reflect an abstract timeless ideal, but rather characteristics of an ancestral species inherited by descendants.[20] This reconceptualization undermined Platonic idealism, explaining "unity of type" as a product of material history, rather than as the impression of an abstract world upon the world of our perceptions. In the aftermath of Darwinism, Platonists were forced to look elsewhere for the imprint of timeless abstractions in nature.

THE PERSISTENCE OF PLATONISM

Before the emergence of the neo-Darwinian modern synthesis, evolutionary theorists (including Darwin himself) were generally pluralistic in their identification of causal mechanisms for evolutionary change and the features of organisms, and did not rely solely on natural selection.[21] In this pluralistic period, D'Arcy Wentworth Thompson (1860–1948), a polymath of exceptional talent, was perhaps the most renowned (although idiosyncratic) representative of the formalist tradition in biology.[22] Gould greatly admired the work of Thompson and sought to extract from his work insights that remained valid, though not uncritically accepting his formalism. Thompson argued that adaptationist explanations of the form of organisms, which are central to the program of those advocating natural selection as the primary force behind evolution, fail to appreciate the structural and mechanical forces that directly shape organisms throughout the developmental process.[23] Although the breadth and sophistication of Thompson's work defies easy classification, in many important respects he was advocating a Platonic approach to the life sciences, in that he saw deep mathematical order in the diversity of nature's products.[24] Ian Stewart, a modern scholar in the tradition of Thompson, explains that a central insight of this perspective is that "some features of the morphology of living creatures are genetic in origin and some are a consequence of physics, chemistry, and the dynamics of growth. One way to tell the difference is that genetic influences have enormous flexibility, but physics, chemistry, and dynamics produce mathematical regularities."[25]

In essence, Thompson argued that spatiotemporally invariant mathematical and physical laws go a long way to explaining the form of organisms, and that functionalist explanations, such as Darwin's, need not be called upon in all, or even most, cases to explain "good design." Thompson's approach ran counter to a fundamental characteristic shared by all other evolutionary theories—it downplayed the importance of phylogeny (evolutionary history) in explaining form, relying instead on ahistorical natural forces. He contended that many similarities of form between the organic and inorganic world were not merely analogous, but rather homologous. For example, similarities of form between geological objects and biological objects often reflect the operation of the same or related physical forces and mathematical laws of form.

One of his most compelling arguments is that the hexagonal shape of honeycombs and corals (and many other organic forms) is not the result of specific genetic encoding for forming such a shape, but rather results from tension among opposing forces in much the same way that nature produces hexagonal soap bubbles in clusters, basalt columns, and cracks in mud, as well as other inorganic structures. Thompson explains, "The hexagonal cell [of a honeycomb] was no more than the necessary result of equal pressures, each bee striving to make its own little circle as large as possible."[26] The hexagonal shape of many organic and inorganic products is the automatic outcome of the close packing of elements of the same basic size and composition, representing a timeless geometric principle, not a contingency of history. Thompson also points to the prevalence of logarithmic spirals in nature.[27] For example, the logarithmic spiral shape of some molluscan shells, ram horns, and other products of the organic world is the result of a growth process that increases the size of an object without changing its shape, reflecting a timeless mathematical regularity. In explaining Thompson's perspective, Gould writes, "We don't invoke any aspect of history or genealogical connection to explain why Cambrian quartz from Asia exhibits the same crystal structure as Recent quartz from America. So why should we not attribute the logarithmic spirals of Paleozoic and modern gastropods to the same spatiotemporal invariance of physical laws?"[28]

One of the most striking examples that Thompson and other formalist biologists have examined, which points to the deep mathematical structure of some biological forms, stems from an old observation that the florets of most flowers, with giant sunflowers providing a prime example, are arranged in two intersecting families of spirals, one clockwise and the other counterclockwise, and the number of spirals of the two families are typically consecutive numbers in the Fibonacci series (the exact pair of numbers depends on the species).[29] The Fibonacci series begins 1, 1, 2, 3, 5, 8, 13, 21, 34, 55, . . . , and has the property that each number after the first two is the sum of the previous two numbers.[30] A fascinating property of the Fibonacci series is that as the series progresses, the inverse of the ratio of consecutive numbers (13/8, 21/13, . . .) converges on the Golden Ratio (often denoted by the lowercase Greek letter phi or φ), which was fundamental to classical Greek design, the value of which is exactly $(\sqrt{5}+1)/2$, or approximately 1.618.[31]

The reason for the ubiquity of this particular mathematical regularity in nature has long fascinated naturalists and mathematicians. A fully satisfactory explanation for why the Fibonacci series and the Golden Ratio are deeply embedded in the natural world did not emerge until recently, although scholars of Thompson's time and before had many important insights about the reasons.[32] To understand this regularity, one needs to focus on the structured nature of plant growth. Gould provides a concise explanation: "The obedience to the Fibonacci series . . . [is] an automatic consequence of initiating each new spiral in a radiating series by setting its founding element into the largest available space at the generating center."[33] This is a prime illustration of the Thompsonian argument that organic form, given the specific character of its material structure, is often the product of mathematical law.

Thompsonian-style explanation fell out of favor, particularly in the Anglophonic world, following the rise of the modern synthesis. But the Platonic tradition persisted and has recently enjoyed some degree of resurgence. Stuart Kauffman, a biologist and the author of *Origins of Order*, is one of the most prominent contemporary scholars in the Platonic-Thompsonian tradition.[34] Following Thompson's assertion that variation across different types of organic form represents the material actualization of "physico-mathematical conditions of possibility," Kauffman points to mathematical regularities in the biological world as evidence of the influence of timeless mathematical and physical laws on organic structures.[35] One of his most provocative suggestions is that a "cell type is an attractor of the genomic regulatory system."[36] In this sense, an *attractor* refers to a state toward which a dynamical system tends. In other words, Kauffman is suggesting that the diversity of cell types observed in organisms is not necessarily a particularistic product of history, but rather the imprint in the material world of the abstract self-organizing principles of dynamical systems. Or, stated differently, observed cell types are a reflection of the set of ideal types of cells that exist in an abstract Platonic reality.

These formalist examples of deep mathematical structure in nature—and there are many other examples[37]—do not necessarily suggest an anti-Darwinian approach to natural history, since the powerful force of natural selection is not denied.[38] However, formalism does point to abstract organizing principles that channel the growth and form of organisms, and that dictate structures in a manner that goes beyond (although does not necessarily contradict) immediate selective necessity. Despite the many examples of such mathematical regularity in nature and the evident influence of basic physical and chemical forces on developmental processes, the biological sciences remain predominantly Darwinian and Aristotelian in nature—and rightly so, since other forces, natural selection foremost among them, play a larger role in determining the features of organisms, particularly multicellular ones, and the pathways of evolution. The lesson to be learned here is that both Platonic and Aristotelian paradigms help direct us to unique insights and encourage us to make a distinction between patterns that reflect the contingencies of history, as in the Aristotelian-Darwinian focus on the fundamental reality of particularistic variation, and patterns that reflect deep mathematical structures, as in the Platonic-Thompsonian focus on ubiquitous regularities of growth and form stemming from timeless mathematical and physical laws.

GOULD'S STRUCTURALISM:
SPANDRELS AND EXAPTATION

As we already discussed, an interest in structural theories was prominent throughout Gould's career, and he worked to develop a pluralistic evolutionary theory that was built on a Darwinian foundation but admitted a diversity of causal explanations. His first technical book, *Ontogeny and Phylogeny* (1977), was an analysis of the structural (formalist) biology tradition developed to a large extent by Continental Europeans in the nineteenth century.[39] Gould, throughout his career, was concerned with criticizing the key assumption of the modern synthesis that natural selection is virtually the only force responsible for evolutionary change and that nearly all characteristics of organisms can and should be interpreted as adaptations. He argues that internal structural constraints of organisms also influence evolutionary change, and, therefore, not all characteristics of organisms are adaptations.

As part of his theorization of the importance of structural forces, Gould criticized the ultra-Darwinian stance that natural selection is the singular force that influences the design of organisms. He notes that the Darwinian argument for the exclusivity of natural selection as the force of evolutionary change is dependent on three central assumptions.[40] First, since natural selection does not directly make anything—serving rather as the executioner of the unfit—and in order for it to act as a creative force through its allowance of a gradual accumulation of favorable characteristics generated by fortuitous variation, variation among units of selection must be *copious*. Without variation, natural selection cannot differentiate among individuals. Second, variation must be *small in extent*, for if variation were large, producing major features in a single step, selection would only serve an auxiliary role of sorting through the features thus produced, but would not contribute to their production. Third, variation must be *undirected*. If variation is more likely in some directions than in others, the nature of variation itself contributes to evolutionary change, undermining the exclusivity of selection.

Gould argues that due to the structural nature of the development of organisms throughout their life course (ontogeny) the conditions for natural selection's exclusivity as the force of evolutionary change are not fully met, particularly the assumption that variation is undirected. The ontogenetic development of an organism occurs in stages and the modification of an early stage can have dramatic implications for subsequent stages. For example, there are no toe genes or nose genes per se, but rather the effect of any gene depends on context (both genetic and environmental) and can affect multiple features of an organism. In this sense, genes do not code for bodies in the manner of a blueprint, which shows an overall picture, but rather in the manner of a recipe, which directs construction in a temporal sequence, where changes in the timing of events can have a great effect on the final outcome. Genes typically have their effect on bodily structure based on the stage of development during which they are expressed. Therefore, the evolved structure of ontogenetic development limits the scope of the types of phenotypic variation that is possible. This constraint does not only exist in the negative sense of limiting the types of variation that are possible, but exists in the positive sense of channeling variation along certain pathways due to the emergent potential typically inherent in complex structures.[41]

Gould's advocacy for recognizing the important role structural forces play in evolution is in large part a critique of the hyper-functionalism and extreme reductionism of ultra-Darwinians who identify all traits of organisms as adaptations. Gould and Richard Lewontin in a famous paper, "The Spandrels of San Marco and the Panglossian Paradigm: A Critique of the Adaptationist Programme," identify the functionalist ultra-Darwinian view as the "Panglossian Paradigm."[42] The Panglossian Paradigm is named for Voltaire's character in his novel *Candide*, Doctor Pangloss (a satirical representation of Gottfried Leibniz), who responded to all misfortunes by saying, "All is for the best in the best of all possible worlds." Gould and Lewontin argued that ultra-Darwinians had come to rely overly on "just so" stories for explaining any and all characteristics of organisms, constructing tales of how each and every trait served some function, regardless of whether sufficient evidence existed to support these claims. Here, there is a tendency to divide an organism into separate traits, assuming that natural selection acts on each trait individually, optimizing it. If the possibility of suboptimality of any trait is raised, hyper-adaptationists argue that there is a "trade-off," where competing demands between traits reach a compromise, which is assumed to be optimal for the organism as a whole. This form of interaction remains focused on particular traits, whereby "just so" stories of a specific purpose for each trait continue to be invoked. In such a situation, there is a strict reliance on functionalist explanations, in opposition to alternatives that incorporate structural constraints.

The danger is that such readily employed explanations are no different than Doctor Pangloss's explanations:

> "It is proved," he used to say, "that things cannot be other than as they are, for since everything was made for a purpose, it follows that everything is made for the best purpose. Observe: our noses were made to carry spectacles, so we have spectacles. Legs were clearly intended for breeches, and we wear them. Stones were meant for carving and for building houses, and that is why my lord has a most beautiful house; for the greatest baron in Westphalia ought to have the noblest residence. And since pigs were made to be eaten, we eat pork all year round. It follows that those who maintain that all is right talk nonsense; they ought to say that all is for the best."[43]

To make matters more difficult, as Gould and Lewontin explain, when "one adaptive argument fails" another is simply invoked as a substitute, without any serious assessment of competing conceptions.[44]

Illustrating the importance of structure, in an article in the scholarly journal *Evolution* and subsequently in an essay in *Ever Since Darwin*, Gould presents the controversy that surrounded the antlers of the Irish Elk, which was actually the largest deer that ever lived, which ranged from China and Siberia in the east to Ireland and England in the west, and became extinct over 11,000 years ago.[45] This deer had antlers with a span up to twelve feet that could weigh ninety pounds. Like other deer, these "antlers were probably shed and regrown annually."[46] After the discovery of fossils of the Irish Elk, debate generally focused on ascertaining what function such large antlers had for the deer, in order to explain why they were developed. In the nineteenth century, it was assumed that antlers were used as weapons against other animals, which increased evolutionary success. It has been suggested that the antlers developed as a means of display for courtship. Likewise, it has been proposed that the antlers were used for display to deter battles and help establish a hierarchy. In contrast to these functionalist "just so" stories, in the 1930s, Julian Huxley proposed that the giant antlers on the deer were simply a consequence of allometry, differential growth rates in the parts of animals. In other words, among deer, antlers grow at a faster rate than body size, so that simply increasing the body size of a deer without altering the relative growth rates of different parts will lead to an animal with very large antlers. Realizing that Huxley's explanation had not been tested, Gould measured the skulls and antlers of eighty-one Irish Elk. He points out that the length of a skull serves as a good measure for size. All of his samples were older in age, so the skulls were fully formed. He found that antlers increased "in size two and one-half times faster than body size from small to large males. Thus, the allometric hypothesis is affirmed. If natural selection favored large deer, then relatively larger antlers would appear as a correlated result of no necessary significance in itself."[47] Thus the exceptionally large antlers of the Irish Elk need not have been adaptive in themselves, and could simply be a side effect of producing a large-bodied deer.[48]

Contrary to the functionalist approach, Gould and Lewontin posited that some characteristics of organisms are merely side consequences of structural forces, and not necessarily adaptive. They illustrate their argument using an architectural analogy. They note that construction of a dome on rounded arches requires the construction of four *spandrels* (the architectural term for spaces left over between structural elements of a building), which set the "quadripartite symmetry of the dome above."[49] The spandrels are therefore a necessary consequence of the structural demand for a dome on rounded arches but serve no function in themselves. Similarly, the nature of ontogenetic development of organisms typically leads to the existence of nonadaptive structural elements (spandrels). For example, as Gould explains in *The Structure of Evolutionary Theory*, "Snails that grow by coiling a tube around an axis must generate a cylindrical space, called an umbilicus, along the axis."[50] Although a "few species use the open umbilicus as a brooding chamber to protect their eggs," the vast majority do not.[51] Evidence suggests that "umbilical brooders occupy only a few tips on distinct and late-arising twigs of the [coiling snail] cladogram [evolutionary tree], not a central position near the root of the tree."[52] Therefore, it appears clear that the umbilicus did not arise for adaptive reasons, although it was later co-opted for adaptive utility in a handful of lineages, but rather arose as a nonadaptive spandrel—a side consequence of a growth process based on coiling a tube around an axis. A key lesson to be drawn from Gould and Lewontin's argument, then, is that "one must not confuse the fact that a structure is used in some way . . . with the primary evolutionary reason for its existence and conformation."[53] With this insight, they stress that functionalist explanations are not sufficient to capture the plurality of forces operating in the natural world.

Stressing the importance of historical assessment, and wary of hyper-adaptationist's explanations, Gould illuminates both the importance of structural influence and its flexibility, given contingent development. Gould and Elisabeth S. Vrba introduce the conception of *exaptation* to understand how complex features evolve.[54] Exaptation refers to the utilization of an existing feature of an organism for a novel functional purpose. In other words, it is important to recognize that "historical origin and current utility are distinct concepts."[55] They

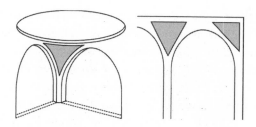

A pendentive, or three-dimensional spandrel (left), forms as a necessarily triangular space where a round dome meets two rounded arches
at right angles. "Classical," two-dimensional spandrels (right), form as
the necessarily triangular spaces between rounded arches and the rec-
tangular frame of surrounding walls and ceilings.

indicate that a particular feature of an organism may have originally
evolved via natural selection as an adaptation for a different reason
than that for which it is currently utilized. Here, within the structural
organization of the organism, a feature is co-opted for a new purpose,
as a type of functional shift. It is also possible that the existing feature
is a spandrel that did not evolve as an adaptation, but was rather a
structural side effect. The important point is that the current utility of
any particular feature need not have been directly produced by natural selection, although it may enhance the fitness of an organism.[56]

The umbilical brooding snails mentioned above represent a prime
example of the latter type of exaptation, where the umbilicus did not
originate for adaptive reasons, but was at some point after its origin
utilized for brooding—a functional purpose. A prime example of the
former type of exaptation is the shift in the primary function of feath-
ers in the bird lineage from thermoregulatory to aerodynamic.[57] At any
one time organisms have a vast "exaptive pool"—that is, many features, both those that evolved under natural selection for the function
they serve (adaptations) and those that are nonadaptive structural side
effects (spandrels)—from which evolution may draw to craft new features as changing conditions dictate. Thus structural forces can generate features, such as the umbilicus of the snail, that potentially provide well-formed starting points for the development of new adaptive

traits. Functional shifts and the exaptation of spandrels can thus explain how the incipient stages of a feature may develop without serving the function to which the feature is later put.

Many features of the human brain illustrate well both spandrels and exaptation.[58] Undoubtedly, the brain has been shaped by natural selection to serve key functions. However, in the process such a complex feature inevitably contains many spandrels that provide a vast exaptive pool, which is far greater than the pool stemming from the adaptations that emerged as part of its initial development. For example, just as a computer designed to perform mathematical calculations has the potential to be co-opted to produce video games, the human mind has the potential to perform many tasks for which natural selection did not directly sculpt it. Thus we have the capacity to read and write, compose sonnets and symphonies, present mathematical proofs, design and build aircrafts, and construct beautiful cathedrals, even though these capacities clearly played no role in the origin of the human brain and were not even actualized for the vast majority of human history. Gould explains, "The human brain, as nature's most complex and flexible organ, throws up spandrels by the thousands for each conceivable adaptation in its initial evolutionary restructuring."[59] Complex features like the brain are inherently ripe with potential and have innumerable emergent properties. Features can nearly always be used in ways other than that for which natural selection produced them. Vrba and Gould propose that exaptive pools, within the structure of an organism, contribute to long-term evolutionary success and contingent changes in complex systems.[60]

Proposing a pluralist conception of evolutionary change (as did Darwin), Gould and Lewontin indicate that it is important to account for how "constraints restrict possible paths and modes of change," dialectically mediating selective forces.[61] Gould noted two types of structural constraints: those stemming from spatiotemporally invariant physical laws and those originating from structures that emerged through the contingencies of evolutionary history but constrain future evolution once they are established. Although Gould focused more on evolved structural constraints that were contingent on the particulars of history, he also often pointed to examples of evolutionary constraint from spatiotemporally invariant physical forces, such as those Thompson identified.

In a particularly informative example, Gould asks: Why is it that no multicellular animals evolved wheels, which seem a potentially efficient form of motility?[62] The hyper-adaptationist perspective that is common among ultra-Darwinians would likely explain the absence of wheels in a functional way: Animals do not have wheels because wheels are not as efficient as other mechanisms for motility. Gould notes, however, that given how useful wheels are to human societies, the functionalist explanation seems to fail. Surely in the vast time animals have been around some would have found wheels to be useful. Gould offers a structural explanation for the absence of wheels that is far more convincing than the functionalist one. Gould reasons:

> If wheel and object are physically linked, then the wheel cannot turn freely for very long and must rotate back, lest connecting elements be ruptured by the accumulating stress. But animals must maintain physical connectedness between their parts. If the ends of our legs were axles and our feet were wheels, how could blood, nutrients, and nerve impulses cross the gap to nurture and direct the moving parts of our natural roller skates? The bones of our arms may be unconnected, but we need the surrounding envelopes of muscle, blood vessels, and skin—and therefore cannot rotate our arms even once around our shoulders.[63]

Gould does note an exception to the general absence of wheels in the animal kingdom: the flagella—long whiplike threads used as propellers—of some species of bacteria. The flagellum rotates freely without a direct physical link to the body of the bacillus. Invoking a spatiotemporally invariant aspect of scale, Gould notes that the reason tiny organisms can have a freely rotating axle lies in the

> correlation of size and shape through the changing relationship of surfaces and volumes. With surfaces (length^2) increasing so much more slowly than volumes (length^3) as an object grows, any process regulated

by surfaces but essential to volumes must become less efficient unless the enlarging object changes its shape to produce more surface. The external boundary is surface enough for communication between the organelles of a single cell with their minuscule volumes. But the surface of a wheel as large as a human foot could not provision the wheelful of organic matter within.[64]

Here invariant physical forces and structural factors influence the development of flagella.

Gould stresses that evolutionary theory, if it is to encompass the diversity of forces that operate in the natural world, must include a focus on evolved structures, including how these structures are constructed and how they change over time, as well as how they restrict types of change. Gould emphasizes the importance of recognizing that "Organisms are integrated entities, not collections of discrete objects."[65] Change is not necessarily piece-by-piece, but involves transformation of a complex package. The evolutionary path that is forged is tied to a *bauplan*, which in part creates a structural legacy.

In *Wonderful Life*, Gould argues that there is a remarkable persistence of basic body plans over millions of years because of evolved structural constraints. Focusing on the Burgess Shale—a fossil site with especially finely preserved fossils from the Middle Cambrian, including fossils of soft body parts—he assesses the significance of the Cambrian explosion to evolutionary history. Over 500 million years ago, there was a rapid burst of diversification of life with the steady appearance of multicellular organisms entering the fossil record. For tens of millions of years, the rate of evolution accelerated as new species originated. Most of the modern phyla emerged, as well as a range of other "anatomical experiments" that became extinct during this period. The species that left descendants that survived to the present embody various "twists and turns upon established designs."[66] Gould suggests that from this pattern, we can gain insights into the workings of history and evolution.

Gould notes that since the phyla Arthropoda and Chordata diverged over 500 million years ago, it was commonly assumed that natural selection would have acted upon each and every feature—including genes—of the subsequent lineages so that no common structural plan would persist to the present.[67] But genetic research has shown that "all complex animal phyla . . . have retained . . . an extensive set of common genetic blueprints for building bodies."[68] Animals from these phyla retain comparable structures that influence evolutionary development. This work provides support for an argument that Geoffroy Saint-Hilaire made in the 1820s. In an attempt to maintain his contention of the structural affinity between arthropod and vertebra, where the nervous system of the former is on their ventral side and of the latter on the dorsal side, Geoffroy proposed an inversion theory, whereby the back of one is the belly of the other. His theory had long been dismissed, but recent research reveals that "the same gene by evolutionary ancestry builds both the dorsal nerve tube in vertebrates and the ventral nerve cords" of arthropods.[69] The dorsal-ventral flip illuminates the inherited architecture, the structural continuance, of two phyla. Within the *bauplan*, "evolution displays enormous ingenuity and versatility in iterating a set of common genes and developmental pathways along so many various routes of ecology and modes of life."[70]

The structural legacies of species constrain the pathways of evolutionary development. In *The Panda's Thumb*, Gould presents how "odd arrangements and funny solutions" can arise from an inherited structure.[71] He notes how pandas appear to use a flexible thumb to separate leaves from the stalk of bamboo, which they consume. Noting how unusual it would be to find an opposable thumb among non-human animals, he points out that pandas have five anatomical digits. The so-called thumb, employed as a sixth digit, is actually an enlarged and elongated bone, known as the radial sesamoid, which is part of the wrist and connected to muscles. It underlies a pad that is separate from another pad under the five proper digits. As a result, pandas are able to insert bamboo stalks in the channel between the pads, and effectively strip away the leaves. Other bears also have a "slightly enlarged radial sesamoid," but in pandas this bone and the surrounding muscles are reconfigured together, refashioning the forepaws for a new function. The thumb "did not arise *de novo*," rather it is entirely composed of existing structures modified over time.

Gould insists that the structure of an organism exerts an internal constraint that also directs evolutionary pathways in relation to natural selection. In fact, he stresses that there are common rules of development due to the deep structure (deep homology) that is shared by different phyla. As mentioned above, Arthropoda and Chordata separated during the Cambrian explosion, yet they have "shared and highly conserved genes regulating fundamental processes of development."[72] The group of conserved and related genes is known as *Hox* genes. Within these genes, there is a DNA sequence (homeobox), which codes proteins that regulate patterns of development, specifically the anterior-posterior axis and segment identity. The sequence of these genes influences the pattern of expression: those at the front of the sequence are expressed in the anterior of the organism; those found toward the end of the cluster are expressed in the posterior. The sequence of these genes specifies the placement of the eyes, antennas, arms, fingers, legs, toes, and so on. Realizing "the high degree of sequence similarity" between these homologs, it has been determined in experiments that there is "interphylum substitutability," whereby "fly *Hox* genes, expressed in vertebrates, usually broker the same developmental sequences as their vertebrate homologs—and vice versa."[73] Here the deep structure constrains morphology, establishing parallels in evolutionary development. For Gould, *Hox* genes illuminated the long persistence of body plans over millions of years.

Gould's view of the structural nature of development, as highlighted by the importance of the *Hox* genes, parallels in informative ways Noam Chomsky's well-known argument about the deep structure of human language.[74] Chomsky famously proposed that there was a deep structure, a generative grammar, that lay behind the great diversity of human languages, a view widely accepted by linguists today. In Chomsky's view, this structural underpinning united all human language, and any particular language was a particular representation of this structure. Similarly, the *Hox* cluster may serve as a generative engine, producing substantial, but constrained, morphological variety.

STRADDLING THE
PLATONIC/ARISTOTELIAN DIVIDE

Raphael modeled his portrait of Plato in *The School of Athens* on Leonardo da Vinci, who had already reached mythic status within his own lifetime. This was an interesting choice, strangely being both appropriate and inappropriate at once. On the one hand, Leonardo had Aristotelian sympathies, rejecting much of the Neo-Platonism of the Middle Ages in his focus on careful observation to answer empirical questions and his criticism of the prevailing Neo-Platonic theory of the origin of fossils.[75] However, on the other hand he remained a medieval Platonist in his conviction that there was a deep connection, even a causal unity, between processes of circulation of water in the earth as a macrocosm and the circulation of blood in the human body as a microcosm.[76] In this he was very much a pre-modern Platonic thinker, seeing "symbolic correspondence across scales of size and realms of matter" that was not merely analogous but deeply meaningful and suggestive of an abstract reality that manifests itself at various scales in the material world.[77]

These dual tendencies are exemplified in his work on the human form, represented in his drawing *The Proportions of the Human Figure (after Vitruvius)*, c. 1490. He followed the classical scholar Vitruvius, who was an architect and engineer in the first century BCE under the Roman Empire, in seeing the proportions of the human figure, with arms and legs outstretched, as fitting precisely within the perfect geometric figures of the square and the circle.[78] In this, he saw a deep connection between human form and the abstractions of geometry, clearly in the vein of Plato and Pythagoras before him. However, as a dedicated empiricist, Leonardo did not assume that Vitruvius's measurements of the human form were necessarily correct—as typical Renaissance scholars likely would have, given their reverence for the authority of the scholars of antiquity—and spent several months systematically measuring the proportions of the human body, utilizing a number of human models.[79]

Thus Leonardo exhibited a willingness to straddle the Platonic/Aristotelian divide, both feeling the allure of the clean, orderly ideal world beyond space and time, and recognizing the importance of a solid grounding in the material world.   Gould, following the Renaissance commitment to humanism as well as science and in his interest in what can be learned from the scholars of antiquity, shares a degree of unity with Leonardo. He open-mindedly recognized the insights that came from both the Aristotelian and Platonic traditions, which aided him in developing a more pluralistic view of evolutionary theory. It was not Gould's intention to argue for the superiority of either the Platonic or Aristotelian view. Debate about these two great paradigms of the nature of reality has continued for over two millennia and will likely continue for millennia to come. Paradigms are not factual or logical assertions, and therefore cannot be ultimately proven either right or wrong. The power of paradigms resides in their ability to both blind us to some things and shed light upon others. This was a fundamental insight of Gould's, and he always tried to illuminate the paradigms that underlie various research programs, knowing that a pluralistic approach and structural theories have much to offer in regard to understanding evolutionary development and history.

CHAPTER THREE

Contingency and Convergence

One important question in the interpretation of patterns of evolution centers on the extent to which history had to turn out the way it did. From before Charles Darwin's time up to the present it has been commonly assumed that history, both human history and the history of life in general, unfolded in a somewhat deterministic manner, that the present was inevitable, either ordained in Heaven or, in the scientific view, mechanically produced by natural laws. This view contrasts with that of the historian: that the quirks, chance events, and particularities of each moment make history, and that the world could have been other than it is. Stephen Jay Gould struggled throughout his career to come to terms with the nature of history and to understand the interplay of general laws and historical particulars, the respective importance of necessity and contingency.[1] He developed a sophisticated and nuanced position that recognized both the importance of general laws and the role of contingency, arguing that natural laws limit the pathways that can be taken, but which of the many available pathways is actually taken depends on many contingent events. Thus the world could not have been just any way, but there are many worlds that are possible, of which we live in just one.

The consideration of history opens up important philosophical as well as political questions, as Gould clearly recognized. It raises questions that have been central to modernist thinking: Is history directional? Is there a continual march to a future that is better than the past? In short, is there progress in human and natural history? The answers to these questions not only have implications for understanding the nature of evolution but political implications as well. If contingency played little part in how history turned out, if the present was inevitable, then it makes little sense to challenge the status quo. However, if contingency dominates history, the future is open, and the world can be another way, as radicals of all types have long believed. Of course, as Gould well recognized, our personal or political preferences should not be imposed on nature—the laws of nature and the patterns of evolution are independent of what we make of them. However, our biases influence how we interpret what we observe in nature. Therefore, it is important to be aware of our biases, both our personal ones and the ones prevalent in society at large.

Questions about the nature of history go to the heart of assumptions in Western culture, and Gould was a major critic of the biases that assume a progressive nature to history and the inevitability of the present. These issues can be seen in the common view in evolutionary theory that each successive wave of species was superior to its predecessors since that species had won out in the struggle for existence. Given human arrogance and the prevalence of progressivist ideology, it is commonly presumed that the emergence of *Homo sapiens* is the inevitable apex of evolutionary processes. Counter to this view, Gould argued that although natural selection led to some degree of "progress" on short timescales in the limited sense that it dialectically adapted creatures to their environments, over longer scales of time there was no direction to the history of life. The fundamental importance of contingency in history was perhaps the most centrally important feature of Gould's thinking.

Gould's view of evolution integrated a recognition of both the importance of spatiotemporally invariant laws and the contingencies of history. Early in his career Gould worked to develop nomothetic (law-like) theory in paleontology, looking for general patterns in nature, as he steadfastly argued that it was not possible to have specific laws that explained how history actually played out.[2] He indicates, "There are nomothetic undertones to the results of evolution—the principle of natural selection is among them—and it is here that our laws must be formulated. They must be based on immanent processes that produce events, not on the events themselves."[3] However, Gould argued that the actual events of history had to be explained in their own terms, recognizing multiple causes. On this point, his views were shared by Ernst Mayr, who notes:

> Generalizations in modern biology tend to be statistical and probabilistic and often have numerous exceptions. Moreover, biological generalizations tend to apply to geographical or otherwise restricted domains. One can generalize from the study of birds, tropical forests, freshwater plankton, or the central nervous system but most of these generalizations have so limited an application that the use of the word *law*, in the sense of the laws of physics, is questionable.... In the physical sciences it is axiomatic that a given process or condition must be explained by a single law or theory. In the life sciences, by contrast, various forms of pluralism are frequent.... The response of a complex system is virtually never a strict response to a single extrinsic factor but rather the balanced response to several factors, and the end result of an evolutionary process may be a compromise between several selection forces. In the study of causation the biologist must always be aware of this potential pluralism.[4]

Gould was clearly interested in invariant natural laws, such as those in physics and chemistry, underlying biological phenomena and constraining all other relationships within the world, including human society.[5] But he argued that much of the order observed within the biological world is due to historically emergent structures, such as the *Hox* genes, which we discussed in the previous chapter and will briefly discuss further below. As a result, biology (as well as other historical sciences, such as geology) attempts not only to understand the general forces that shape natural phenomena, but also to explain how and why history developed as it did. (The social sciences share a similar orientation in their own specified context, seeking to comprehend forces that influence social phenomena.) Gould saw the importance of assessing the available pathways to a specific end in order to develop a proper explanation. Here the particularities of biological systems and their history need to be understood in their own terms.

THE WEDGE OF PROGRESS
AND THE PARADOX OF THE FIRST TIER

As a consummate student of Darwin, Gould often returned to Darwin's writings to work out difficult issues in evolutionary theory. In trying to understand the patterns of evolutionary history and the question of whether there was a progressive trend in that history, Gould reflected on Darwin's thinking on the issue:

> No question troubled [Darwin] more than the common assumption, so crucial to Victorian Britain at the height of industrial and imperial success, that progress must mark the pathways of evolutionary change. Darwin clearly understood that the basic mechanics of natural selection implied no statement about progress, for the theory only speaks of local adaptation to changing environments. . . . To resolve this troubling discordance between the mechanics of his basic theory and his fundamental impression of pattern in life's history, Darwin called up [an] ecological principle encompassed by the metaphor of the wedge.[6]

Explaining this wedge metaphor, Gould highlighted a passage from Darwin's unpublished long manuscript, the shortened version of which became the *Origin of Species*, that gives a clear presentation of the worldview that Darwin had developed regarding the struggle for existence:

> Nature may be compared to a surface covered with ten thousand sharp wedges, many of the same shape, and many of different shapes representing different species, all packed closely together and all driven in by

incessant blows: the blows being far severer at one time than at another; sometimes a wedge of one form and sometimes another being struck; the one driven deeply in forcing out others; with the jar and shock often transmitted very far to other wedges in many lines of direction.[7]

Gould notes, "The *Origin of Species* contains several passages about progress in the history of life, and all are validated, not by the bare bones mechanism of natural selection, but by the second principle of the wedge, the vision of a full world ruled by overt competition among organisms."[8] He goes on to quote a passage from the *Origin of Species* in which Darwin demonstrates his commitment to the idea of progress (although he struggled with this view, also arguing against inappropriate progressivism):

> The more recent forms must, on my theory, be higher than the more ancient; for each new species is formed by having had some advantage in the struggle for life over other and preceding forms. . . . I do not doubt that this process of improvement has affected in a marked and sensible manner the organization of the more recent and victorious forms of life, in comparison with the ancient and beaten forms.[9]

In considering the extent to which a progressive trend could emerge in the history of life, Gould recognized that different processes occur at different temporal scales. He argued that it is useful to think of evolutionary processes unfolding across three tiers of time. The first tier is "normal" ecological time: the day-to-day struggle of organisms to survive and reproduce. This is the tier of time in which natural selection in the traditional Darwinian sense operates, and this is the tier of time that has been the focus of the modern synthesis in biology. Supporters of the modern synthesis have typically assumed that all long-term changes in organic evolution can be extrapolated from processes happening in this first tier. Gould, however, argues that processes also occur on two other tiers of time, which disrupt any trajectory that may emerge from processes occurring on the first tier. The second tier is normal geological time *between* episodes of mass extinction. This is where Niles Eldredge and Gould's theory of punctuated equilibrium addresses the deployment of species and origin of trends over long stretches of time. As we explained in the introduction and chapter 1, the theory of punctuated equilibrium says that speciation events and differential survival of species that are not reducible to natural selection in ecological time (that is, the first tier) explain a substantial degree of patterns in geological time. Thus the second tier is dominated by processes independent of the first tier, such as those stemming from the characteristics of lineages that lead to different rates of speciation.

The third tier of time is dominated by mass extinction events that are due to processes not reducible to the first or second tiers, such as the asteroid impact that led to the Cretaceous extinction. Gould notes that these extinction events appear to operate with their own rules, and are thus independent of processes occurring in the other two tiers. At the same time, events, such as those causing mass extinctions, influence evolutionary processes and history. He conceives of mass extinctions as "a separate process, and a cardinal shaping force for patterns of life's history" that disrupts the "accumulated achievements at lower tiers."[10] Emphasizing this decisive power, as well as its potential, he explains, "Mass extinctions are not unswervingly destructive in the history of life. They are a source of creation as well, especially if the . . . view of external triggering is correct. . . . Mass extinction may be the primary and indispensable seed of major changes and shifts in life's history. Destruction and creation are locked in a dialectic of interaction."[11]

Gould succinctly summarizes these three tiers:

> The first tier includes evolutionary events of the ecological moment. The second encompasses the evolutionary trends within lineages and clades that occur during millions of years in "normal" geological time between events of mass extinction. . . . [Mass extinction represents] a third distinct tier with rules and principles of its own.[12]

Gould indicates that the logic of Darwin's argument, particularly with regard to the power of natural selection and the wedge metaphor, did suggest that there could be some form of "progress" in ecological time, but only in the limited sense of species becoming more adapted to their local environments, which over the course of time are subject to change. However, despite long-standing assumptions to the contrary, no clear directional trajectory can be found in the history of life indicating some form of overall progress. Gould refers to this failure to find a progressive signal in life's history as the *paradox of the first tier*:

> The Dilemma of the modern synthesis for paleobiology lay in its claim that all theory could be extrapolated from the first tier, thus converting macroevolution from a source of theory to a simple phenomenology. . . . But if the tiers of life create pattern by emergent rules not predictable from processes and activities at lower tiers, then paleobiology adds its special insights without contradicting principles for lower tiers.[13]

Gould concludes, "A theory of mass extinction would largely resolve the paradox of the first tier. If anything like progress accumulates during normal times (and punctuated equilibrium casts doubt even upon this proposition), the vector of advance may be derailed often and profoundly enough to undo any long term directionality."[14] This recognition of emergent rules across different tiers of time is an important part of Gould's thinking on the hierarchical nature of causality, and we will return to it in the next chapter.

WONDERFUL LIFE: LESSONS FROM THE CAMBRIAN

Over 500 million years ago, *Pikaia*, a two-inch-long worm-like creature, swam in the Cambrian seas. It was not particularly common, nor in any way would it have appeared especially remarkable to a hypothetical naturalist surveying the fauna of the time. However, despite its apparent lack of distinctiveness, *Pikaia* went on to great evolutionary success, whereas many of its contemporaries left no descendants that survived to the present. *Pikaia* is the first known chordate, the phylum to which *Homo sapiens* and all other vertebrates belong. As Gould posited in one of his most renowned books, *Wonderful Life*, an exceptional level of human arrogance is necessary to argue that *Pikaia* was superior to its many contemporaries who either went extinct or, through the vagaries of history, dwindled to obscurity.[15] Yet despite the absurdity of it, there is such a common social bias viewing history as a march of progress leading inexorably to the present that many natural historians have long argued that evolution on Earth unfolded in a predictable, progressive manner, with the emergence of humanity, or at least a conscious intelligent being, as its inevitable outcome. This view fits well with the perspective of the dominant classes of various historical ages that asserts that the hierarchical social order is both natural and inevitable, the point toward which history had been striving.

A similar, although ahistorical, notion was embodied by the medieval conception of the "great chain of being," which long provided a scheme for ordering the universe—from God at the top down to "simple" organisms at the bottom. In its original presentation, the great chain of being was anti-evolutionary, as the world was determined to be static and unchanging. God designed each creature and assigned a specific place within the hierarchy of life. It should come as no surprise that the supposed preordained order in nature was commonly seen within the social world as well, as the king reigned above the serf, according to inherent and just design. Arthur Lovejoy, the historian of ideas, explains that in the nineteenth century it was popular to translate the great chain of being into an evolutionary conception that presented the ladder of evolutionary "advance" from the amoeba to humans. All too common, given the social and racial inequalities that have marked human history, were attempts to rank and order the human population, using a chain-of-being argument, whereby whites were seen as the most highly evolved human population, and blacks typically seen as of the lowest order.[16] Gould warns that though the racism that marked these arguments is somewhat less evident today, the commitment to natural hierarchy remains a deep conviction in Western (as well as other) societies.

The belief in progress is at the heart of the modern Western worldview, so it is not surprising that it finds its way into theories of natural history. Darwin developed his theory during what was perhaps the height of progressivist thinking, the Victorian era, and, ever since, his theory has been widely interpreted as suggesting that organisms improve over the course of evolutionary history.[17] Gould worked to counter the long-established view, dating back to before Darwin, that evolution was directional and progressive. As discussed above, Darwin himself, although much more sophisticated and nuanced in his thinking than many of his subsequent acolytes, argued that there should be some degree of progress in evolution, at least with regard to adaptation to the local environment. But he was skeptical of such claims in regard to historical progress, as indicated in his correspondence with U.S. paleontologist Alpheus Hyatt, who contended that there was necessary progress. Darwin, in some degree of contradiction with the passage quoted above from the *Origin*, in a letter dated December 4, 1872, wrote, "After long reflection I cannot avoid the conclusion that no inherent tendency to progressive development exists."[18] Nonetheless, the progressive view became central to the modern synthesis. Gould points out:

> Progress is not merely a deep cultural bias of Western thought . . . it is also . . . the explicit expectation of all deterministic theories of evolutionary mechanism that have ever achieved any popularity, from Darwinian selection to Lamarckism to orthogenesis. I do not, of course, mean progress as an unreversed, unilinear march up the chain of being; Darwin did away with this silly notion forever. But even Darwinism anticipates that an imperfect, irregular, but general ascent should emerge from all the backing and forthing inherent in a theory based on a principle of local adaption to changing circumstances.[19]

The popular view of "survival of the fittest" indicates that the unfit are the ones weeded out over time. Is not extinction, after all, a mark of failure?[20] Aren't dinosaurs, for example, of an intrinsically lower grade than mammals, as evidenced by the persistence of the latter to the present? Running counter to much of prevailing thought, as we noted above, one of Gould's central themes is that of historical contingency—events (such as those characterized by the third tier of time), often occurring effectively by chance and that are not predictable beforehand (although they may be rendered sensible in hindsight), may change the course of history, foreclosing some options and opening others. The trilobites—marine arthropods that flourished before their disappearance in the greatest of all mass extinctions, which ended the Permian period approximately 250 million years ago—surely did not vanish due to inherent inferiority. After all, they had thrived for 300 million years, longer than mammals have been around and over one thousand times longer than *Homo sapiens* has trod upon the earth. But their existence blinked out likely due to bad luck in an unpredictable, and still unexplained, global shake-up that took with it over 90 percent of all species then extant.[21] Likewise, it is hard to imagine that the descendants of *Pikaia* made it through this bottleneck due to anything but good fortune. Furthermore, had an asteroid not collided with the earth 65 million years ago, at the close of the Cretaceous period, the dinosaurs almost surely would have persisted in their dominance over the inconsequential rat-like ancestors of mammals, and our lineage would have taken a different path. There is every reason to suspect that if this contingent event had not occurred, dinosaurs would have survived to the present and humans would never have evolved. Dinosaurs and mammals, after all, appear in the fossil record at approximately the same time, coexisting for over 100 million years, with dinosaurs arguably being more successful than mammals. Gould stresses, "*Dinosaur* should be a term of praise, not of opprobrium. They reigned for 100 million years and died through no fault of their own; *Homo sapiens* is nowhere near a million years old and has limited prospects, entirely self-imposed, for extended geological longevity."[22]

Gould pointed to Mark Twain's sarcastic derision of the notion of progress and purpose in evolution as an insightful critique.[23] Drawing upon the science of his time—such as Lord Kelvin's estimate of Earth's age—Twain pointed out that the world had existed for hundreds of millions of years (the best estimate today is around 4.5 billion years), but *Homo sapiens* had been present for well less than 1 percent of this time. Nonetheless, it was commonly assumed that all of history was directed toward preparing the world for the eventual rise of human beings. Twain mockingly explained, following this logic of argument, that if the present was simply meant to be, many important steps were necessary to set the stage for current needs. For instance, "Man would have to have the oyster," so "preparation was made for the oyster." But such a process is not easy, as all of the oyster's ancestors would have to be made first, so a variety of invertebrates had to precede the oyster. Twain explained that many of the invertebrates

> will die and become extinct, in the course of the nineteen million years covered by the experiment, but all is not lost, for the Amalekites will fetch the homestake; they will develop gradually into encrinites, and stalactites, and blatherskites, and one thing and another as the mighty ages creep on and the Archaean and the Cambrian Periods pile their lofty crags in the primordial seas, and at least the first grand stage in the preparation of the world for man stands completed, the oyster is done.

To drive the point home, he added:

> An oyster has hardly any more reasoning power than a scientist has; and so it is reasonably certain that this one jumped to the conclusion that the nineteen million years was a preparation for *him*; but that would be just like an oyster, which is the most conceited animal there is, except man. And anyway, this one could not know, at that early date, that he was only an incident in a scheme, and that there was some more to the scheme, yet.[24]

After dealing with oysters, Twain, with wry wit, detailed how the preparation of the earth for humans required fish, and of course such a cuisine needed coal to fry it. So the history of the earth also involves millions of years where forests grew only to be buried within the earth to create fossil fuel, awaiting the eventual evolution of *Homo sapiens*. To symbolically represent the human haughtiness that conceived of the history of the earth in this light, Twain wrote sarcastically: "If the

Eiffel Tower [the tallest human-built structure in the world at the time] were now representing the world's age, the skin of paint on the pinnacle-knob at its summit would represent man's share of that age; and anybody would perceive that the skin was what the tower was built for."[25] This quote summarizes Gould's view of history and human arrogance well. It is no more reasonable to assume that humans were the necessary outcome of evolution than it is to assume that the Eiffel Tower was built to put paint on top of it.

Due to the dominance of contingency in natural and social history, the world of the present is only one of the many worlds that are possible; it does not represent a foreordained order. Or to use Gould's powerful metaphor, if we were to "replay the tape of life," a different history would unfold, almost surely without the appearance of humans or any creature especially similar to us; a history that would appear just as sensible and even as "inevitable" as the history that actually occurred. At each moment in history we stand at a gate of worlds, and although it is not predictable where any path will ultimately lead, our actions nonetheless influence the path along which we travel, and the organization of the larger world will influence what constraints and possibilities we will confront as a new present emerges and eventually becomes history.

THE QUESTION OF CONVERGENCE

One of the important issues in debates that Gould had with other scholars centered on the extent to which the evolutionary principle of convergence made the outcome of history inevitable in its broad features, if not in its particulars. Convergence refers to the fairly common phenomenon where two species from lineages that are not closely related will come to share common features, such as the morphological similarities between marine mammals, like dolphins, and fishes, since they face common selection pressures due to shared environmental constraints. Gould, like other evolutionary biologists, fully recognized the ubiquity and importance of convergence and its illustration of how natural selection shapes organisms to fit their environments. However, as we discussed in the previous chapter, Gould also was leery of hyper-adaptationist assumptions that attributed all similarities across species to selection, noting that many examples of convergence may reflect common structural underpinnings, such as the *Hox* genes shared by many phyla. In particular, although Gould accepted the importance of convergent evolution, he was highly skeptical of what might be called *meta-convergence*, the argument that the overall patterns of evolution and the structure of the modern biotic world necessarily had to be as they are.

Gould presents a sophisticated view of evolutionary change, which, as we detailed in the last chapter, includes the structural, historical legacies of organisms. He points out that organisms are not mere putty to be sculpted over the course of their phylogeny (evolutionary history) by external environmental forces, but rather their structural integrity constrains and channels the variation on which natural selection operates.[26] In this, Gould challenges the notion that phenotypic variation is isotropic, equally likely in all directions. Although mutation produces genetic variation that is random relative to selective advantage, this does not mean that phenotypic variation is not more likely in some directions than in others. Gould notes that the structural nature of the development of an organism throughout its life course (ontogeny) limits the types of phenotypic variation that is possible, because changes at one stage of the developmental process have consequences for later stages. Therefore, many characteristics of an organism cannot simply be modified without having substantial ripple effects throughout the whole organism. For example, as explained in the previous chapter, enlarging the body of a deer leads to disproportionately enlarging the antlers. The inherited patterns of development do not readily allow for all types of modification—for example, it would be difficult (although not necessarily impossible) for natural selection to make a larger deer with smaller antlers since this would require a restructuring of the development process. Hence the evolutionary process is a dialectical interaction between the internal (inherited structural constraints) and the external (environmental selection pressure), just as the ontogeny (development over the life course) of individual organisms is a dialectical interaction between their genes and the environment. Such an understanding helps restore the organism as a concept in biology—"an integrated entity exerting constraint over its history," situated in a specific environmental context.[27]

The structural nature of development has consequences for patterns of change. To illustrate this point, Gould makes use of a metaphor: Galton's polyhedron.[28] As he frequently does, Gould draws upon the arguments of various historical figures involved in the debate on evolutionary theory to build his own. Francis Galton, who was Darwin's cousin (Erasmus Darwin was grandfather to both), was deeply impressed by Darwin's work on evolution, but he disagreed with Darwin's assumptions about the nature of variation. He was especially concerned with the "stability of types." He developed a metaphor to challenge aspects of Darwin's conception of natural selection and the nature of change. Adopting Galton's conceptual insight, Gould explains that in the idealized Darwinian formulation species are metaphorical spheres (such as marbles) that roll freely on any phylogenic course through morphospace that the external world pushes them along—that is, they do not have a structural integrity that offers resistance to pressure from the external environment, and thus, move readily wherever environmental forces direct them via natural selection. Alternatively, in the metaphor of Galton's polyhedron, species are polyhedrons, multisided solid objects that have flat faces (such as dice), whose structure prevents them from rolling freely when only slightly perturbed and limits the paths they can follow after receiving a sufficient push from the external world. In other words, "change cannot occur in all directions, or with any increment." Polyhedrons can switch the facet on which they rest, but they cannot simply rest in any given position (for example, they can rest on a face but not on a corner). In contrast with a sphere, which may roll smoothly with a light tap, the polyhedron will resist minor perturbations, but given sufficient force will switch facets abruptly—potentially generating changes "that reverberate throughout the system." Thus species cannot perfectly track changing environments because of the structural interconnections they develop over the course of their phylogeny that limit and, potentially, direct the type of change possible. The metaphor of the polyhedron illustrates well the nature of punctuated change, structural constraint, and the nature of contingency emerging from these phenomena.

Gould emphasizes the importance of both recognizing the reality of structural constraint and also that structures have historical origins.[29] Here he helps unite insights from both sides of the age-old debate between functionalist biologists, such as Darwin and Jean-Baptiste Lamarck, and formalist (structuralist) biologists, such as Étienne Geoffroy Saint-Hilaire and Johann Wolfgang von Goethe. The functionalists typically stressed that features of organisms existed for utilitarian reasons (they were adaptations to their environments), and formalists underscored the structural unity of type common across similar organisms. Formalists often denied the possibility of evolution because they believed that only superficial change was possible, not fundamental change of underlying structures. This division was undermined when Darwin and subsequent evolutionists recognized that structures had evolved, although after their emergence these structures may indeed constrain the evolutionary pathways available to organisms (as how the metaphorical polyhedron rolls is affected by the number and shape of facets it has). In this, Darwin fundamentally reoriented the functionalist-formalist debate by adding a new dimension to the functional (active adaptation) and formal (constraints of structure) dichotomy: history (contingencies of phylogeny).[30] Galton's polyhedron illuminates two important themes from the formalist tradition that need to be part of evolutionary theory: "discontinuous evolution, and internally generated pathways."[31] Structural forces mediate the emergent reality, restricting possible pathways, but the state of the world does change, and inherited structures themselves can evolve. Thus the current conditions are not immutable, given historical contingency, and the future remains indeterminate.

Gould made a case for what might be called *contingent convergence*, whereby one of the reasons convergence is observed is because distantly related lineages share common structural features that are resistant to change, but whose emergence is the result of historical contingencies. Recalling the parallel between the generative potential of the *Hox* cluster and the generative grammar underlying human languages as theorized by Noam Chomsky, it is important to recognize that the shared view of these two theories is that structures, once they have emerged, constrain and channel diversity but are themselves products of history that could have been otherwise. Up to the Cambrian period, the world was relatively underoccupied by metazoans (multicellular animals), providing the space for a bounty of evolutionary experiments to emerge. Early in the evolutionary history of metazoans, before developmental pathways were set, mutations could more fundamentally alter the development of organisms and produce widespread diversification. New body plans could emerge more readily than after deep structures became firmly established. And, just as contingency played an important role throughout history, the particularities of these structures (such as the *Hox* genes) were not inevitable. Although these structures, once established, might lead to considerable convergence due to the constraints they place on developmental pathways, their origin was contingent.

Recognizing the profound importance of contingency, and wary of cultural biases leading others to see history as a march of progress, Gould in his book *Full House* provided one of his most compelling critiques of the assumption that evolution inevitably proceeds in a progressive manner, moving from simple to complex.[32] Gould argues there is no predisposition toward evolutionary progress; that is, there is no general trend in the history of life whereby organisms typically become more complex, intelligent, or otherwise "superior" to their ancestors. Rather, there has been simply an increase in the *variability* of the complexity of organisms since the origin of life—that is, the history of life has been one of *diversification* not "improvement" per se.[33] Bacteria, the simplest form of life, have remained the most common form of life throughout history.[34] Although the most complex organism at any particular time in the past was less complex than the most complex organism alive today, the modal level of complexity has remained unchanged.

Gould argues that the typical lineage is just as likely to become simpler over geologic time as it is to become more complex. This is because, as per the paradox of the first tier, natural selection adapts creatures to their immediate environments, and complexity does not necessarily convey greater adaptive fitness than simplicity. The prime examples of lineages simplifying over evolutionary time are of those adopting a parasitic way of life. Since parasites typically live on the body of other organisms, they tend to become simplified eating structures, losing many of the complex features of their ancestors. Why then are there more complex species alive today than there were one billion years ago, before the rise of metazoans? Simply because over time there are more chances to get successive net shifts toward complexity in some lineages (as there are, likewise, more chances to get successive net shifts toward simplicity). In the same sense that if you flip many different coins (metaphoric lineages) many times each (with each flip being a metaphorical unit of time), some particular coins will almost surely come up with substantially more heads than tails compared to other coins, simply due to chance, and the more times each coin is flipped (the more time that passes) the more opportunities for a particularly large absolute number of heads (shifts toward complexity) in excess of tails (shifts toward simplicity) on some coins. Note that this process does not lead to a change in the central tendency of the proportion of heads and tails (that is, it should remain around 50 percent), but does lead to a much wider range (variability) in the absolute number of heads in excess of tails (complexity).

It is important to note that Gould does not argue that organisms evolve due to chance processes alone. He is only pointing out that in adapting creatures to their local environments, natural selection is approximately as likely to make any particular lineage more simple as more complex. That is to say, there is no particular reason to believe that complex organisms are generally fitter, in the Darwinian sense, than simple organisms, as evidenced by the remarkable enduring success of single-celled organisms. In one set of circumstances selection pressure may favor simple organisms, and in another it may favor complex organisms.

So, although the most complex organism extant at any one time is generally more complex the closer we are to the present (due to more opportunities for metaphoric flips of the complexity coin), there is no general trend toward complexity, only increasing variability in the level of complexity across organisms. The specific twist to the history of life is that since, by necessity, life originates as the simplest form, there is not room to vary in the direction of even less complexity at the left side of the frequency distribution of complexity. However, other than at the very simplest end, the complexity of any particular lineage is approximately as likely to drift in one direction as in another.

Gould's position is best understood when contrasted with thinkers who are prone to interpreting evolutionary history as directional, notably a diverse group including Richard Dawkins, Daniel Dennett, Robert Wright, and Simon Conway Morris. These thinkers have varying backgrounds and credentials, but agree that there is some degree of progress in evolution. What is telling here is that they agree on the idea of progress in evolution while sharing fundamentally different assumptions about the nature of the world.

The general ethos of the progressive position is well represented by journalist Robert Wright's argument that both social and natural history have a trajectory that moves from simple to complex. His belief in what we have called meta-convergence is so strong and his view that society is moving in a progressive direction is so deeply held that the subtitle of one of his books is *The Logic of Human Destiny*.[35] He writes: "When you look beneath the roiled surface of human events . . . you see an arrow beginning tens of thousands of years ago and continuing to the present. And looking ahead, you see where it is pointing," which of course is to a more advanced (in the sense of being further along the imagined road of progress) society, since "change in the structure of societies is more likely to raise complexity than to lower it."[36] Wright has little original to say and mostly draws on the work of Dawkins and other scholars, but he is noteworthy for his popularity in certain circles, demonstrating that he presents a position that fits well with the preferences of mainstream culture and the social elite.

Richard Dawkins, undoubtedly one of the most distinguished con-temporary evolutionary theorists, clearly represents the Darwinian tradition in his views on the nature of evolution. He is a strict materi-alist and a believer that, due to convergence, the larger patterns, although not the particulars, of evolutionary history were to a large extent inevitable. He explains that "a progressive trend is one in which there are no reversals; or if there are reversals, they are out-numbered and outweighed by movement in the dominant direction," following a particular anatomical trend from early to intermediate to late. He pro-poses that "evolution exhibits progress" that is "value-free" (neutral) as well as "value-laden." The latter entails a progressive evolutionary direction that is desirable, in some general sense, as far as "*somebody's* value system*." Relying on the metaphor of the arms race, which is very similar to Darwin's wedge argument, Dawkins argues that species gen-erally progress through history due to competition.[37] Here micro-level events generate evolutionary changes that can be seen at the macro level, with a tendency toward convergence.

Daniel Dennett, a philosopher of science and biology, presents an argument that is similar to Dawkins:

> There aren't *global* pathways of progress, but there is incessant *local* improvement. This improvement seeks out the best designs with such great reliability that it can often be predicted by adaptationist reasoning. Replay the tape [of life—a reference to Gould's metaphor] a thousand times, and the Good Tricks will be found again and again, by one lineage or another.[38]

Dennett's argument is that there are a limited number of ways for organisms to survive in the world, and over time natural selection will explore all of these options, finding again and again the best solutions to the challenges the environment throws up. Thus, although the particularities of the history of any lineage may be largely contingent, there will be considerable meta-convergence, where the larger patterns of history are constrained to have unfolded generally as they did. And this pattern is characterized to some degree as being one of progress to more finely adapted organisms. Dawkins and Dennett are materialists who make sensible arguments. However, they do not effectively counter Gould's case since they do not demonstrate a proper understanding of the contingent nature of many instances of convergence.

For example, Dawkins has argued that the independent evolution of the eye in multiple lineages is a prime example of evolutionary convergence, suggesting that eyes are to some degree inevitable features of the natural world.[39] It is indeed true that various types of eyes have emerged in divergent species and that the characteristics of these eyes are constrained by the physics of light, and thus similarities in eyes across distantly related species to some degree reflects convergence. However, what Dawkins fails to appreciate is that the convergence of eyes is also to some degree a *contingent* convergence, in that eyes across species, even those from different phyla, are built using some of the same developmental genes, indicating that eyes in different phyla are in part *homologous*, not simply analogous. As Gould explains, discoveries in the 1990s showed that different phyla use homologous developmental pathways to build eyes, controlled by shared *Pax* genes, most notably the *Pax-6*, and that amino acid identity shared between mammalian and insect *Pax-6* sequences is over 90 percent.[40] Thus, although complex eyes emerged independently in different lineages, they are built using a shared underlying structure, and that structure is an *evolved* one—that is, a product of *history*. The *Pax* genes did not evolve originally to produce eyes, since the eyeless common ancestors of multiple phyla shared them. The *Pax* genes could not have been produced by natural selection for their ability to build complex eyes. However, once they emerged, for whatever particular reasons that led to their development at the time, they provided a structure that could be co-opted to produce eyes. Without this historically produced structure, complex eyes as we know them may not have evolved. After all, distantly related species use the same developmental structure, rather than each having a uniquely evolved one. This illustrates Gould's point that structures constrain developmental pathways and can lead to convergence, but the structures themselves may be *contingent* products of history. Eyes, while clearly good examples of convergent evolution, are also good examples of the *contingent* nature of that convergence. The *Pax* genes, along with the *Hox* genes, illustrate the importance of historically constructed structures and—counter to Dawkins's interpretation—show the profound effects of contingency on subsequent evolution. If early in the evolution of metazoans, developmental structures other than the *Pax* and *Hox* genes had evolved and become dominant, the subsequent history of life on Earth may have been dramatically different.

Simon Conway Morris, who was one of the paleontologists who did important work on the Cambrian Shale fossils, makes an argument for meta-convergence that goes beyond the more mundane (and fairly sensible, if limited) one made by Dawkins and Dennett. Bizarrely for a modern scientist, Conway Morris is actively hostile to materialism and takes a stance in favor of a kind of theistic evolution.[41] Although he does not argue for divine intervention in evolution, separating him from the more absurd supporters of "intelligent design," he clearly assumes that there is some design in the universe that structured it to lead to the emergence of humanity. One of his most prominent books carries the rather extraordinary subtitle *Inevitable Humans in a Lonely Universe*, clearly demonstrating that he not only sees the broad features of evolution as largely inevitable (similar to Dawkins and Dennett) but even the particulars of humans as inevitable.[42] In this book, he itemizes the many examples of convergent evolution throughout history, including eyes across phyla, but also many particular features across different branches of the arthropod phylum, arguing that the ubiquity of convergence points to the inevitability of our present world. This is an extreme example of viewing history as unfolding in a progressive manner leading to a predetermined outcome. Conway Morris's views come close to the absurd caricature of faulty reasoning that Twain mocked, which would lead one to conclude that the Eiffel Tower was built so that it could have a layer of paint on its top. According to Conway Morris, if the tape of life was replayed, evolutionary structures and constraints would lead to the inevitable return of *Homo sapiens* or a form very similar to present humans. In other words, from a specific evolutionary starting point, given the existing material and the course of development, there is a highly restricted range of options as far as evolutionary pathways.

Interestingly, contrary to Dawkins and Dennett, and half in line with Gould, Conway Morris sees evolution as controlled by underlying structures, which lead to the ubiquity of convergence. However, unlike Gould, he fails to recognize the *historical* emergence of many of these structures, assuming that they represent a more general underlying order to nature. In a more recent book—the title of which is *The Deep Structure of Biology: Is Convergence Sufficiently Ubiquitous to Give a Directional Signal?* (a question clearly answered in the affirmative)—Conway Morris and his fellow contributors rely on examples of convergence based on underlying structures to make the case for progress in evolution and, sometimes implicitly, sometimes explicitly, design in the universe.[43] In his own contribution to this volume he is clear that he sees metaphysical implications stemming from convergence.[44] In fact, in the closing essay in this volume, theologian John F. Haught ends with the claim that the history of life may be "pregnant with the promise of ultimate meaning. If so, there may still be abundant room, alongside of science, for a theology of evolution."[45] It is worth noting that this book is published by Templeton Foundation Press, which, as expressed on the back jacket of the book, aims to help "intellectual leaders and others learn about science research on aspects of realities, invisible and intangible. Spiritual realities include unlimited love, accelerating creativity, worship, and the benefits of purpose in persons and in the cosmos."

It is particularly remarkable that Dawkins, a prominent atheist and vocal critic of theistic arguments, largely endorses Conway Morris's argument, without acknowledging that it is based on anti-materialist premises.[46] Dawkins does acknowledge that Conway Morris's structuralism sits in tension with his own functionalism, but declares himself in this instance somewhat convinced of Conway Morris's argument. Dawkins's willingness to accept an argument based on theistic premises since it agrees with his own conclusion about directionality in evolution is perhaps indicative of a strong bias in favor of seeing progress. Gould often noted, in his examination of the history of science, that many metaphysical interpretations of nature remain unchanged even when the scientific understanding of the relevant phenomena fundamentally changes. This persistence in interpretation despite radical change in evidence suggests a cultural bias rather than a logical inference from the facts of nature.

For example, Gould has noted that Alfred Russel Wallace, who discovered natural selection independently of Darwin, believed, unlike Darwin, that the universe was pervaded by mind and that human life was no accident. Wallace made the all too common error of imposing his desire for meaning onto nature, which is basically the same error Conway Morris makes in finding meaning in the history of life. Gould writes:

> Wallace examined the physical structure of the earth, solar system, and universe and concluded that if any part had been built ever so slightly differently, conscious life could not have arisen. Therefore, intelligence must have designed the universe. . . . Wallace's argument had its peculiarities, but one aspect of his story strikes me as even more odd. During the last decade, like cats and bad pennies of our proverbs, Wallace's argument has returned in new dress. Some physicists [notably Freeman Dyson] have touted it as something fresh and new [the "anthropic principle," the idea that intelligent life lies foreshadowed in the laws of nature and the structure of the universe]. . . . To me it is the same bad argument. . . . The central fallacy of this newly touted but historically moth-eaten argument lies in the nature of history itself. Any complex historical outcome—intelligent life on earth, for example—represents a summation of improbabilities and becomes thereby absurdly unlikely. But something has to happen, even if any particular "something" must stun us by its improbability.[47]

Gould then goes on to explain that Wallace's understanding of the universe was radically different from our modern understanding, and thus Wallace and Dyson, like Conway Morris, manage to reach the same conclusion—that there is some form of design in the universe—based on profoundly divergent conceptualizations of the natural world. Gould suggests: "If the same argument can be applied to such different arrangements of matter, may we not legitimately suspect that emotional appeal, rather than a supposed basis in fact or logic, explains its curious persistence?"[48]

We find it particularly interesting that both Conway Morris and Dawkins, the theist and the atheist, respectively, who have fundamentally different conceptions of the universe—the former believing that it reflects an underlying intelligence and the latter being an ardent materialist—both see some form of progress and inevitability in the history of life. Conway Morris sees this as a sign of divine intent, while Dawkins sees this as a reflection of deterministic natural laws. Following Gould's perspective, we suggest they are both wrong. Perhaps they both see progress in evolution and believe that the present was inevitable because of a pervasive cultural bias rather than because of a clear signal from nature. Hope as we may, intelligent life was not inevitable, but rather it is a contingent outcome of history.

Conway Morris and others like him make a common error in equating what we value most in our world with what is necessary or inevitable. As Gould himself commented, "There's a common tendency to equate importance with necessity. Just because something is important—which consciousness clearly is to the history of the planet—doesn't mean it was meant to be. There's never anything in the history of life that's had such an impact on the earth as the evolution of human consciousness, but that doesn't mean it was meant to be. It could still be accidental."[49] Gould emphasized the importance of contingency because it is a reality of the natural world and the history of life on Earth, and he criticized the belief in progress, as justified by faith in the powers of meta-convergence to inevitably lead to the conditions of the present, because it represents an inaccurate characterization of natural history. He sought to show that biology is a *historical* science that cannot be reduced to a set of mechanical, deterministic laws. However, he also focused on contingency and the critique of progress to make a larger point about science and society. The belief in progress is a prime example of how social biases can distort science. Gould aimed to show that the natural world does not conform to human aspirations. Nature does not have human meaning embedded in it, and it does not provide direction to how humans should live. Instead, we live in a world that only has meaning of our own making. Rather than seeing this as disheartening, Gould saw it as liberating because it empowers us to make our own purpose. Gould stressed, similar to Karl Marx and other radical thinkers, that we make our own history and that the future is open.

CHAPTER FOUR

Emergence, Hierarchy,
and the Limits of Reductionism

The emergence of a new general theory of evolution involves challenging the constraints of established evolutionary thought. The hardening of the modern synthesis restricted questions on how the causal processes behind evolutionary changes may vary across levels of aggregation.[1] As discussed in chapter 1, a commitment to gradualism has dominated evolutionary theory. The microevolutionary perspective that is at the heart of the modern synthesis embraces this approach, focusing on how small changes accumulate in the gene pool of a population due to natural selection on individual organisms or genes over long stretches of time. From this perspective, macroevolution is merely a phenomenon caused by micro-processes.

Stephen Jay Gould contended that the modern synthesis provided an inadequate explanation of the breadth of processes and phenomena that have occurred over evolutionary history. He spent many years developing a hierarchical approach to macroevolution, disputing the narrow level of analysis within much of evolutionary research, which focused purely on selection among individual organisms or genes. He was not rejecting the fundamentals of Darwinian evolutionary theory or questioning the importance of natural selection. Rather, he was attempting to forge a pluralistic evolutionary perspective that recognized multiple causes of evolution. Such reasoning, Gould pointed out, was in line with Charles Darwin's thinking, given that the latter recognized multiple forces producing evolutionary change. Just as developmental structures can channel variation, as discussed in chapter 2, processes happening on levels other than the gene or the organism affect evolution. An uncritical evaluation of the modern synthesis has constrained evolutionary thought. Gould worked to open up this realm to a more sophisticated research project. This venture involves a critical assessment of the role of reductionism within science, the level of aggregation at which various causal processes occur, and the importance of emergence, all of which remain concerns in the natural and social sciences.

THE POWER AND POVERTY OF REDUCTIONISM

While Gould did not identify as a Marxist per se, he was clearly influenced by this tradition. He shared with Karl Marx and Frederick Engels a critical, though also appreciative, view of reductionism, the long-standing tradition in the natural sciences that sought to understand wholes by examining their parts. In *Anti-Dühring*, Engels wrote:

> The analysis of nature into its individual parts, the grouping of the different natural processes and objects in definite classes, the study of the internal anatomy of organic bodies in their manifold forms—these were the fundamental conditions of the gigantic strides in our knowledge of nature that have been made during the last four hundred years. But this method of work has also left us as legacy the habit of observing natural objects and processes in isolation, apart from their connection with the vast whole; of observing them in repose, not in motion; as constants, not as essentially variables; in their death, not in their life. And when this way

of looking at things was transferred by Bacon and Locke from natural science to philosophy, it begot the narrow, metaphysical mode of thought
peculiar to the preceding centuries.[2]

Engels captures well the power and poverty of reductionism. The
Cartesian method of investigation assumes that a complex whole or an
integrated system—such as an ecosystem, an organism, or a cell—can
be understood by examining the parts that compose the whole. This
line of reasoning proposes that there are distinct parts with unique
properties that exist independently of one another and that precede
the whole. Higher levels of organization simply represent the properties of the parts aggregated. While interaction exists in the assembly of
the parts, causation is rooted in the lowest level.[3] This methodological approach has yielded important insights in the natural sciences,
especially in physics and chemistry. For example, reductionistic
research contributed to a variety of scientific advances, from establishing the properties of atoms to discovering the structure of DNA.
However, a problem arises when we assume "that the world is like the
method," separate parts existing in static isolation.[4]

Rooted in his understanding of natural history and the history of
science, Gould held a view similar to Engels. Gould insisted that different insights could be gained from distinctive styles of reasoning and
analysis. As a result, he had a deep appreciation for the power of
reductionism. However, as someone who focused on understanding
macroevolution, large-scale patterns of evolution over geological time,
rather than focusing on microevolution, the changes in gene frequencies in populations that occur over ecological time, he was interested
in the emergence of the properties of systems that need to be understood on their own terms and that cannot be fully explained by simply
looking at the parts of the systems. Gould supported a hierarchical
theory of evolution that appreciated diverse causal processes occurring at different levels of aggregation, such as genes, organisms, demes
(a locally interbreeding population), and species. The level of organization always remained an important consideration for Gould, especially in complex systems. Gould stated:

I believe that reductionism—a powerful method that should be used whenever appropriate, and that has been employed triumphantly throughout the history of modern science—must fail as a generality (both logically and empirically). . . . I do not believe that reductionism can come even close to full success as a style of explanation for levels of complexity (including several aspects of evolutionary biology, and then proceeding "upward" in intricacy toward cognitive and social systems of even greater integration and interaction) for two basic reasons. . . . First, *emergence*, or the entry of novel explanatory rules in complex systems, laws arising from "nonlinear" or "nonadditive" interactions among constituent parts that therefore, in principle, cannot be discovered from properties of parts considered separately. . . . Second, *contingency*, or the growing importance of unique historical "accidents" that cannot, in principle, be predicted, but that remain fully accessible to factual explanation after their occurrence. The role of contingency as a component of explanation increases in the same sciences of complexity that also become more and more inaccessible to reductionism for the first reason of emergent principles.[5]

We discussed the importance of contingency in Gould's thinking in the previous chapter, so here we focus primarily on the importance of emergence and the error of narrow reductionism when assessing causation.

As stated in the quote above, Gould emphasized that the role of contingency increases when considering complex structures, which are generally characterized by emergent properties at higher levels of organization. He pointed out that it was through engaging the humanities and social sciences that he gained a greater appreciation for the importance of contingency in history—whether it is natural or social history.[6] Thus it is ironic that a number of perspectives—even seemingly divergent research traditions, such as rational choice theory and postmodernism—within the humanities and social sciences suffer from various forms of reductionism. Rational choice theory proposes that the behavioral patterns in society simply reflect the choices of individuals, who engage in cost-benefit analysis to maximize personal gain. From this perspective, which employs a particular type of reductionism known as methodological individualism, social institutions are perceived to be the result of the actions of individuals, and therefore the characteristics of society at large can be explained by the traits of the individuals that compose society. Rational choice theory is widely employed in economics, sociology, and political science.[7] The pervasiveness of this logic is evident in the "consumer sovereignty" model in economics, which proposes that all economic decisions are driven by the demands of consumers, who therefore determine the direction and function of the economy. John Kenneth Galbraith, the iconoclastic economist, dismissed this conception as a form of fraud, as it ignored that the economy, as well as society, had higher levels of organization.[8] He pointed out that concentrated power shapes economic operations. Corporations work to ensure their protection and to maximize profit. Massive marketing campaigns are constantly employed to act as a form of coercion to manage individual behaviors.[9] Thus the explanation of consumerism and other social phenomena cannot be properly explained by focusing on individual people.

The rejection of higher levels of organization is also apparent within postmodernism. Given that this tradition encompasses a substantial variety of intellectual positions used in different ways, it is hard to give a definitive characterization of it. However, there are clear features common to various forms of postmodernism. Postmodernism is often defined in regard to what it rejects, such as objective truth, totalization, utopianism, and metanarratives. Often it advocates plurality and contextual analysis. It is concerned with language, discourse, and culture. Some variants of postmodernism, such as those associated with Jacques Derrida, reduce reality only to the text, dismissing the existence of an objective external reality. In this situation, the only reality that exists is that provided by language—the physical world is filtered through a multitude of narratives, each potentially as valid as another. Social relations are thus merely reflections of these constructs. The existence of larger material structures is typically denied by postmodernists, and all phenomena are reduced to the subjective experiences of individual humans. An extreme position views ecological crises, such as global climate change, as merely social constructs, residing in people's perceptions, not in an external reality. In general, there is a focus on fragmented narratives within postmodernist historiography. Rather than attempt to establish an integrated historical narrative within the larger world context, a focus is placed on the scattered pieces of a subjective experience to discern new patterns and meanings.[10] Thus postmodernism, like rational choice theory, ultimately rejects the reality of emergent structures at higher levels of organization than the individual person.

We, following Gould, are not denying the importance of plurality, diverse voices and experiences, or contextualization. In fact, like Gould, we see the value in these efforts, and do not view them as the exclusive domain of postmodernism. Historical specificity has long been a central component of the Marxist approach.[11] Also the challenge that postmodernism incorporates into its perspective to notions of a grand historical purpose is important, as we have already noted in this book. But what we do find problematic is the reductionistic tendency to view society as simply the result of the subjective experiences of individuals. Experiences are not simply isolated events independent of the larger whole of society. Instead, experiences emerge from social interactions in a concrete world, in which the social and natural are part of the materialist properties of reality. There are higher levels of organization that channel experiences. Language has meaning in relation to physical reality; it does not stand on its own outside of the material world.[12]

Clearly, it is not only the natural sciences that have suffered from a narrow reductionism, but the social sciences as well, and this may reflect general tendencies in society. Social psychologists have identified a particular form of reductionism among the general population, known as the fundamental attribution error. This error refers to the tendency of individuals to explain the behavior of another person in terms of that person's individual characteristics, rather than the circumstances in which he or she acts.[13] For example, it is common to assume that another person who trips does so because he or she is clumsy, not because the ground is uneven or the lighting is poor. The important point here is that there is a common failure to recognize that individuals are immersed in a larger world that influences behavior and the consequences of behavior. Many features of the circumstances in which a person acts may contribute to a particular behavior.

The problem with narrow reductionism, whether it is in the social or natural sciences, is that it fails to describe and understand the emergent properties of complex, dynamic systems. Gould explains that complex systems include non-linear and non-additive interactions among the constituent parts. The operating laws cannot be determined from studying the properties of the parts considered separately and in isolation. Although reductionism works by breaking down the complex structure into separate parts to determine the laws regulating the parts, it

> won't give you a full explanation of the higher level in terms of these lower-level parts because, in constructing the higher-level item, these parts combine and interact. Thus one must also include these interactions as essential aspects of an adequate higher-level explanation. How, then, can reductionism work if interactions among lower-level parts must figure prominently in any higher-level explanation?[14]

New properties, which do not appear at any other level, develop from interactions in complex systems. "If these emergent properties (as they so often do) become central principles of explanation at the higher level," Gould notes, "then reductionism has failed, and the higher level must be studied in its own totality if we hope to achieve satisfactory scientific explanation."[15]

BOOKKEEPING AND CAUSALITY:
A HIERARCHICAL THEORY OF SELECTION
AND THE FALLACY OF THE SELFISH GENE

Following Darwin, the modern synthesis held that the organism is the single, or at least the primary, unit of selection, and that all or nearly all trends in evolution at higher levels of aggregation (such as demes or species) are simply a product of lower-level causation. This microevolutionary tradition sees macroevolutionary phenomena simply as the result of natural selection's cumulative influences on the gene frequencies in populations from the day-to-day interactions of organisms. More recently, hyper-reductionists such as Richard Dawkins have tried to push the level of causation to an even lower level than the organism, that of the gene.[16]

Dissatisfied with the limitations of microevolutionary explanations, Gould challenged the narrowness of the modern synthesis, opening up evolutionary theory to a plurality of explanative principles. If evolution is simply a reflection of changes in gene frequencies driven by natural selection on genes, the particulars of history and the characteristics of organisms and species are rendered largely meaningless. But if a variety of evolutionary casual forces operate, in different ways, on distinctive levels of organization, which are the result of past historical processes, then historical considerations are paramount.[17] Taking a position that is consonant with much of sociological thinking, Gould asserts that a comprehensive causal explanation cannot be reduced to a single level. Following Gould, recent scholarship increasingly stresses the shortcomings of the modern synthesis and narrow reductionism.[18] Gould's primary case is a defense of a hierarchical theory of selection, particularly species selection, although his general case is a critique of (narrow) reductionism and an argument for the importance of emergent characteristics, forces, and processes at higher levels of aggregation. His argument is closely tied to his theory of punctuated equilibrium.

The question of where in the hierarchy of nature the causal forces behind evolution operate is a complex and challenging one, which has required a great deal of theoretical, empirical, and philosophical analysis to sort out. One of the central concerns in developing a hierarchical theory of selection is determining what constitutes an "individual" in nature upon which selection and other causal forces can operate. It was a concern to which Darwin dedicated considerable thought, and it has been a difficult and controversial subject since his time. This is a topic that Gould considered "both exceedingly difficult and enormously important." He noted: "I have struggled with this issue all my professional life, and have often wondered why the questions raised seem so much more recalcitrant, and so much more cascading in implications, than for any other major problem in Darwinian theory."[19] To work out this subject Gould collaborated with other scholars, including Elisabeth A. Lloyd, a philosopher. His massive tome, *The Structure of Evolutionary Theory*, includes a detailed presentation of a hierarchical theory of selection.[20]

In developing his theory, Gould focused on the question, "Are species individuals or classes?" He is not only concerned with species as individuals but also with the individuality of other units.[21] He explains that in vernacular usage, to qualify as an individual, a material entity must have (1) a discrete and definable beginning; (2) a distinct and determinable ending; and (3) a sufficient degree of stability and coherence throughout its lifetime.[22]

Although each of these criteria has gray areas, it is important to recognize that we never doubt the individuality of a particular organism, such as a human being, even though there is ambiguity about (1) when it began, e.g., conception versus birth; (2) when it ends, e.g., people have been revived after being considered clinically dead, and a person's body may continue to function on life support systems even after conscious parts of the brain are effectively dead; and (3) the continuity of material existence, e.g., humans change form throughout their life course from infant to adult and so forth, and their material composition is constantly in flux as the atoms that compose human bodies are continuously replaced by other atoms. This understanding presents many philosophical questions about the extent to which we are the same person throughout our lifetimes, although typically no one questions each person's individuality. Gould noted that meeting these vernacular criteria is a necessary, but not a sufficient, condition for identifying an entity as an evolutionary "individual."[23] To be a Darwinian actor on the evolutionary stage, an individual must also be able to reproduce, have attributes that are inheritable by its "offspring," and vary from other individuals in some ways, so that selection may operate.

Gould's argument is that at different levels in nature's hierarchy there are units not limited to genes and organisms that qualify for status as individuals by both the vernacular and Darwinian criteria, including cell lines, demes, species, and clades (a group of biological taxa or species that share features inherited from a common ancestor). His argument for this, particularly for the individuality of species, is based on his and Niles Eldredge's theory of punctuated equilibrium, which asserts that species typically emerge rapidly and go extinct suddenly in terms of geological time (the punctuations), but change fairly little between their time of emergence and their extinction (the equilibrium). Gould argues that due to the pattern generated by punctuated equilibrium, species meet the vernacular criteria for individuality. Although there is certainly some fuzziness on each criterion for species, as we have already noted, the same is true for organisms. Species also meet the criteria necessary to operate as Darwinian individuals, since they reproduce (that is, spawn other species); their offspring inherit many of their attributes; and species vary from one another in ways that affect their long-term survival, and thus serve as units on which selection can operate.

Gould does not make an argument for species selection in the old functionalist sense, where individual organisms are seen as having characteristics for the good of the species. Rather, he argues that species have emergent characteristics and fitness that are separate from those of the individual organisms that make up species, just as organisms are more than merely the summation of their genetic characteristics.[24] These species-level characteristics will affect the survival of species through geologic time. For example, species with wide geographic distribution will be less likely to become extinct than species with a restricted distribution because they will be less susceptible to local disturbances (such as volcanic eruptions) that can wipe out local populations.[25] Note that geographic distribution is a characteristic of a species, not an individual organism. Individual organisms in a widely dispersed species may have very restricted geographic ranges. For example, many insect species are spread over large areas, but the individual organisms that make up the species may never travel very far over the course of their lifetimes. In this situation, then, species have emergent features that are not directly derived from the characteristics of individual members.

Similarly, population size is a function of geographic range and population density, which are features that characterize populations, not individual organisms—for example, an individual organism does not have a population density.[26] Species with small populations are, all else being equal, more prone to extinction than species with large populations. Smaller populations have more restricted gene pools, and therefore, all else being equal, they will typically have less absolute genetic diversity to draw on in the course of evolution. Variability within a species is vital for the long-term survival of that species, since it provides more evolutionary options in the face of changing environmental conditions.[27] In addition to the diversity of the gene pool, large absolute numbers convey certain advantages. If, for example, a species has 1,000 members and some event (such as the impact of an asteroid or the spread of a disease) wipes out 99 percent of these individuals, there will be only 10 members left, which would not likely serve as a viable population and could easily be finished off by a secondary minor event (such as a drought). Contrarily, even if 99 percent of individuals in a species with a population of 100 million are killed off, there will still be a million individuals remaining, more than enough to reproduce successfully even in the event of a secondary event. Note that the advantages conveyed by having a large population are not simply due to a characteristic of the individual organisms that compose the species or of any particular gene in the gene pool but are based on the species-level feature of population size. Of course, organism-level characteristics affect population sizes. Large animals, like elephants, tend to have smaller populations than small animals, like mice, because of obvious differences in the amount of biomass they need to consume to survive. However, although population size is *affected* by the characteristics of the organisms (such as mass) that compose the population, it is not entirely *reducible* to these characteristics. Species of large animals are on average more prone to extinction than species of small animals not because the individual organisms that compose them are unfit—elephants and other large animals may be well adapted to their environments—or because they have unfit genes, but rather because of a species-level characteristic, small population size, which, among other things, limits the size of the gene pool.

In articulating his argument, Gould does not frame it as macroevolution versus microevolution. Rather, he proposes that evolutionary theory must be reformulated to incorporate the existence of macroevolution, where distinct forces operate on separate levels. Thus, microevolution and macroevolution are not the same but are "bound together by extensive feedback" due to the nature of emergent systems.[28] Gould indicates that the necessity for this expansion of evolutionary theory is "a contingent fact of the empirical world." A higher order of sorting takes place at the level of species due, in part, to punctuated evolutionary moments, as "species arise (in geological time) with their differences established from the start" which are maintained during the period of stasis. Stressing this point, Gould and C. Bradford Calloway pointed out:

> Evolution works on a hierarchy of levels, and some causes at higher levels are "emergent." These causes must be sought in phenomena—like speciation—that cannot be rendered as an extrapolation of sequential changes in gene frequencies within local populations. This claim that paleontology can have an independent theory (within a unified system of evolutionary thought) is not mere sectarian politics on our part, but a reflection of a world arranged as a hierarchy of levels, not entirely as a smooth continuum.[29]

Gould's argument, therefore, is that various forces operate at different levels of aggregation, and one level is not necessarily more important than others. An important implication of the hierarchical theory of selection is that these diverse forces operating at distinct levels may reinforce, counteract, or simply be orthogonal to one another. Gould illustrates this point by considering interdemic selection.[30] If, for example, a deme (group) of organisms within a species has members that behave altruistically—that is to say, some individuals take actions that reduce their own likelihood of reproductive success but increase the success of the group as a whole—that deme will have a competitive advantage over other demes, and, therefore, interdemic selection will favor demes with some altruistic members. However, within demes, individuals who behave altruistically—at the expense of their own reproductive success—will be selected against and will, therefore, decline in frequency within the group, making it unlikely for demes to contain altruistic members.[31] This straightforward example illustrates that a characteristic (altruism, in this case) has different (contradictory, in this case) consequences for selection at different levels of aggregation. Some characteristics will, of course, have similar consequences for selection at different hierarchical levels and are therefore particularly likely to be perpetuated.

The hyper-reductionist view, advocated by Dawkins, Daniel Dennett, and others, that tries to limit all evolutionary explanation to the lowest level, the gene, is based on an error of reasoning that Gould refers to as the "fallacy of the selfish gene" stemming from the confusion of bookkeeping with causality.[32] An important distinction that sheds light on the problem with gene selectionism is that between replicators and interactors—a distinction recognized but not properly appreciated by George Williams, one of the founders of gene selectionism, Dawkins, and other gene-centric theorists.[33] In *The Selfish Gene*, Dawkins justifies his focus on genes with the argument that they are the transmitters of evolutionary information, the replicators that provide the continuity across generations. Gould does not disagree that genes are the units of replication that make evolution possible. However, following other scholars, such as David Hull, Gould argues that interactors, not replicators, are the units of selection, and therefore interactors are the sites of causal explanation.[34] An interactor is an entity that interacts with its environment so that differential replication is possible. Genes for the most part interact with the environment through other entities, organisms and species being of particular interest here, and it is the outcome of these interactions that leads to selection and evolutionary change (or stasis).

As Gould and others have pointed out, it is interactors, not replicators per se, that mate, live, and die. Thus it is interactors that are selected for or against by the environment. Genes, the replicators, merely record the outcome of these interactions.[35] Thus focusing on the genes themselves confuses bookkeeping with causality. As Gould writes:

> Changes recorded at the genetic level do play a fundamental part in characterizing evolution, and records of these changes (bookkeeping) do maintain an important role in evolutionary theory. But the error [of gene selectionism] remains: bookkeeping is not causality; natural selection is a causal process, and units or agents of selection must be defined as overt actors in the mechanism, not merely as preferred items for tabulating results.[36]

THE IMPORTANCE OF EMERGENCE

The world is complex and composed of emergent levels of organization. Too often in attempts to understand the ways of nature, such as with the application of the Cartesian method, we divide the world into pieces, assuming the isolated parts explain the whole. Although useful for many investigative purposes, such reductionism is not able to capture emergent properties and higher levels of organization. Gould sought to challenge the narrow reductionism present in the modern synthesis and other arguments focused solely on gene-centric selection. He proposed that evolutionary action takes place on multiple levels. Whether the hierarchical theory of evolutionary selection proves to be especially important within the larger body of evolutionary theory remains to be seen. But regardless of the ultimate assessment of the hierarchical theory, Gould made well-reasoned arguments about the limitations of reductionism and the importance of emergence. It is clear that, as Gould argued, the level of causation is not necessarily the same as where change is recorded. This error is evident throughout both the natural and social sciences. Just as with many branches of the natural sciences, economics, psychology, and sociology are often guilty of confusing bookkeeping with causality. Social changes are often "recorded" in transformations in the beliefs and behaviors of individual people, but that does not necessarily mean that causal processes operate at the level of the individual person alone, in the absence of higher levels of organization. Sociologists in general argue that society is more than the aggregation of individuals, and therefore sociology is not reducible to psychology. This point is even relevant within disciplines, as assessing the consequence of a factor at one level of aggregation does not necessarily allow for the inference that the factor has the same consequences at other levels of aggregation. Furthermore, no one level of aggregation is necessarily a more appropriate level of analysis than any other (depending on the specific nature of the research, of course). Gould's argument for hierarchical causation—having much in common with other fields of inquiry that study complex systems—presents a number of insights for investigations of the complex, multifaceted world. Given the richness of the world and its history, it is important not to limit our potential conceptualizations of emergent systems.

PART TWO

Science and Humanity

CHAPTER FIVE

Debunking as Positive Science

Physicist Alan Sokal laid a trap for postmodernists and anti-science scholars on the academic left when he submitted his article, "Transgressing the Boundaries: Toward a Transformative Hermeneutics of Quantum Gravity," to *Social Text*, a left-leaning cultural studies journal. The trap sprang when the journal unwittingly published the article in its 1996 spring/summer issue. The article was intended to parody the type of scholarship that had become common in some sectors of the academy, which substitutes wordplay and sophistry for reason and evidence. Sokal purposefully included in his article a variety of false statements, illogical arguments, incomprehensible sentences, and absurd assertions, including the claim that there was in effect no real world and all of science was merely a social construction. He submitted the article to test whether the editors of *Social Texts* had any serious intellectual standards. They failed the test, and the scandal that ensued has become legend.[1]

It is sad to say, but nonetheless true, that some scholars on the academic left have renounced materialism and strayed into a postmodern wonderland in which there is no objective reality and any one factual claim is as good as the next. Such scholars deserve the criticism to which they have been subjected, and one cannot blame Sokal, a leftist himself who taught mathematics at the National University of Nicaragua under the Sandinista government, for exposing them as intellectual frauds. However, one of the misconceptions that has emerged out of the Sokal affair is that the left is dominated by anti-intellectualism, and by implication, that the right is the defender of reason. Nothing could be further from the truth. Although some on the left veered toward philosophical idealism as the twentieth century unfolded, materialism has been maintained and advanced by many radical intellectuals, including Rachel Carson, Noam Chomsky, Albert Einstein, Stephen Jay Gould, Richard Levins, Richard Lewontin, Barbara Ehrenreich, and Bertrand Russell— just to name just a few prominent scholars. It is, therefore, a sad irony that the left has been identified as having anti-scientific leanings. The right, to a large extent, is based on an anti-scientific foundation. This is most apparent in the silliness peddled by Christian fundamentalists, such as the oxymoronically named "creation science" and its progeny, "intelligent design."[2] It is also evident—and unfortunately influential— in right-wing denial of anthropogenic climate change. Conservative ideology has long focused on mystical and obscurantist doctrines that deny materialism and reason.

In the finest intellectual traditions of the Enlightenment, Gould, nearly three decades ago, published the first edition of his landmark book, *The Mismeasure of Man*.[3] More than in any other of his books, in *Mismeasure of Man* Gould demonstrates his commitment to scientific analysis in the public interest and his philosophy of how intellectuals should engage scientific debates. For this reason, *Mismeasure of Man* deserves a particularly close look. In it Gould provides a devastating critique of the right-wing (pseudo) science of classifying individuals on a one-dimensional scale of supposed inherent intellectual worth. Ironically, the revised edition of this work was published the same year as Sokal's article in *Social Text*, and, with additional essays criticizing Richard Herrnstein and Charles Murray's *The Bell Curve*, demonstrated the presence of a critical science committed to realism, objectivity, and reason, which countered rightist ideology thinly disguised as science.

The power of Gould's analysis lies in his focus on particulars. Rather than attempt a grand critique of all "scientific" efforts aimed at justifying social inequalities, Gould performs a well-reasoned assessment of the errors underlying a specific set of theories and empirical claims. As Gould writes in the introduction to the revised edition, "*The Mismeasure of Man* treats *one particular form* of *quantified* claim about the ranking of human groups: the argument that intelligence can be meaningfully abstracted as a single number capable of ranking all people on a linear scale of intrinsic and unalterable mental worth"; it "is a critique of a *specific* theory of intelligence often supported by *particular* interpretation of a *certain* style of mental testing: the theory of unitary, genetically based, unchangeable intelligence."[4] This approach is emblematic of Gould's style: He does not attempt to tackle the great questions head-on in an abstract and general way, but instead sneaks up on these questions by a careful analysis of the details of particular cases—here examining the work of the historical originators of this form of biological determinism.

His tight focus makes his critique all the more devastating, leaving the research tradition behind such works as *The Bell Curve*, which contended that social class positions were a reflection of innate differences between people as assessed by IQ scores, in shambles. In the process of critique, he also illustrates the power of leftist science properly applied. He does not start by denying factual claims because of a distaste for their political implications. Rather, recognizing that factual claims must be tackled based on reason and evidence, not ideology, he undertakes an analysis of the reasoning underlying specific claims about the nature of human inequality and the evidence used to support such claims. In this way, he allows the insights of the critical tradition to alert him to instances of ruling-class ideology embedded in scientific theories, but he does not expect left ideology to dictate the answers to empirical questions. Gould recognizes that our ideological commitments and intellectual allegiances alert us to questions that need to be asked, but they do not provide the answers to these questions. Only reasoned analysis can do that.

Here we focus on some of the key lessons of *Mismeasure of Man* about how the ideas of the ruling elite become embedded in scientific theories, which are then used to legitimate prevailing social inequalities, and how to look for the telltale signs of the dogma of the dominant class in supposedly objective research. We follow Gould's own style in focusing on the particulars of his arguments, from which we, like he, develop general lessons about the sciences and social justice. Of course, the most blatant manner in which the powerful sculpt research findings to conform to their ideology is by the purposeful fabrication of data or dishonest presentation or suppression of research results, tasks made all the easier by the fact that a substantial share of all scientific research is done by people from socially privileged backgrounds or by people supported by corporations or other elite interests. The pernicious influence of the powerful on scientific inquiry was particularly blatant during the presidency of George W. Bush in the United States, where the administration altered reports on scientific findings by government researchers, notably those working on global climate change, and attempted to intimidate other scholars into silence.[5] However, while the flagrant distortion of scientific knowledge by the Bush administration is particularly noteworthy for its prominence, there are many other subtle ways that science is manipulated that can have an even more insidious effect. As Gould shows, the noxious influence of reactionary ideology permeates work in a number of ways.

Before delving into the ways in which science is distorted by ideology, it is important to note that although blatant academic dishonesty is presumably uncommon, one of the foundational studies used to support the claim that intelligence is highly heritable and that the social environment has little influence on the abilities of individuals is based on manufactured data. Gould retells the widely known story of Sir Cyril Burt (1883–1971), an influential British educational psychologist who reported analyses of the IQ of fifty-three pairs of identical twins separated at birth and reared apart. His analyses found a high correlation between the IQ scores of the twins, and this provided the basis for his widely touted claim that IQ was not much influenced by the environment. Arthur Jensen, an educational psychologist, in his notorious 1969 article in the *Harvard Educational Review*, used Burt's analyses to support his argument that differences in intelligence between whites and blacks in the United States were innate and ineradicable. As the investigations by Princeton psychologist Leon Kamin and the medical correspondent for the London *Sunday Times*, Oliver Gillie, revealed in the 1970s, Burt not only fabricated his data, he manufactured two "collaborators."[6]

Of course, purposeful dishonesty is the most obvious way to manipulate research to support a political agenda. More interesting, and presumably more common, are distortions that emerge from the unconscious bias of researchers. These are the types of biases to which we are all subject, since none of us can fully remove ourselves from our social context and see the world from a God's eye view. However, although all researchers, including the most honest and progressive, are subject to unconscious biases, this type of manipulation of research findings often serves to perpetuate the ideology of the ruling class because research is so frequently conducted by scientists who come from, are funded by, or otherwise pander to the social elite. An interesting example of such bias that Gould examines in detail comes from Samuel George Morton, a nineteenth-century practitioner of craniometry—the specialty that focuses on measuring human skulls. Morton claimed that his study of differences across race in cranial capacity showed that whites have larger brains than people of other races, particularly those of African ancestry. This naturally fit well with the view that whites were ordained to rule over other races and served to justify slavery and other institutions of racial inequality.

Gould, recognizing the potential for unconscious bias in the analysis of data and the importance of rational scrutiny of scientific findings, did not take Morton's reported statistics at face value, but rather chose to reanalyze the raw data (which Morton faithfully published) himself. Gould notes: "Morton's [statistical] summaries are a patchwork of fudging and finagling in the clear interest of controlling a priori convictions. Yet—and this is the most intriguing aspect of the case—I find no evidence of conscious fraud; indeed, had Morton been a conscious fudger, he would not have published his data so openly."[7] In brief, Gould found Morton's distortions fell into four general categories. First, "Morton often chose to include or delete large subsamples [within racial groups] in order to match group averages with prior expectations."[8] That is to say, the data to be analyzed was influenced by his prior biases rather than strict rational criteria. This is an important point, because it shows that how scientists select and organize data can have a profound effect on research findings. Second, Morton would measure cranial volume by filling skulls with seed, and then pouring out the seed and measuring its volume. Seed, however, can be packed to differing densities, so that measurement has a subjective element—that is, the measurer (Morton in this case) decides when a skull is full and the seed is packed to the "correct" density. Subsequent re-measurement of the same skulls Morton measured using lead shot, which cannot be packed, instead of seed showed Morton systematically underestimated the volumes of the skulls of non-whites relative to those of whites.

Third, Morton failed to perform what would seem to be obvious procedural corrections for differences in sex or stature across samples. Brain size is most meaningful not in an absolute sense, but relative to body size—that is, people with large bodies have, on average, large brains relative to people with small bodies, although intellectual abilities do not appear to be related to body size. Controlling for gender is highly important because women have, on average, smaller bodies than men and, therefore, smaller brains (although no smaller relative to body size). Morton never controlled for differences in gender composition or average stature across samples, and thus his findings of differences in cranial size across racial groups reflect to a large extent differences in gender composition and body size across groups in his sample. For example, "Morton used an all-female sample of three Hottentots to support the stupidity of blacks, and an all-male sample of Englishmen to assert the superiority of whites."[9]

Fourth, Gould found that in all the instances of miscalculations and apparently accidental omissions made by Morton, the results favored the inflation of cranial size estimates for whites and the deflation of cranial size estimates for non-whites. Gould, once again, found no evidence of purposeful fraud: "All I can discern is an a priori conviction about racial ranking so powerful that it directed his tabulations along preestablished lines."[10] Gould's careful reanalysis of the original data provides powerful evidence of how scientists can sculpt data to fit their a priori convictions without intentionally committing fraud.

In a similar case, Robert Bennett Bean, a Virginia physician following in the craniometric tradition at the beginning of the twentieth century, studied the brains of cadavers. He identified the key indicator of intellectual ability as the ratio of the genu, the front part of the corpus callosum, to the splenium, the back part. Based on his research, he argued that whites were superior to blacks and men to women in intellectual ability based on his finding of relatively larger genu in whites and men. The fact that he focused on this criterion, rather than the more traditional brain *size* preferred by other craniometrists, is striking. "The reason for this neglect [of brain size]," Gould explains, "lies buried in an addendum: black and white brains did not differ in overall size" in the data he collected.[11] Thus Bean sought an alternative avenue for explaining inequalities.

Bean also made measurement errors reminiscent of those made by Morton. Bean's mentor at Johns Hopkins, Franklin P. Mall, became suspicious of Bean's data because it was simply too good, fitting Bean's expectations so neatly as to be implausible. Mall repeated Bean's work and found quite different results. Unlike Bean, Mall attempted to be more objective by making his measurements of brains *before* he knew the race of the person from which each had come (Bean knew the race of the person from which each brain had come before he measured it). In his study, Mall found no clear difference between the brains of whites and blacks or between those of men and women. Furthermore, he examined 18 brains (10 whites, 8 blacks) from the sample Bean had examined and found that Bean's measure of the genu was larger than his in the case of seven whites, but only one black, and that Bean's measure of the splenium was larger than his for seven out of the eight brains of blacks. Bean's biased expectation had clearly influenced his measurements, thus allowing him to construct a finding of differences between the brains of blacks and whites and men and women where likely none existed.

As reactionary scientists failed to establish valid biophysical explanations for social inequality by measuring skulls both on the outside (using calipers and rulers) and the inside (using mustard seeds and lead shot), they moved into the realm of measuring "the content of brains by intelligence testing."[12] It is here the error that perhaps receives the bulk of Gould's attention is found: *reification*—the process of treating as a real entity something that is in fact an abstract concept. Cyril Burt and current advocates of the notion that intelligence is literally a one-dimensional feature of the brain that is measurable by psychometric tests are guilty of reifying their own construction. They argue that there is a general underlying intellectual ability in each of us, g, that is measured reasonably well by IQ tests, in spite of the evidence suggesting that g is a product of the tests themselves, a statistical creation, not a genuine mental attribute.

In an unflinchingly rational manner, Gould devastates this "IQ as indicator of general intelligence" interpretation by showing it to be a creation of the statistical procedures used and the a priori convictions of the researchers. The general intelligence factor emerges from factor analysis of a variety of mental tests. Factor analysis is a statistical procedure that attempts to explain the covariance (correlation) among variables (various mental tests in this case) by "extracting" one or a few "latent factors" (statistical creations that may or may not represent a factor in the real world) that can account for the observed inter-correlations (individuals' scores on different tests tend to be positively correlated with one another—that is, people who do well on one type of test tend to do well on other types). IQ proponents have long argued that only one factor is necessary to explain observed correlations among a variety of mental tests, which they take to indicate the existence of a general intelligence that is an actual characteristic of the brain. However, as Gould explains, factor analysis does not work magic; it is entirely based on the observed correlations among tests. The belief that a factor extracted via factor analysis is a real entity is based on the assumption that the variables under analysis (perfor-

mance on various mental tests in this case) are connected by an underlying causal regime (stemming from a feature of the brain). This
assumption is not and cannot be established by statistical methods
alone and is only valid to the extent that correlation is indicative of
causation. Although demonstrating correlation among hypothesized
cause and effect is *necessary* for establishing a causal relationship
among variables, it is not *sufficient*. Factor analysis alone cannot adju-
dicate the matter of causality, nor establish whether a factor corresponds with a real entity.

Gould points to the work of psychologist L. L. Thurstone in the
first half of the twentieth century that unveiled the error of equating a
factor extracted via factor analysis with an actual characteristic.
Thurstone showed that the types of mental tests included in the factor
analysis greatly affected the results of the analysis. That is to say, altering the set of mental tests included in factor analysis may change the
factor structure the analysis produces. Furthermore, Thurstone illustrated that a variety of different factor structures could be produced
from the same data depending on the specific statistical method used
in the analysis, so there was no objective reason to prefer the assertion
that a single mental ability underlay performance on a variety of tests
to the assertion that multiple and distinct abilities were the determi-
nants of test performance. It is, of course, also important to recognize
that none of these types of tests and statistical analyses served to establish whether intellectual performance was primarily due to innate
characteristics or was the product of social privilege.

The most general error of the biological determinist research that
Gould reviews centers on the proclivity of scholars to interpret
ambiguous evidence in a manner that confirms their prior convictions. This is a more general error than that represented by the miscalculations of Morton, the fabrications of Burt, and even the reification
of factor analysts. We are faced with a complex world where there is no
single clear and unambiguous piece of evidence that can answer many
of our most pressing questions and resolve our intellectual disputes.
In these circumstances, people are forced to survey a breadth of information and attempt to reach a reasoned conclusion. However, given

the complexity and ambiguity inherent in such circumstances, even well intentioned researchers are prone to searching out evidence that supports their prior beliefs, neglecting evidence that contradicts them, and interpreting ambiguous information in their own favor—a tendency that is often referred to as "confirmation bias."[13] Gould provides several fascinating examples of this phenomenon from the history of biological determinist mental testers.

In particular, there are examples both of the application of ad hoc explanations and special pleading by researchers to maintain their preferred theories when evidence contradicts their expectations and of shifting the data to be examined as theories change so that while the specific grounds on which claims for inequality were based become discredited, the general conclusions remain unchanged—e.g., the dominant class, race, and/or gender are superior to everyone else. The work of Paul Broca, perhaps the most renowned craniometrist, and his followers illustrates well the reliance on ad hoc explanations to preserve a preferred view in the face of contradictory evidence. As Gould explains, Broca made efforts to measure the brains of eminent men after their deaths, expecting that the most renowned men would have brains much larger than average.[14] Although some of these candidates did have large brains, others had merely average-sized brains, and some even had brains strikingly below average. Undeterred, Broca relied on a variety of tactics to explain away "anomalous" findings. For example, where eminent men were found to have average or smaller than average brains, Broca explained away the inconsistency between achievement and brain size by arguing that these men had especially convoluted brains, which he took as an indication of intelligence. In other cases he argued variously that the subjects had died very old and their brains had thus degenerated, the brain was poorly preserved, or the person in question was of small stature and thus had a respectably sized brain for his body. (Of course, none of these types of special pleading were applied to excuse a small or average brain size of a person who Broca had not a priori judged superior.) Perhaps the most peculiar tactic, when all else failed, was to argue that men of great achievements who had small brains must not have been so great after all.

The application of the recapitulationist theory of evolution to assessments of a presumed racial hierarchy provides a striking example of scholars picking and choosing among which pieces of evidence to focus on so as to fit the facts to their preconceived notions. German zoologist Ernst Haeckel, an early convert to Darwinism, but with his own idiosyncratic take on evolutionary theory, developed the position that "ontogeny recapitulates phylogeny"—that is, as individuals develop from an embryo to an adult (ontogeny) they go through all of the stages of adult form from their evolutionary history (phylogeny). This now discredited view was much in vogue at the end of the nineteenth and at the beginning of the twentieth centuries. The theory assumed there was a progressive nature to evolution, where "advances" were made by speeding up early stages of development and adding on new stages. Based on this view, adults of less "advanced" races were expected to be similar to children of more "advanced" races. For example, E. D. Cope, a well-known American paleontologist and supporter of this view, identified four inferior groups: women, non-whites, whites of lower social class, and southern European whites. Supporters of this position claimed a variety of anatomical and physiological characteristics that marked the adults of these supposedly inferior groups as being like upper-class white male children of northern European ancestry.

The theory of recapitulation collapsed by the end of the second decade of the twentieth century. Following this, the Dutch anatomist Louis Bolk developed a theory of exactly the opposite view of development. He proposed that humans had diverged from apes not by speeding up developmental processes, but slowing them down, so that juvenile traits of ancestors become the adult traits of descendants—a phenomenon referred to as neoteny, or "holding on to youth."[15] He noted that adult humans have many features in common with juvenile apes, including a large brain relative to body size. Thus, after decades of supposedly objective scientific work had proclaimed that "inferior" groups such as non-whites were childlike, this new theory implied that the more childlike a group was, the more advanced in mind it was. At this point, Gould explains,

Bolk reached into his anatomical grab-bag and extracted some traits indicating a greater departure for black adults from the advantageous proportions of childhood. Led by these new facts to an old and comfortable conclusion, Bolk proclaimed . . . : "The white race appears to be the most progressive, as being the most retarded."[16]

Here we see most clearly the smoking gun of ideology imposed on the world. When theory suggested that being childlike was a mark of inferiority, oppressed groups of people were identified as being childlike based on supposedly objective analysis. However, when a new theory emerged that suggested that being childlike indicated superiority, new data were found to support the contention that the dominant social group was the most childlike.

It is fascinating that among the many efforts to establish inherent differences across race, gender, and class in mental ability, the indicators of intellectual ability that have been utilized were never established to actually measure an innate and immutable intellectual ability. As Gould points out, not only has it still to this day not been firmly established that races systematically differ in average cranial size, there is little evidence that cranial size is even especially related to intelligence within a species, with the exception of extreme cases where the brain fails to develop properly. The degree to which IQ measures an innate ability remains highly contested, and the extent to which it is heritable is still not firmly established. As Gould's close colleague Richard Lewontin points out in *Biology as Ideology*, all existing studies of twins reared apart have methodological flaws that undermine their conclusions; for example, separated twins are often raised by close relatives, so that twin pairs frequently share similar socioeconomic and cultural circumstances. It is remarkable, then, that the base assumptions behind much of biologically deterministic research—cranial size corresponds to intellectual ability, IQ measures a real and innate property of mind—go unquestioned and are merely asserted as true without sufficient supporting evidence.

What is remarkable about *Mismeasure of Man* is that it provided a definitive critique of the reasoning behind *The Bell Curve* thirteen years before the latter was published. As Gould remarked, "The critique of biological determinism [is] both timeless and timely," and it is of utmost importance given how biological determinism is used "as a social weapon."[17] The recurrence of biological determinist arguments is a sociopolitical manifestation related to periods of "political retrenchment and destruction of social generosity."[18] The revised edition of *Mismeasure of Man*, published in 1996, extended the original by including essays that explicitly criticize *The Bell Curve*. Gould shows how Herrnstein and Murray committed virtually all of the same errors of reasoning committed by earlier biological determinists. As Gould explains with razor sharpness, Herrnstein and Murray accept without thoughtful reflection that IQ tests measure a singular, one-dimensional intelligence that is highly heritable and largely immutable, although the balance of existing evidence does not support this view. They then march ahead, with this dubious presumption unquestioned, to argue that IQ is a key factor determining where individuals end up in society, that IQ varies across social classes due strictly to merit-driven stratification, that blacks are typically on the lower rungs of society because they have on average lower IQs than whites and other races, and that all of these "facts" taken together indicate that social programs aimed at improving the lot of the poor are a waste of effort, since the poor occupy their social position due to their inherently inferior intellects. All of these dubious claims are established by a highly selective reading of existing evidence, where findings suggesting interpretations counter to their own—e.g., IQ is influenced by social position, therefore lower IQs among the underprivileged are the *effect*, not the cause, of inequality—are ignored, by wild speculation in the absence of appropriate evidence, and by reifying IQ in the same unthinking manner as their biological determinist predecessors.[19]

It would be hard for any sensible person after seriously considering Gould's critique, even if she or he is unsympathetic to the left, to accept *The Bell Curve* as representing anything but a politically motivated effort to interpret ambiguous evidence so as to support an a priori preferred position, in spite of the fact that much of the evidence cries out for an opposite interpretation. *The Bell Curve* is perhaps one of the best examples in recent times of right-wing ideology dishonestly presented as objective science. As Gould recognized, eternal vigilance and scientific investigation are necessary to disarm the ruling class of their ideological weapons and scupper their attempts to justify social inequality.

One of the most important lessons we can learn from Gould is that we should neither reject the ideal of seeking objective knowledge of the world nor assume that scientists operate in an objective manner, conveying the truths of nature unsullied by social preconceptions. Although none of us can be truly objective, we can strive toward this ideal by recognizing our own preconceptions and engaging in thoughtful, reflexive self-critique. In this, we become embedded in a process of confronting the world and our own biases, as well as those of other people. Gould closes the original edition of *Mismeasure of Man* with an argument that debunking can serve as positive science. He notes that debunking is often seen only in a negative sense, as tearing down ideas and claims, not as a positive intellectual activity that builds our understanding of the world. Counter to this view, Gould argues that we can learn a great deal from studying where researchers go wrong, and therefore debunking can help improve our understanding of the world and, particularly, how humans go about trying to understand it. In this, Gould is establishing a perspective that sees the sociology of science as leading to insights that can help refine scientific inquiry, rather than as denying the intellectual foundations of science as postmodernists would have it.

The dialectic of argument and counter-argument is central to the advancement of knowledge. Since the scientific establishment remains dominated by those sympathetic to the concerns of the economic elite, rationally debunking flawed research should be a central part of the left's intellectual agenda. However, radicals should not slip into the anti-intellectualism that Sokal criticized—intellectual dishonesty in service of a just cause is dishonesty nonetheless. The rejection of reason will only serve to undermine the ability of the left to speak truth to power. As Gould recognized, we will be best served by sticking to the intellectual roots established in the Enlightenment and adopted by a long tradition of leftist scholars, Karl Marx among them. In this tradition, the left stands for a commitment to reason and fights the vapid dogma and pernicious ideology endlessly pedaled by the right. Gould's work serves as an example of how the light of reason can lay bare the false claims of those who wish to perpetuate injustice and inequality and can lead us to a better understanding of the material world in which we live and struggle.

CHAPTER SIX

The Critique of Biological Determinism

One of the overarching projects to which Stephen Jay Gould had a serious commitment throughout his life was the critique of biological determinism. His book *The Mismeasure of Man*, discussed in the previous chapter, was his single most prominent contribution to this project, but he took on biological determinism in a variety of manners and venues. Starting in the 1970s he criticized the biological deterministic character of sociobiology, and his engagement with the ideas from sociobiology remained important to much of his work. Gould's efforts to critically assess sociobiology are best understood when considered along with the work of a group of dialectical biologists he was close to who sought to address misapplications of evolutionary theory to society. The critique that they collectively present continues to serve as a basis to challenge biological determinism. At the same time, it illustrates a commitment to humanism that maintains a dedication to the scientific endeavor.

Evolutionary biologist and geneticist, and Gould's colleague and collaborator at Harvard, Richard Lewontin explains how when attempting to describe the natural world, it is almost impossible not to rely on metaphors, given that we are trying to explain phenomena that we often cannot directly perceive or detect. René Descartes's statement that the world is a machine has served as a powerful metaphor for explaining the organization of the natural world. But the danger arises that we risk "confusing the metaphor with the thing of real interest. We cease to see the world *as if* it were *like* a machine and take it to *be* a machine." The very power of some metaphors leads to their reification, influencing the questions that are asked as well as the traits that are assigned to objects or processes. The metaphor that sees nature as a machine encourages a narrow reductionism within science, as can be seen in common assumptions about genetic determinism. Even the term "*development* is a metaphor that carries with it a prior commitment to the nature of the process" whereby it is assumed that the present state is simply the latent expression of genes—that is, the unfolding of a predetermined order.[1]

Gould's associates Hilary Rose and Steven Rose, a sociologist and a neuroscientist respectively, stress that there has been a "spread of the evolutionary metaphor far outside its biological domains, above all in the repeated attempts to at least tame and limit—and at worst eradicate—the social in theorizing humanity, and thus to biologize the human condition."[2] A crude biological conception of evolution, divorced from what is actually happening within evolutionary science itself, has been constructed as a "universal acid" to dispose of other theories, assuming that biological arguments offer a type of certainty for the state of the world.[3]

Richard Lewontin and Richard Levins point out that "with the waning of religion as the chief source of legitimation of the social order, natural science has become the font of explanation and justification for the inevitability of the social relations in which we are immersed. Biology . . . plays a central role in creating an ideology of the inevitability of the structure of society."[4] The basic operation of the capitalist world system generates vast social inequalities in wealth and power, yet the "ideology of equality" remains fundamental to "bourgeois social theory." Here biological and genetic determinism help justify the status quo, suggesting that social inequalities are merely "the consequence of unequal distributions of temperament, skill, and cognitive power, manifestations of genetically determined differences between individuals, races and sexes." They critically note that this explanation is often combined with a story that invokes natural selection in order to naturalize social relations and particular behaviors. As a result, it is then proposed that social change goes against the inherent order of the world.

Biological justifications for social inequality are a mainstay of supporters of sociobiology and its descendant evolutionary psychology, which represents sociobiology applied specifically to humans. For example, in the same year he published his influential book *Sociobiology* (1975), the Harvard biologist Edward O. Wilson argued for a biological predisposition for the gendered division of labor:

> In hunter-gatherer societies, men hunt and women stay at home. This strong bias persists in most agricultural and industrial societies and, on that ground alone, appears to have a genetic origin.... My own guess is that the genetic bias is intense enough to cause a substantial division of labor even in the most free and most egalitarian of future societies.... Even with identical education and equal access to all professions, men are likely to continue to play a disproportionate role in political life, business and science.[5]

Such essentialist views are hardly new even if arrayed in fashionable clothing. The argument that social inequalities are a reflection of an immutable natural order pre-dates the formalization of sociobiology in the latter part of the twentieth century. Similar conceptions were employed to justify imperialism and slavery, since the emergence of the capitalist world system. The particular form and character of the biological argument has changed, depending on the state of biological knowledge and the specific social relations within society. Nevertheless, as Gould emphasizes, "biological determinism" is used "as a social weapon—for 'others' will be thereby demeaned, and their lower socioeconomic status validated as a scientific consequence of their innate ineptitude rather than society's unfair choices."[6] Biological explanations are invoked as justification of social inequality, whether between classes, sexes, or ethnic groups, veiling the long history of social inequalities that contribute to contemporary social relations and differences between groups of people.

Gould insightfully recognized:

> The reasons for recurrence are sociopolitical, and not far to seek: resurgences of biological determinism correlate with episodes of political retrenchment, particularly with campaigns for reduced government spending on social programs, or at times of fear among ruling elites, when disadvantaged groups sow serious social unrest or even threaten to usurp power. What argument against social change could be more chillingly effective than the claim that established orders, with some groups on top and others at the bottom, exist as an accurate reflection of the innate and unchangeable intellectual capacities of people so ranked?[7]

It is not a surprise that those in power invoke crude biological arguments as a justification of social inequality and that this invocation receives considerable public attention, helping shape the dominant ideology.

The persistence of biological determinism did not shock Gould, but it did capture his ire. As part of his commitment to science and humanism, he devoted himself (along with many of his aforementioned colleagues) to a critique of sociobiology and its descendant evolutionary psychology. In particular, this critique illuminated two conceptual errors within sociobiology: an adherence to narrow reductionism and the uncritical acceptance of functionalist, hyper-adaptationist assumptions of cruder versions of the neo-Darwinian program.[8] Here the biological basis of human societies and the fundamental truths of Darwinism were not being denied. Instead, Gould and other critics sought a more sophisticated understanding of the interactions between the biological and sociological, as well as the processes within biological systems.

Both the natural and social sciences are founded on a critique of natural theology, which helped open up the world to social inquiry and materialist explanations.[9] Concerns with organization—whether it was zoological taxonomy, the ontogenetic development of animals, or social communities—characterize scientific research. The borders between disciplines have always been tenuous at best. Interactions between the realms of study are a long-standing and important practice that helps to further understanding of the world. Insights from other fields of study only become more important once we accept that humans are both social and biological creatures, influenced by forces from each realm through a complex set of relationships. Thus interdisciplinary work holds much promise for enhancing our ability to comprehend the processes and relationships that bind social and natural history. In contrast to the sociobiology tradition, Gould and his colleagues offer a dialectical approach for assessing the connections between biology and culture, and at the same time highlight the dynamic nature of biological relations.

It is important to recognize that the sociobiology tradition has developed over time, in part due to various challenges that it has confronted within the scientific community. At the same time, it is necessary to situate the general perspective of this tradition. In his book *Sociobiology*, Wilson proposes that "the organism does not live for itself." Instead, "it reproduces genes, and it serves as their temporary carrier." With information regarding "the behavioral constraints imposed by the genetic constitution of the species," it is possible, he contends, "to predict features of social organization." As a result, "each phenomenon is weighed for its adaptive significance and then related to the basic principles of population genetics." His argument employs the development metaphor, which portrays genes as an innate plan inscribed inside a body that unfolds to determine both human being and social organization. Wilson asserts that the social sciences and humanities "are the last branches of biology waiting to be included in the Modern Synthesis."[10] Here he asserts "total knowledge" can be found by driving "right down to the levels of the neurons and the gene. When we have progressed enough to explain ourselves [*Homo sapiens*] in these mechanistic terms, the social sciences come to full flower."[11] More recently, Wilson has explicitly called for the social sciences to be subordinated to the biological sciences.[12]

Early work in sociobiology, when aimed at analyzing humans, claimed that every social manifestation imaginable (such as conformity, male dominance, xenophobia, entrepreneurism) was an adaptation.[13] Here it is assumed that specific behaviors exist because they have proved to be evolutionarily successful and they are established in the genetic makeup. This early incarnation of sociobiology was more prone than recent versions to claiming that behavioral differences across human cultures could be explained by cross-cultural genetic variation.[14] In its crudest versions, as represented by the 1994 book *The Bell Curve*, it was asserted that class positions were simply a reflection of innate differences that could be explained by individual-level genetic differences.[15]

Evolutionary psychology has abandoned some of the discredited and/or unsubstantiated claims made in earlier sociobiological work. It seeks to establish cultural universals—that is, characteristics shared by all humans. It also attempts to recognize the importance of contextual factors in determining the ultimate expression of genetic traits, such as the concern with "norms of reaction," which we will discuss further below. This partial reorientation, which has in part come about due to the influence of critiques, has led to more nuanced work that addresses such varied issues as parental investment, family structure, sexuality, morals, values, altruism, aggression, sexual domination, socioeconomic position, friendships, and social capital.[16]

Evolutionary psychology has become a prominent realm of study within sociobiology, with its specific, stated focus to study "universal human nature, which is a collection of domain-specific evolved psychological mechanisms."[17] Evolutionary psychologists link behavioral patterns to genes, based on the argument that natural selection has shaped psychological mechanisms. They also assert that cognitive tools arose in response to specific selection pressures, giving them particular forms and rules of operation.[18] More specifically:

> An *evolved psychological mechanism* is an information-processing procedure or decision rule with which evolution by natural and sexual selection has equipped humans in order to solve a particular adaptive prob-

lem (a problem of survival or reproduction). . . . Adaptive problems during the course of human evolutionary history are expected to have led to the evolution of the brain. . . . Individuals who possess certain psychological mechanisms live longer (because the psychological mechanisms help them survive) and reproduce more successfully (because the psychological mechanisms help them find mates). Those with particularly adaptative psychological mechanisms out-reproduce those without them in each generation, and more and more individuals come to possess the selected psychological mechanisms over generational time. Eventually, all individuals come to possess them, and they become part of universal human nature. Evolved psychological mechanisms are thought to engender desires, values, preferences, emotions, and other internal states that serve as proximate causes of behavior.[19]

These psychological mechanisms are assumed to operate primarily behind conscious thinking. Successfully solving particular adaptive problems eventually allows for universal traits to characterize human nature. (It is interesting to note that the proposed universal in regard to humans in evolutionary psychology is rather peculiar, given that much of what is published is actually focused on determining so-called "innate, evolved sex differences" between men and women.)[20]

Evolutionary psychologists explain that there is nothing special about *Homo sapiens*, because they are "just like other animals" and "there is nothing special about the brain as a human body part."[21] It is proposed that the human brain, like the rest of the human body, was shaped "to perform certain tasks." Leda Cosmides and John Tooby, two prominent evolutionary psychologists, elaborate on this point:

> The brain can process information because it contains complex neural circuits that are functionally organized. The only component of the evolutionary process that can build complex structures that are functionally organized is natural selection. . . . Cognitive scientists need to recognize that while not everything in the design of organisms is the product of selection, all complex functional organization is.[22]

Thus the brain has specific devices for forming social contracts, engaging in mate selection, acquiring language, and so on.

Importantly, Joanne Savage and Satoshi Kanazawa indicate that the shape and functions of the brain have not changed much in 10,000 years, since the end of the Pleistocene epoch, which is the environment for which humans are properly adapted. Given that human psychological mechanisms were adapted to a life in a past environment, it cannot be expected that they always produce evolutionary optimal behaviors in the contemporary world due to how radically different the environment is today.[23] Evolutionary psychologists employ psychological mechanisms to explain organized human behavior, but at the same time provide an out, in that they claim that our distance from our ancestral past and the different environment in which we live explains deviations from "rational" behavior.[24]

Underlying this perspective is a commitment to genetic determinism—sometimes it takes a strong form, other times a weak form. Although it is important to recognize that evolutionary psychology is not a monolithic, unified perspective, it is necessary to highlight the specific aspects of this work that have raised concerns among critics, especially as they relate to biological science itself and its application to other realms.

Too often sociobiology, or evolutionary psychology, is presented as the natural nexus between the biological and social sciences (or the logical appendage of a unified field of biology), as if there are no other alternative conceptualizations. Or it is asserted that the failure to embrace sociobiology is due to "ignorance of evolutionary biology" and "bioilliteracy." Certainly the social sciences, humanities, and the public have a great deal to learn from the natural sciences. But biology, like other sciences, is filled with debate. Furthermore, the most important critiques of sociobiology have emerged from within the biological sciences.

It is important to point out that all participants in these debates, both those critical of and those supportive of sociobiology, profess their belief that genes and culture both play a role in determining human behavior. In a review of Charles J. Lumsden and Wilson's book on sociobiology, *Promethean Fire* (1981), Gould writes:

Every scientist, indeed every intelligent person, knows that human social behavior is a complex and indivisible mix of biological and social influences. The issue is not *whether* nature or nurture determines human behavior, for these factors are truly inextricable, but the degree, intensity, and nature of the constraints exerted by biology upon the possible forms of social organization.

No one doubts that biological universals exist. We must sleep, eat, and grow older, and we are not about to give up procreation; almost all our social institutions are influenced by these imperatives. Therefore, the simple listing of imperatives by Lumsden and Wilson, and the specification of the epigenetic rules they establish, is . . . no vindication of sociobiology. We must ask instead how shaping and constraining are the universals that can be specified? The answer, at least from the list provided by Lumsden and Wilson [which Gould lists as: "avoidance of brother-sister incest; learning of color vocabularies; preference of infants for objects . . . corresponding to the abstract form of a human face . . . ; the universality of certain facial expressions; preference of newborns for sugar over plain water and for sugars in descending order of sucrose, fructose, lactose, and glucose; anxiety of very young children in the presence of strangers; and phobias, particularly those that respond to ancient dangers (like snakes, running water, and thunderstorms)"], is not very much at all. I therefore find this particular invocation of genetics as a determinant of social behavior both trivial and uncontroversial.[25]

Lewontin, Steven Rose, and Leon Kamin make a similar point, also pointing out that the problems with the sociobiology tradition are not simply associated with application to human societies. They stress that what sociobiology

has to say about human society is more wrong than what it says about other aspects of biology because its simplifications and misstatements are the more gross. But this is not because it has developed a theory applicable only to nonhuman animals; the method and theory are fundamentally flawed whether applied to the United States or Britain today, or to a population of savanna-dwelling baboons or Siamese fighting fish.

> There is no mystical and unbridgeable gulf between the forces that
> shape human society and those that shape the societies of other organisms;
> biology is indeed relevant to the human condition. . . . Humanity cannot be
> cut adrift from its own biology, but neither is it enchained by it.[26]

The most important criticisms of sociobiology, then, are not based on claims regarding the irrelevance of biology to the social sciences or on inaccurately characterizing sociobiologists as denying the importance of human culture. Rather, the focus is on the broader conceptual errors underlying the tradition. As Gould makes particularly clear in the quote above, in its watered down form sociobiology is uncontroversial, making claims that are trivially true. This tendency is apparent in an article by Richard Machalek and Michael W. Martin, where each of their claims—about evolved learning adaptations in humans, existence of human instincts, a norm of reaction in relation to sociocultural heterogeneity, "degrees of flexibility [in social behavior] probably designed to maximize the fitness-enhancing value of the adaptation in variable environments," gene-culture coevolution, and the maximization principle for human behavior—of what sociobiology has to offer sociology appear of minor importance and are sufficiently vague so as to be indemonstrably either true or false.[27] Perhaps the only seriously controversial point on this list is the sixth and last one about the "maximization principle," but even this point is a basic assumption of the rational actor paradigm that has long been part of the social sciences and capitalist ideology. Even in this article, social forces still provide the dominant influence on human societies.

Natural scientists, such as Gould, Lewontin, Levins, Steven Rose, Niles Eldredge, and others, ground their critique of sociobiology in the biological sciences. As noted above, two of the most prominent conceptual errors of sociobiology and evolutionary psychology include an adherence to a narrow reductionism and overextended adaptationism. Consideration of these errors becomes all the more important if sociobiology is to be taken in its stronger form (that genes dominate culture), rather than its weaker, uncontroversial form, where it takes the position that humans are evolved biological creatures who depend on the natural world for survival and whose behavior emerges from a complex interaction of social and biological influences. In the weak form, sociobiology is mundane, since few would disagree with these claims.

REDUCTIONISM, DIALECTICS, AND EMERGENCE

Gould argues that just as the anatomical and physiological features of organisms typically require explanations from the realm of biology, rather than physics, most features of societies require socio-historical explanations, rather than biological ones. Although it is true in some sense that sociology is connected to biology through psychology, as biology is connected to quantum physics through chemistry, each field must be understood in its own terms, rather than through a reductionism of one field to another, because new forces emerge from the interaction of components. Certainly there is a causal chain that runs from quantum physics through chemistry, biology, and psychology to sociology. As a materialist, Gould and other scientists accept this and contend that the world must be explained in terms of itself. At the same time, Gould recognized that there are emergent phenomena at each level, which makes each field of study non-reducible to a lower level.

Ernst Mayr, a central figure in the development of the neo-Darwinian modern synthesis in the mid-twentieth century, has long been critical of hyper-reductive tendencies among some traditions in biology. Pointing to the importance of understanding emergent phenomena in their own right, he writes: "Systems almost always have the peculiarity that the characteristics of the whole cannot (not even in theory) be deduced from the most complete knowledge of the components, taken separately or in other partial combinations."[28] Mayr has strongly argued for the independence of biology from the physical sciences, recognizing that though biological phenomena are ultimately emergent from the laws of physics and chemistry, biology cannot be usefully subsumed by the physical sciences.[29] Few biologists accept that biology should be subsumed by physics and chemistry, even though, of course, it cannot contradict physical laws. Likewise, although biology can help further our understanding of some of the workings of societies, it can no more replace social explanations of social phenomena than physics can replace biological explanations of biological phenomena.

Although reductionism is a powerful scientific approach for gaining knowledge of the world, in which the properties of a complex whole are explained in terms of the pieces that compose it, a narrow reductionism fails to appreciate the dialectical interaction between the whole and its parts as well as the emergent properties created by the totality.[30] For instance, even if we knew everything there is to know about hydrogen and oxygen, we could not predict the behavior of water from the properties of these two elements. Water must be understood in its own right, and its properties cannot be discerned by reducing analysis to the individual atoms that compose it. The point is, as Gould indicates, that "knowing the properties of each part as a separate entity . . . won't give you a full explanation of the higher level in terms of these lower-level parts because, in constructing the higher-level items, these parts combine and interact. Thus one must also include these interactions as essential aspects of an act."[31]

Biology, chemistry, and physics cannot be collapsed into a single field without sacrificing explanatory power and an understanding of emergent properties at various levels. The same is true in the social sciences; sociology cannot be reduced to psychology or biology. Steven Rose insightfully points out, "A commitment to a belief in the ontological unity of the biological and social dimensions of our world never reduces the social to the biological, never privileges one type of explanation over another, but continues to search for ways of learning the translation rules between the two languages."[32] Disciplines can and must inform each other, and the relationship between the levels must be investigated. We do not oppose such efforts—indeed, we encourage them—but the application of a narrow reductionism, where one discipline is subsumed under another, in a form of disciplinary imperialism as proposed by Wilson, will likely hinder our scientific understanding of the world.[33]

The sociobiology position continues to develop, attempting to redefine itself in response to critics. Part of this refinement has been to invoke a "norm of reaction" argument, to highlight how environmental influences can create variation in the expression of the same group of genes.[34] Nonetheless, a reductionism pervades the perspective. Following Richard Dawkins, some sociobiologists point out that genes "do three things: (1) replicate; (2) direct the synthesis of protein; and (3) regulate the activity of other genes."[35] In this account, genes specify and direct the phenotypic traits of an organism. Genetic influence on behavior is indirect in the sense that it prescribes "the design properties of cells, tissues, organs, and organ systems," and through this role it influences behavior. It is recognized, wisely, that organisms develop as a result of both genetic and environmental influence, otherwise known as epigenesis.

However, though sociobiologists, when it is convenient, take the position that culture dominates genes, the importance of genes in explaining social behavior remains an underlying point. It is commonly argued that variability in a trait can be broken down into the percentage due to heredity and the percentage due to the environment.[36] Gould explains that it is in these cases that "the errors of reductionism and biodeterminism take over."[37] If the influence of interactionism is taken seriously, it does not permit such arguments. "The adult being," he indicates, "is an emergent entity who must be understood at his own level and in his own totality."[38] Emergent properties make narrow reductionism inappropriate to the study of the world—whether it is the social or natural world. A holistic account of the world demands a dialectical conception, as Levins and Lewontin explain: "Contradiction is not only epistemic and political, but ontological in the broadest sense. Contradictions between forces are everywhere in nature, not only in human social institutions."[39] Thus it is important to recognize that reductionism can illuminate certain relationships, but this approach must be transcended in order to grapple with emergent properties and tendencies throughout the material world.

Counter to what many sociobiologists seem to think, the "norm of reaction" does not strengthen their position.[40] Instead it points to the profound limitations of their perspective. If properly understood, the fact that the interaction among genes and culture leads to a wide variety of emergent phenomena indicates the need to understand these interactions and emergent phenomena in their own right rather than by reductionism, which when assessing human relationships increases the necessity for dialectical and sociological insights. A dialectical approach runs counter to reductionism, as it assesses the interaction between levels and the emergence of life and new forms (and states). It "does not ascribe intrinsic properties either to individuals or to societies but stresses the interpenetration of individual and social properties and forces."[41] It does not conceive, as reductionism does, that "the world is broken up into tiny bits and pieces, each of which has its own properties and which combine together to make larger things."[42] Lewontin contends that in spite of its name, sociobiology is really a theory of individual causation, rather than social causation, due to its narrow reductionism.[43] Furthermore, in its ahistorical, non-dialectical approach, it even fails to grapple with the lives of individuals in their development, as this takes place in a world filled with history and contradiction.[44]

The genetic determinism that is all too pervasive in society is enhanced by the mythology that surrounds the DNA molecule, which is seen as the "absolute monarch" responsible for all inheritance.[45] DNA is commonly presented as both self-reproducing (allowing for its own duplication) and self-acting (imposing a specific form on an organism due to its internal structure); it is "the cause of itself and the cause of all the other things."[46] Through the unwinding of the double helix, nucleotides (that is, adenine, cystosine, guanine, and thymine) match up with complementary nucleotides on the exposed strand of DNA to form a new strand of DNA. In this, it is simplistically assumed that DNA re-creates itself. Lewontin explains that though the story is correct as far as the details, it is incorrect in what it claims to explain.[47] DNA is not the ghost in the machine. Too often we fail to recognize that "DNA did not create life; life created DNA."[48] DNA cannot self-reproduce; "genes can *make* nothing."[49] Instead, DNA "is a dead molecule" that is produced by the cellular machinery of proteins. Rather than producing proteins, it is protein enzymes that produce DNA. "Only whole cells may contain all the necessary machinery for 'self'-reproduction," because no molecule is self-reproducing by itself.[50]

Genetic differences, Lewontin indicates, can serve as an explanation for why lions look different from lambs, but they are not sufficient for explaining "why two lambs are different from one another."[51] In fact, genes may be irrelevant for some characteristics. Genes only serve as models for more genes, because DNA holds information that is utilized by the cell machinery in its own productive process to determine the sequence of amino acids that will produce a protein and where and when a protein will be made. But even here, code sequences of nucleotides may be exactly the same, yet the code can have more than one meaning (that is, it could be instructions to insert the amino acid valine in a protein, or it could be a spacer in a sequence). It is not known how the cell chooses between the possible interpretations presented by code sequences. Furthermore, the same genes can express a wide range of variation in their outcomes. For instance, the left and right side of a fly has the same genes, but the number of hairs on one side can be different than the other. "The variation between sides of a fly is as great as the average variation from fly to fly."[52] To complicate matters even more, Gould points out that "some genes can excise themselves from a chromosome and move to other locations in the genome; if these 'transposable elements' operate as regulators to turn adjacent genes on and off, their movement to new places (near different genes) can have major effects on the timing and control of development."[53] The genome is not simply a "one-way flow of information." Instead, Gould stresses, it must be conceived as a dynamic system "with the potential for rapid reorganization and extensive feedback from their own products and other sources of RNA." As a result, rearrangement, interaction, and mobility become important issues in regard to the genome. Contingency is a powerful aspect of development, as chance molecular events within cells and random cellular movements influence the expression of internal information. These influences are part of the reason that fingerprints between our left and right hands are different, just as the fingerprints of "identical" twins are different.

Protein-forming machinery makes the proteins of the cell, and proteins make other proteins. Both DNA and cell machinery are composed of proteins. The relationship between the various components is important, as is realizing how the whole operates in and of itself. "When we refer to genes as self-replicating," Lewontin warns, "we endow them with a mysterious, autonomous power that seems to place them above the more ordinary materials of the body."[54] And all too often, in discussions of genes, the organism disappears. To understand the evolutionary development of life, we need to focus on how "a living organism at any moment in its life is the unique consequence of a developmental history that results from the interaction of and determination by internal and external forces."[55]

As discussed in chapter 4, Gould explicates how natural selection operates on many units, including at the level of the gene, organism, and species. Natural selection in Darwin's conception functions on the level of the organism. Sociobiologists, including Richard Dawkins, advocate a narrow reductionism at the level of the gene. Gould indicates that such a focus would be appropriate "if genes built organisms in a one-to-one fashion" and their influence was simply additive. But, he stresses, the interaction between genes is non-additive. There are "emergent characteristics at the level of organisms, which cannot be explained in terms of individual genes." At each higher level of organization, new properties arise from the interaction and combination of the parts.[56] Thus organisms are selected, not traits.[57] Counter to narrow reductionism, Gould stresses that it is more appropriate to understand an organism as a totality, one that is composed of parts integrated into a number of systems, all shaped by history and structure.[58] Reflecting on the failure of genetic determinism, as an adequate explanation of complex systems and life, Gould indicated:

The collapse of the doctrine of one gene for one protein, and one direction of casual flow from basic codes to elaborate totality, marks the failure of reductionism for the complex system that we call biology—and for two major reasons.

First, the key ingredient for evolving greater complexity is not more genes, but more combinations and interactions generated by fewer units of code—and many of these interactions (as emergent properties, to use the technical jargon) must be explained at the level of their appearance, for they cannot be predicted from the separate underlying parts alone. So organisms must be explained as organisms, and not as a summation of genes.

Second, the unique contingencies of history, not the laws of physics, set many properties of complex biological systems. Our thirty thousand genes make up only one percent or so of our total genome. The rest—including bacterial immigrants and other pieces that can replicate and move—originated more as accidents of history than as predictable necessities of physical laws. Moreover, these noncoding regions, disrespectfully called "junk DNA," also build a pool of potential for future use that, more than any other factor, may establish any lineage's capacity for further evolutionary increase in complexity.[59]

The organism is a site of interaction between genes and the environment. At the same time, the organism is a force that is active in its own construction, as well as that of the environment, as it transforms the material world. An organism cannot be reduced to computing itself from DNA. As Lewontin makes clear, "If we take seriously the proposition that the internal and external codetermine the organism, we cannot really believe that the sequence of the human genome is the grail that will reveal to us what it is to be human" in all of its development.[60] Instead, as the dialectical-materialist approach suggests, an organism is the consequence of

a historical process that goes on from the moment of conception until the moment of death; at every moment gene, environment, chance, and the organism as a whole are all participating. . . . Natural selection is not a consequence of how well the organism solves a set of fixed problems posed by the environment; on the contrary, the environment and the organism actively codetermine each other.[61]

Here organisms are more than the summation of their genetic characteristics, and species by this reasoning—as Gould emphasizes—are more than a collection of individuals. The interaction and relationship between levels is an important aspect of biological and social development. New properties arise at different levels. Here the world is a dynamic place, filled with change, some of which is unpredictable, some of which is structured.

Organisms are both subjects and objects within the world. They are active agents involved in complex relationships and interactions, as they actively transform the world in which they are immersed, are influenced by a world filled with historical forces and contingency (such as environmental conditions, global climate change, pollution), and confront the influence of their own historical-structural development. Life is neither a consequence of a free-flowing, hodgepodge series of independent events nor of genetic determinism. Instead, it emerges from the complex interactions that are constantly taking place. Life activities influence the development of an organism, as external signals influence physical developments, such as temperature changes affecting the concentration of sugar in one's blood.[62] These life activities are also a necessary part of forging space within the world for existence. Ecological niches do not simply exist, and organisms do not simply fill a niche in nature. Nothing is preordained; environments are constantly changing. Organisms create niches for themselves in relation to the properties of the larger world. Foraging for food and the use of the environment are necessary activities that organisms engage in, and in the process they contribute to the construction of their world.[63] This is a universal characteristic, as life is a process of becoming.

In day-to-day operations, any number of materials (rocks, water, trees, etc.) may exist in nature, but organisms interact with other organisms and with the physical environment, utilizing a small portion of what is available. Thus in their patterns of life they determine what is relevant to their development. In the process of obtaining sustenance, organisms must interact with their environment, and in so doing they transform the external world—both for themselves and other species. Their consumption of parts of the external world is also the production of new environments. The conditions of the environment are not wholly of a species own choosing, given that there are natural processes independent of a particular species. Previously living agents have historically shaped nature, and coexisting species are also engaged in altering material conditions—such as the destruction of natural habitat by urban sprawl. The conditions of the natural world are also a consequence of geological influences and billions of years of life, actively transforming the environment in the process of living.

Organisms convert the physical signals from the external environment into information that causes physical transformations in the organisms themselves. The biology of a species will determine if and what information it receives. Ultraviolet light helps lead bees to food; for humans it can cause skin cancer. The value and use of existing information varies among species. The "traits" selected are influenced by the dynamic organism-environment relationship. What becomes useful is a consequence of a long historical process—one that is subject to change. An organism is the result of complex interactions between its genes and environment—"the dialectical relations between parts and wholes"—where the organism takes part in the creation of its environment and its own construction. In this, it sets, in part, the conditions of its natural selection.[64] In the process of developing, new properties emerge in this dynamic world, thus the particular, historical development of organisms is important.

"The more we learn about complex systems," Gould stresses, "the less we can sustain a belief that classical reductionism might work, and the more we must suspect that emergence and contingency will enter in ever more important ways as we mount the scale of complexity in nature's material reality."[65] For example, Lewontin argues that culture has provided the ability to overcome individual limitations. No individual can fly using his or her own body mechanics alone. But through "social organization" people have produced the means to fly, via engineering, the plane, the pilot, fuel, and so on.[66] Likewise, humans have fundamentally altered the world, changing the conditions of life. By mining the earth to remove stored energy (fossil fuel derived from plants that existed long ago) to fuel machines of production, capitalist production has "broken the solar-income budget constraint, and this has thrown [society] out of ecological equilibrium with the rest of the biosphere."[67] Additionally, "most of the chemical reactions produced by humans have never before taken place because the reactants have never been in contact."[68] The growth of the global economy has incorporated much of the world into its operations, fundamentally changing natural process and cycles and undermining ecosystems. We cannot understand the world or society in a simple, reductionistic manner, but must, rather, understand the emergent properties particular to the present historical context.

It is here that sociobiology confronts a difficult position. If culture largely dominates genes and we accept the critique of narrow reductionism, sociobiology offers us little in understanding the development of an organism, much less the social world. However, if sociobiology continues to claim that genes are dominant, then the critiques of genetic determinism are relevant to consider. We support efforts to investigate the connections between levels within organisms and the world, yet we contend that biological determinism is no substitute for sociology in regard to describing the workings of the social world.

Furthermore, as Gould details, complex systems are not simply additive. New properties develop from interaction in complex systems and become "central principles of explanation at the higher level."[69] Historical uniqueness of events remains an issue, ignored in the reductionist approach, as unpredictable developments present themselves. Only with historical hindsight can we explain an event such as a mass extinction due to an asteroid crashing into the surface of the earth. The more we learn about complex systems the more contingency and emergence become necessary for explaining relationships. The critique of sociobiology starts by showing the failures of a narrow reductionism within the biological sciences and revealing how the errors only compound as one moves to the realm of the social world.

FUNCTIONALISM AND ADAPTATION

The second conceptual error that underlies the sociobiology tradition is its overreliance on adaptationist explanation for features of organisms—that is, the assumption that all features of an organism evolved *for the function they currently serve or for the function they served in a previous environment*. Natural selection does indeed lead organisms to become adapted to their environments. Charles Darwin's brilliance shows through in devising a functionalist explanation of the form of organisms that relies only on a blind materialist mechanism, which contrasts with the mystical processes invoked by most functionalist explanations. There is no question that natural selection leads to adaptation, but it should also be recognized that natural selection is not the only cause of evolutionary change—as noted by Darwin. Furthermore, there is considerable debate, as we discussed in chapter 2, about the extent to which each and every feature of an organism evolved for the function it currently serves. The singular focus on adaptation, Gould stresses, leads to a lack of appreciation for the flexibility inherent in most structures, which thus limits the degree to which biology constrains society.

The invocation of adaptationist explanations for characteristics of humans is common, and this use of adaptationism is often coupled with an argument that human behavior is constrained and channeled by the adaptive origins of characteristics. This type of argument is well illustrated by psychologist Simon Baron-Cohen's claim that men's brains (which are supposedly good at systematizing) and women's brains (which are supposedly good at empathizing) are substantially different from each other and that these differences emerged for adaptive reasons (hunting versus caregiving). He then contends that these variations in brain structure explain differences in behavior across the sexes.[70]

As noted above, some evolutionary psychologists propose that human beings and their brains are properly adapted to the conditions that existed over 10,000 years ago, at the end of the Pleistocene epoch. The era before the emergence of agriculture is referred to as the "environment of evolutionary adaptedness" (EEA). In attempting to provide adaptationist explanations for human features, the EEA is invoked as the proper context in which "adaptedness" is to be assessed.[71] So when some human behaviors do not seem optimal in the present, evolutionary psychologists argue that such psychological mechanisms were selected for in the distant past. For example, Robert Wright makes the banal and uncontroversial suggestion that a "sweet tooth" was an adaptation that arose in the context of fruit being available, but before an era of candy production. In the past, a sweet tooth was beneficial, but now it is unhealthy.[72] Part of this discussion is predicated on the notion that cultural change far outpaces the rate of biological change.

Ian Tattersall, a paleoanthropologist, indicates that there is a fundamental flaw in this line of argument: there was no single EEA.[73] In other words, a universal EEA never existed. Environments are always in flux, and the period from when human ancestors emerged in Africa up to end of the last ice age (about 10,000 years ago) was particularly chaotic climatically and thus ecologically. What may be adaptive in one environmental context may not be so in another. Features in modern humans cannot be assessed against a single mythical EEA to determine the adaptive reason, if any, for their origins.

Hilary Rose and Steven Rose find it problematic that evolutionary psychologists propose "that human nature is an evolved property" and then employ "the profoundly un-Darwinian assertion that this [human nature]—by contrast with the rest of nature—was fixed in the Pleistocene, and that there has not been enough evolutionary time for human nature to change subsequently."[74] In contrast, they specify that culture has produced biological changes in humans in "digestive physiology and brain structure." For example, in Western societies that have domesticated cattle for thousands of years, a mutation has spread widely, allowing adults to digest lactose without complications.

In *The Structure of Evolutionary Theory*, Gould applauds the recent recognition by proponents of evolutionary psychology that the historical origin and current utility of a human trait do not necessarily correspond to one another. In fact, some traits may be maladapted to the current context. But he does criticize them for their conventional insistence that we must find the origin of such traits in the EEA, assuming that there has to be an "adaptive value" found in the context of our gather-hunter ancestors. In practice, the evolutionary psychology approach (as well as the strong adaptationist position in general) usually involves pure speculation and attempts to construct plausible stories. Though not denying the importance of adaptation, Gould insists that we must also recognize the importance of "constraints and nonadaptations in the initial construction of the cognitive and emotional modules and attributes that we collectively designate as 'human nature.'"[75]

Gould and Lewontin penned one of the best-known critiques of the "adaptationist program"—the effort to construct purely functionalist explanations for all characteristics of all organisms.[76] They pointed out that in such explanations, the adaptive nature of any particular characteristic was typically an *assumption*, not a finding. Hence they suggested that much of the adaptationist program was based on "just-so" stories in the tradition of Rudyard Kipling. Gould and Lewontin do not deny the important role natural selection plays in the evolution of form, but they question whether natural selection is the sole force influencing form. They suggest that many features, what they call *spandrels*, of organisms may be side consequences of development, without adaptive function. In this, evolution produces "organisms full of nonadaptive parts and behaviors."[77]

Gould and Elisabeth S. Vrba expanded on this critique, arguing that many features that may indeed be useful to an organism may have originated for reasons other than their current utility, and subsequently were co-opted—exapted—for a new purpose.[78] This may reflect a functional shift, where a feature was sculpted by natural selection for one purpose, but then proved to be useful for another (a point Darwin himself recognized). Spandrels—features that did not originally serve any function—may be likewise co-opted by evolution to serve a function. One of Gould and Vrba's central arguments is that there is no necessary logical connection between current utility and the reasons for historical origin.

The prevalence of exaptation has a clear and important implication concerning the constraining role of evolutionary history on the flexibility of biological features: rather than dramatically limiting options or determining behavior, many evolved features can potentially be utilized in multiple ways, many of which may be entirely novel. Gould uses this simple insight to undermine the arguments of biological determinists, where specific behaviors "must be interpreted as adaptations of organisms."[79] He argues: "Human sociobiology is fundamentally wrong because . . . ultra-Darwinism, especially in its commitment to adaptationism, is fallacious (or at least overextended)—not because many of us do not like its political implications."[80] In particular, the human brain, along with other human features, though they are surely the products of materialist evolutionary forces, are greatly flexible and can be used in ways other than those for which natural selection has historically honed them.[81] For example, the ability to read and write is dependent on the brain's capacity to understand symbolic representation and language, the acuity of the eye, and the dexterity of the hands. However, none of these features evolved for reading and writing, abilities that only emerged in the past few thousand years, and which have only been widely used by a substantial proportion of humanity within the past one hundred years. Likewise, nearly all of the major features of modern societies—such as living in cities, driving cars, utilizing electronic devices—rely on human abilities that evolved for other reasons. Thus Gould argues that evolutionary history does not dramatically constrain human potential, but, rather, our bodies and minds are remarkably flexible.[82] This point undermines claims made by Wilson about the impossibility of gender-egalitarian societies, and other types of biological determinism.

Humans engage in a great many behaviors that cannot be explained based on adaptationist principles. The most striking of these is the voluntary restriction of fertility. Billions of the world's people purposefully limit their fertility, in spite of the fact that many of them could support more children. In many developed countries, many people voluntarily have no children and average fertility in these countries is well below replacement level. Restricting fertility fundamentally goes against any supposed Darwinian drive. The reasons for this, of course, do not undermine Darwinism, but rather show how different contexts can lead to different behavior. Through most of human history, humans had only restricted ability to limit their fertility, so the desire for sex was a sufficient mechanism for ensuring human fecundity. However, in the context of the modern world where humans have developed effective birth control, they can use their cognitive capacity for assessing life decisions to restrict their fertility. Clearly there is no evolved brain structure that pushes humans to desire a great many children. The point to be learned here, then, is that simply because selection pressure sculpts all organisms, it does not necessarily undermine the ability of organisms to behave in ways quite different from how they did historically.

THE DIALECTICAL WORLD

A proper understanding of natural history requires an evolutionary perspective, as does an ecological conception of the world. In this, biology is fundamental in explaining human development, but the human condition and the social order, like the conditions of nature, cannot be reduced to genetic explanations or biological determinism, as proposed by sociobiology. The social and natural worlds are not machines determined by innate instructions that unfold over the course of time. Gould and his colleagues from throughout the natural sciences, employing a dialectical approach, illuminate the dynamic relationships that emerge throughout the natural world. In this, their science and critique of sociobiology stands in stark contrast to crude biological arguments, which do not reflect the debate and state of biological science, but are widely applied to all parts of society, attempting to preempt social theory and analysis. Their critique illustrates the shortcomings of evolutionary psychology and other approaches that rely on narrow reductionism and the uncritical acceptance of functionalist adaptationism.

Gould advocated a pluralistic view to "put organisms, with all their recalcitrant, yet intelligible, complexity, back into evolutionary theory."[83] This approach is not limited to conceptions within biology or the natural sciences in general. It opens the door to pluralistic conceptions. The interaction of genes and culture leads to emergent phenomena that demand different approaches and explanations. The same can be said about human behavior, as well as culture. This recognition of different non-reducible levels is part of what makes scientific and interdisciplinary work so important and exciting. It also becomes the source of power to counter attempts to justify the status quo. Social inequalities in wealth and power are not based on innate differences, due to natural selection. Rather, they are the consequence of contingent, social-historical relationships. As Darwin lamented, in *Voyage of the Beagle*, "if the misery of our poor be caused not by the laws of nature, but by our institutions, great is our sin."[84] The natural and social sciences can help us understand why the world is the way it is, but they also indicate that the course of human history is, in part, in our hands.

CHAPTER SEVEN

Homo Floresiensis and Human Equality

The discovery by a team of Indonesian and Australian researchers of the remains of a previously unknown species of hominin, *Homo floresiensis*, on the Indonesian island of Flores was characterized by some scholars as the greatest discovery in anthropology in a half-century and was selected by *Science* magazine as the leading runner-up for the 2004 "breakthrough of the year" (first place went to the discoveries of the Mars Exploration Rovers that indicate Mars was once wetter than it is today and potentially capable of supporting life).[1] The discoverers of the new species note that it was a particularly small hominin, with an adult stature of approximately 1 meter and an endocranial volume of about 400 cm^3, less than one-third that of the typical modern human and even small relative to its body size.[2] They argued that it was most likely a descendant of *Homo erectus* that evolved in long-term isolation, with subsequent endemic dwarfing. Subsequent opinion has varied, with it sometimes being suggested that the ancestors of *Homo floresiensis* may have diverged from the line leading to modern humans early in human history, perhaps before the emergence of

Homo erectus.[3] Another interesting aspect of the find is that *Homo floresiensis* apparently lived until at least 18,000 years ago (and likely until 12,000 years ago or even more recently) and was, therefore, a contemporary of anatomically modern humans.[4] Recent evidence even suggests that the modern humans who replaced *Homo floresiensis* may have learned some of their stone flaking techniques from their smaller cousins.[5] Many scholars were shocked by both the small stature of and late date attributed to the new hominin, with some moved to question whether the remains were not merely those of a deformed modern human, a suggestion that its discoverers and a growing list of scholars reject as unsupported by the evidence.[6]

Despite the unusual character of this find, should we be completely surprised that our genus, *Homo*, spawned a dwarf species that was contemporaneous with *Homo sapiens* for a long stretch of our evolutionary history? Stephen Jay Gould would surely have said no. What we see as a surprise can reveal a great deal about our underlying, and often unconscious, assumptions about the world. The discovery of *Homo floresiensis* is surprising from perspectives grounded in the paradigmatic assumption that history necessarily unfolds in a progressive manner, leading inexorably to our contemporary world. As we have discussed previously, Gould was one of the sharpest critics of this worldview. He surely would have both welcomed the discovery of *Homo floresiensis* and been to some degree unsurprised by it (although he would no doubt have been fascinated by the particular, unusual features of *Homo floresiensis*). Gould would almost certainly have written about *Homo floresiensis* if he was still with us. Nevertheless, his insights remain invaluable to the maintenance and development of a dialectical science of human origins. Here we interpret the finding of *Homo floresiensis* in the manner we believe Gould himself would have done to illustrate the powerful insights produced by his worldview. Gould's perspective helps us to recognize the important implications of the discovery of *Homo floresiensis*, implications that may be missed by less critical scientists.

As we have noted throughout this book, a theme that runs through nearly all of Gould's work is that the present is the product of innumer-

able contingent events, and therefore we live in only one of many possible worlds.[7] Gould argued that the unfolding of natural history, and by
extension human history, over the long haul is not properly characterized by a progressive, directional trend, but rather as a wandering across
the landscape of possibility governed predominantly by happenstance.[8]
Although natural selection adapts creatures to their local environments
over ecological time, the contingencies of geological history typically
undermine long-term trends (the paradox of the first tier). From early in
his career, Gould emphasized the importance of recognizing that the
evolutionary process was best characterized as a metaphorical bush,
with copious branches, rather than by a ladder, with its implication of
clear directional progress to a higher status. Applying this point to
human evolution, he argued that the evolutionary development of our
species was not a linear march to our current form, but rather a process
of diversification of hominin species and subsequent pruning of lineages
through extinction, with the present point in time, where we are the only
extant hominin, being historically atypical.[9]

Gould's writing has already proven prophetic at least once, when
evidence was reported in 1996 that suggested *Homo erectus* survived
on the island of Java until perhaps as recently as 27,000 years ago, and
therefore may have shared the world with *Homo sapiens* for well over
100,000 years.[10] This find prompted Gould to note that perhaps as
recently as 40,000 years ago there were at least three coexisting human
species, *Homo neanderthalensis* in Europe, *Homo erectus* in Asia, and
Homo sapiens spreading out of Africa into other parts of the inhabita-
ble world.[11] The discovery of *Homo floresiensis* adds a fourth member
of our genus to this same period, with its discoverers suggesting that
the remains of still further species of hominins might be found on
other islands in the East Indies. The mass of accumulated evidence
suggests, quite forcefully, that Gould called it correctly long ago: modern humans are not the product of a linear march of progress, but
rather one twig on the hominin bush that merely had the good fortune
to survive to the present.

While the discovery of a new species of *Homo* from the recent past
in and of itself disturbs the linear progressionist view of history, since

it suggests that at least three other human species may have been the contemporaries of our own species, the dwarfism of *Homo floresiensis* further indicates that there is no necessary direction in the evolution process. Since our genus *Homo* apparently spawned not only large-brained and tall-statured modern humans, but also a descendant that had a small body and a remarkably small brain (even smaller than would be expected based on its diminished physical stature), there was clearly no inherent evolutionary drive toward larger brains among our ancestors. As the prominent scholar Jared Diamond has noted, we should not be particularly surprised by the apparent fact that our *Homo* brethren spawned a "micropygmy" population, since it is well known that "large mammals colonizing remote small islands tend to evolve into isolated populations of dwarfs," with examples including pygmy hippos and elephants.[12] Humans clearly are not exempt from the evolutionary forces that affect other animals. It is only because of the widely held notion that the modern world is the inevitable outcome of a natural progressive drive that the bushiness of our family tree and the small physical and cranial stature of one of our evolutionary cousins come as a surprise at all.

If the recent argument that there is continuity between the stone-flaking techniques of *Homo floresiensis* and the *Homo sapiens* that replaced them, with its suggestion that perhaps modern humans learned from *Homo floresiensis*, holds up, we are presented with a distinct piece of evidence that challenges our common assumption that we modern humans are unambiguously superior to our ancestors. Big brains are not everything. Our dwarfed cousins on Flores may have known a thing or two that modern humans found worthwhile to learn. It is also worth noting that modern humans do not even win out if we focus on brain size alone. *Homo neanderthalensis* actually had somewhat larger brains than *Homo sapiens* and the brains of modern humans appear to have shrunk over the past 10,000 years.[13] As Gould would have expected, rather than our evolutionary history showing a march of progress toward our modern form and abilities, we see a bushy diversity of human forms and behaviors, with each species having its own distinct features, and none better than the others in a universal sense.

The *Homo floresiensis* find should also draw our attention to the remarkable unity of all contemporary humanity, since it sheds further light on the origin of modern humans. Scholars in the *multiregionalist* tradition have long claimed that modern human populations descended from regional populations of *Homo erectus* that evolved in parallel over hundreds of thousands of years, with modest genetic exchange across populations.[14] Multiregionalists adhere to the position that the division of humans into distinct groups (races) is very old, which implies there may be substantial biological differences among contemporary races. This view parallels a common position before the rise of Darwinism known as *polygenism*, which asserted that each human race was the product of a separate divine creation, and that therefore human races are in fact separate biological species.[15] This position was often invoked to justify imperialism and social inequalities. After evolutionary theory became widely accepted, the polygenist view eventually collapsed. Subsequently, multiregionalism emerged as a scientific proposition about human origins, with some noteworthy similarities to polygenism. It is important to note, however, that most contemporary supporters of multiregionalism deny any support for racist views or policies and acknowledge the high level of genetic similarity among human populations.[16] Nonetheless, the multiregionalist position does reify the division of humans into distinct biological races (if not species).

The combination of paleontological and genetic evidence has made the multiregionalist explanation of human origins increasingly untenable, supporting, rather, the argument that all modern humans share a very recent (in geological terms) common ancestor who lived in eastern or southern Africa approximately a quarter of a million years ago and whose descendants spread out of Africa around 100,000 years ago, eventually replacing all other human groups.[17] As some anthropologists have observed, the find of *Homo floresiensis* "puts yet another (the last?) nail in the multiregional coffin," since it demonstrates the recent existence of human groups in various regions of the world that were entirely distinct from modern humans and could not have exchanged genes with our recent ancestors. The weight of current evidence points to the conclusion that regional populations of *Homo erectus, Homo neanderthalensis,* and *Homo floresiensis* did not slowly blur into regional populations of *Homo sapiens,* but rather were distinct contemporaries of modern humans until very recently. Therefore regional populations of modern humans do not share a continuous ancestry with the populations of *Homo erectus* that spread out of Africa one to two million years ago, but rather with *Homo sapiens* who migrated out of Africa only a geological eye-blink ago.[18]

In our present world where humans increasingly dominate the global environment and many other species have been driven into extinction or have become endangered, we are faced with fundamental ethical dilemmas about how to value other species. Human actions are threatening the survival in the wild of our closest relatives, chimpanzees and bonobos, and apes in captivity are often subjected to treatment—such as in medical experiments—that would constitute torture if inflicted on humans. The common justification for the exploitation of other species is that they are not equal to humans, in at least two senses. First, other animals are *qualitatively* different from humans. Although similar to us in many ways and clearly related to us, chimpanzees are clearly not the same as humans. Second, there is also the common assumption that other creatures are unequal to humans in a hierarchical sense, being of lesser moral value. This second assumption is clearly based on social prejudice, since nature provides no moral hierarchy. It is humans who *rank* people, animals, and so forth from "better" to "worse," not the laws of nature. Although there is no necessary logical reason why the first justification, the qualitative inequality of humans and other animals, should justify the second hierarchical moral inequality, it has long been common to rationalize the production of a hierarchical order based on the existence of qualitative inequality. This creates a moral challenge, since other species are indeed qualitatively different from humans. At the same time, these qualitative differences are consequences of an evolutionary process whereby variation is "the primary expression of natural reality" and there remains continuity—even in the minds and emotions, as products of this history—between human beings and other animals due to the descent of all species from common progenitors. Unfortunately, human arrogance and ideology make it difficult to rise to this challenge.[19] Within the human family, however, we are not faced with such a dilemma.

As Gould argued two and a half decades ago, human equality is a contingent fact of history.[20] We could have lived in a world where divisions among human groups occurred long ago, and therefore races were truly biologically distinct. For much of human history, a variety of hominin species of distinct character coexisted. If that reality had continued to the present, we would be faced with the ethical dilemma of how to deal with other groups of humans who were not qualitatively equal to us (or where we were not qualitatively equal to other groups, depending on one's vantage point). We hope that in such a world humans of all types would come to recognize that qualitative inequality does not and should not suggest hierarchical inequality, but that may not have been the case. We do not, however, now live in such a world due to the quirks of history, and we do not face this dilemma. We live in a world where all humans are remarkably similar genetically and where race as a biological reality is an illusion. We should rejoice in our unity. Gould expressed the lesson well:

> If our current times are peculiar in substituting the bushy richness of most human history with an unusual biological unity to undergird our fascinating cultural diversity, why not take advantage of this gift? We didn't even have such an option during most of our tenure on Earth, but now we do. Why, then, have we more often failed than succeeded in the major salutary opportunity offered by our biological unity? We could do it; we really could. Why not try sistership; why not brotherhood?[21]

CHAPTER EIGHT

Art, Science, and Humanism

British scientist and novelist C. P. Snow delivered the 1959 Rede Lecture in Cambridge where he identified a growing divide between what he called the "two cultures," the sciences and the humanities.[1] This presentation has been highly influential, and his description of the two cultures has become a common way to describe the divisions among intellectuals. The divide he pointed to is apparent as a generality, where scientists often have highly specialized technical training, while lacking broad knowledge of literature, art, and other humanistic pursuits, and humanistic scholars frequently are not well versed in the sciences or mathematics. The two cultures are the product of modernity, with the divergence beginning during the scientific revolution of the seventeenth century, and generally widening ever since. Whereas Renaissance scholars famously took all knowledge as their purview, it is rare to find today a scholar with advanced knowledge and talents in multiple fields, and it is, of course, impossible now for anyone to have a grasp on all human knowledge, given its ever-growing vastness. Stephen Jay Gould was that rare scholar who, although a specialist of a sort, had a broad and well-rounded education, with sophisticated knowledge of the sciences, where he was a professional, and the humanities, where he was an amateur, but in the positive sense of the term—someone who studies out of love for the subject. Gould gave considerable thought to the separation of the two cultures and worked to make connections across what he saw as an unnecessary divide.

In *The Hedgehog, the Fox, and the Magister's Pox*, one of his last books, Gould took on the goal of "mending the gap between science and the humanities," as the subtitle of the book states.[2] He aimed to show how the gap developed in the first place and presented a defense of both the ways of science and the ways of the humanities. As Gould explained, Renaissance scholarship was entirely in the humanist tradition, focusing on the rediscovery of classical knowledge through the examination of texts. This approach to knowledge—textual analysis— contrasts with that of a "modern" scientific approach, which bases knowledge on empirical evidence. Early modern scholars in the seventeenth century, such as Francis Bacon, argued for the importance of empirical analysis over the authority of the great scholars of antiquity. In Gould's telling, the gap between the sciences and the humanities first originated here. The emerging field of science was concerned with the factual conditions of the natural world and therefore, rightly in Gould's view, privileged empirical evidence over textual authority. Nascent scientists in a sense were trying to carve out a legitimate domain for science as independent from the humanities. Gould argued that whereas the tension between science and the humanities was a natural consequence of the birth of science and its claim to territory previously controlled by the humanities, such a tension has become entirely unnecessary and in fact harmful given that science is now a firmly established and entrenched tradition. Consequently, science does not need to worry about being displaced.

Gould contended that the sciences and the humanities are both great traditions that, though having independent domains, abut and complement each other. Although, as we noted in chapter 5, some scholars in the humanities have taken an oddly anti-science stance, Gould made great efforts to show that such a position is not typical. Humanistic scholars and artists are not generally hostile to science and share many common concerns with the sciences. There is no need for conflict between the humanities and sciences. Rather, both traditions can be enriched by a lively dialogue. The empirical world is the domain of science, whereas aesthetics, ethics, and human meaning fall in the domain of the humanities. Neither of these domains is more important than the other and knowledge of one domain cannot replace knowledge of the other. The findings of science can inform the humanities, just as insights from the humanities can enlighten science. Gould stressed that though the sciences and the humanities have legitimate separate domains, they are not nearly as dissimilar as popularly conceived, with both traditions requiring creativity and reason. Similarly, Gould also emphasized that scientific products can have artistic value, just as works of art can make scientific contributions. To understand Gould's views on the relationship between the sciences and the humanities, it is useful to contrast his position to that of Edward O. Wilson, the famous Harvard entomologist, who sought to merge science and the humanities in an unequal fashion.

TOWARD A CONSILIENCE OF EQUAL REGARD

In *The Hedgehog, the Fox, and the Magister's Pox*, Gould offered a focused critique of Wilson's book *Consilience*, in which the latter attempted to provide a foundation for unifying all knowledge. Wilson proposed that "all tangible phenomena, from the birth of the stars to the workings of social institutions, are based on material processes that are ultimately reducible however long and tortuous the sequences, to the laws of physics."[3] He indicated that reductionism serves as a powerful means to establish "cause-and-effect explanations across levels of organization."[4] He then suggested that the same strategy should be applied to the realm of social inquiry, unifying the natural sciences with both the social sciences and humanities.

Gould commended Wilson for helping rescue the great philosopher of science William Whewell's word *consilience* from obscurity. Consilience means the "jumping together" of "disparate facts into a unitary explanation."[5] Charles Darwin's theory of evolution is perhaps the greatest example of utilizing consilience as a method of theory development, as a vast range of information—in this case, specific facts about natural history, ranging from biogeography to paleontology—was organized under a coherent explanation of relationships in the material world.[6] Thus Gould recognized consilience as an important approach for scientific inquiries. He argued, however, that Wilson made an error of equating consilience with reductionism. In his excessive commitment to strict reductionism, Wilson failed to properly appreciate the distinctive concerns of the humanities. As a result, Gould suggested, Wilson incorrectly extended consilience to the humanities.[7]

Wilson uses reductionism as the basis for collapsing science and the humanities into one field of inquiry.[8] He indicated that a reductionist approach can identify the genetic and, by extension, evolutionary basis of human aesthetics and ethics, thus subsuming the humanities under the domain of science. Although Gould acknowledged that reductionism is a powerful method and must be utilized whenever appropriate, he argued that it cannot be applied as a generality (as we discussed in chapter 4).[9] He indicated that Wilson's approach does not properly address the humanities because the primary concerns of this field of social inquiry go well beyond factual claims about why humans have the ethical systems and aesthetic preferences they do. For example, an anthropology of morals might tell us what types of ethics are common across human societies, and perhaps even establish some evolutionary reason for these patterns, but it cannot tell us what types of moral codes we should follow.[10] Employing philosopher David Hume's distinction between the "is" and the "ought," Gould argued, "The 'is' of the *anthropology of morals* (a scientific subject) just doesn't lead me to the 'ought' of the *morality of morals* (a nonscientific subject usually placed in the bailiwick of the humanities)."[11] Gould's point is that science can contribute to our understanding of common features of ethical codes across societies, but it cannot speak to what ethical codes we *ought* to follow. It can help us comprehend why things are the way they are, but this does not determine how things *ought* to be. Likewise, science can certainly shed light on the human mind and our perceptual appa-ratus, which can help us understand how we experience the world and what types of features we commonly interpret as aesthetically pleasing, but this does not explain beauty itself or detract from the intangible talent it takes to create great art.

Rather than hammering the sciences and the humanities together through reductionism, Gould argued for a recognition that the sci-ences and humanities are different ways of knowing and that we can "utilize the two domains to our maximal benefit when we recognize the different light that each can shine upon a common quest for deeper understanding of our lives and surroundings in all their com-plexity and variety."[12] We must seek a "*consilience of equal regard*" that recognizes the inherent differences and embraces the distinct worthi-ness of the forms of knowledge that comprise wisdom.[13] These two traditions of knowledge can and should inform each other. But at the same time the interaction between the sciences and the humanities requires critical reflection and constraint. In encouraging and advanc-ing this dialogue, Gould warned us that we should neither impose our values and morals on nature, nor try to derive our morals and values from nature.[14] The effort to end inequality and injustice is not dependent on distorting nature's truths and denying the reality of the objective world.

NO SCIENCE WITHOUT FANCY,
NO ART WITHOUT FACTS

Gould had a long-standing interest in art, which became more pro-nounced toward the end of his life, especially following his co-found-ing in 1998 with his second wife, the artist and sculptor Rhonda Roland Shearer, the Art Science Research Laboratory (ASRL)—a nonprofit organization that aimed to further interdisciplinary research on art, science, and the humanities.[15] An important feature of some of Gould's work was a commitment to recognizing the overlap in talents between artists and scientists, a recognition of the scientific contributions of artists (particularly in his work connected with the ASRL), and an appreciation of the artistic contributions of science.

In an essay examining the connections between art and science in the work of Vladimir Nabokov, who, though best known as a novelist, was also a professional taxonomist specializing in butterflies, Gould quoted Nabokov's elegant statement from a 1966 interview:

> The tactile delights of precise delineation, the silent paradise of the camera lucida, and the precision of poetry in taxonomic description represent the artistic side of the thrill which accumulation of new knowledge, absolutely useless to the layman, gives its first begetter. . . . There is no science without fancy, and no art without facts.[16]

Like Nabokov, Gould saw connections between art and science and challenged the simplistic caricatures of each field, where sciences like taxonomy are seen as uncreative drudgery lacking fancy, and the arts are seen as grounded in personal idiosyncrasy and as indifferent to factual accuracy and analytic coherence. Fancy and facts are required to do good work in both art and science. Gould frequently stressed that creativity is a central part of science, where in struggling with the complexity of the natural world, scientists must not only document facts accurately, but must also be able to look beyond superficial appearances in new and nuanced ways if they are to find the path from observation to understanding. Likewise, artists must be analytically astute and know facts, particularly those dealing with the human perceptual system, the nature of materials, and, in the case of some artists, the substance of natural phenomena they explore in their work.

As an example of art concerned with natural history, Gould pointed to the works of the great landscape painter Frederic Edwin Church, in particular his widely admired *The Heart of the Andes*, exhibited in New York in 1859—and incidentally the year that marked both Darwin's publication of *On the Origin of Species* and the death of the great scientist Alexander von Humboldt, who did foundational work in natural history during a five-year journey in South America at the turn of the nineteenth century. In this and other canvases, Church, who was inspired by Humboldt's aesthetic and scientific appreciation of nature (as was Darwin), sought to accurately portray the diversity of life that abounded in the tropics, and how this was pronounced across gradations of elevation, particularly in the Andes, while also producing an aesthetically pleasing work of art that would spur in people a love of nature. Gould explained: "Church did not doubt that his concern with scientific accuracy proceeded hand in hand with his drive to depict beauty and meaning in nature."[17] Critics praised Church for the "intricate botanical details in his foregrounds and for geological forms in his backgrounds."[18] In his attempt to present the unity and diversity of nature, and to evoke a deep feeling of grandeur, Church's tropical paintings present "idealized vantage points" that encapsulate everything from lowlands to snow-covered peaks—presentations of the world that are not actually possible to see. Nonetheless, Gould asserted, such paintings were able to present in a single picture the vast connections and continuity of reality. In this, Church's artwork, through an artistic alternation of pure observation, presents important insights about the natural world. Gould suggested that artwork such as Church's might be even more important today, given the fragmentation of the world and the drive of specialization within intellectual practice.[19]

Gould also highlighted the artistic character of many scientific products. The German biologist Ernst Haeckel, an early enthusiast for and popularizer of Darwin's theory of evolution, had considerable artistic talent. Providing a parallel with Church, the artist who aimed for scientific accuracy, Haeckel was a scientist who endeavored to render his illustrations of natural objects in an aesthetically pleasing fashion that conformed to the prevailing artistic style of his era, Art Nouveau.[20] Haeckel's *Kunstformen der Natur* (Artforms in Nature), a volume with one hundred plates of illustrations of natural objects published in 1904, was explicitly presented with a goal of combining art and science. Haeckel indicated:

> The primary purpose of my *Artforms in Nature* was aesthetic: I wanted to provide an entry, for a wider circle of people, into the wonderful treas-

ures of natural beauty hidden in the depths of the sea, or only visible, as a consequence of small size, under the microscope. But I also wanted to combine these aesthetic concerns with a scientific goal: to open up a deeper insight into the wonderful architecture of the unfamiliar organization of these forms.[21]

Haeckel's plates show beautiful illustrations of, for example, creatures such as octopuses and squid, presented with accurate anatomical detail, but with tentacles undulating into graceful swirls that conform to the style of Art Nouveau—improbable poses of these creatures in nature. Thus Haeckel presented scientific illustrations of real creatures from nature while taking artistic license to enhance aesthetic enjoyment. His work is simultaneously both artistic and scientific in character.

Gould himself participated in efforts to combine art and science in a single project. Beginning in the 1980s, he collaborated with photographer Rosamond Wolff Purcell to produce three books of photographs of scientific objects, which were taken as artistic objects as well.[22] These books present Purcell's photographs of objects from various museum collections, principally fossils and preserved animals (including humans) and animal parts, with Gould's accompanying comments and short essays. The overarching goal of these collaborative works is to explore where science and art meet, but there is a particular concern with not only showing the beauty of the natural objects humans have collected over the centuries but with showing how, in their displays of natural objects, scientists have often imposed their own aesthetic preferences. In the introduction to *Illuminations*, the first book in the series, Gould noted:

> The standard tradition in natural history tries to capture organisms as they "are" in nature—and it favors the beautiful and pleasant, rather than the disturbing or ugly. Its conceit is factuality and separation from human concerns—nature as she is, away from the corruptions of civilization. Its twin claims are *objectivity* and *beauty*. [In contrast, this book] is about a particular mode of *interaction* with organisms. . . . This book gathers its materials from the back rooms of museums; it captures attitudes

expressed in the way we store and collect organisms that are *not* on public display. This book is about information lost in partial preservation, and dimensions added by treatment that exposes, in ways all the more telling because unconscious, our intimate connections with all life.[23]

These collaborative books are an artistic examination of science, in that the photographs are aesthetic delights and genuine works of art, as well as an analysis of the products of science: an examination of what objects in nature humans select for collection and display, or more commonly determine to be not worthy of display, and how they modify, store, and present them. Although collection and display of natural objects are generally assumed to be based purely on principles of scientific interest, Purcell and Gould show how they are also based on the aesthetic judgments of scientists, thus providing instruction in how humans perceive and evaluate nature.

In addition to arguing that the skills and interests of scientists are not so very different from those of artists, and that products of nature and how scientists present them have artistic merit, Gould was concerned with the scientific contributions of art. He asserted that "art, at its best, can add a dimension to our perceptions."[24] Similar to how Church's paintings from idealized vantage points show real patterns in nature, with regard to scientific illustration of natural objects, such as fossils, good illustrations can add "increased clarity and instruction" by not presenting perfect literal representations of the objects under study but by enhancing the prominence of relevant features less apparent, particularly to the untrained eye, in the original object.[25] For this reason, Gould remarked, "To this day, most naturalists prefer drawings to photographs for presentation of anatomical complexity and detail—and good scientific artists remain in high demand."[26]

However, Gould recognized that scientific contributions of artists extended well beyond those of scientific illustrators. In an essay in a book on the art of Alexis Rockman, Gould wrote:

> Art and science mingle best when the special attributes of one discipline aid the other in ways that cannot be accessed by tools of the enterprise

receiving help. If artists, for example, reach an impasse over attribution by style, scientific data on the chemistry of pigments or the dating of woods may fix provenance in a persuasive manner. The aid rendered by art to science, however, tends to be more subtle, but often far more comprehensive and globally enlightening.[27]

Gould saw Rockman as a prime example of an artist who showed a deep understanding of science and whose work made a scientific contribution in that it interrogated the categories and boundaries humans impose on nature and challenged anthropocentric views of the natural world. Rockman produced many works of art that portray scenes of nature, typically in careful and accurate detail, but that also modify and blend features to make artistic and scientific points. Gould insisted that Rockman contributes

> to the dialogue between art and science [by] use of artistic fancy to fracture and amalgamate the mental categories employed by scientists and falsely accepted by them as objective identification of nature's real distinctions. . . . [Through examining Rockman's work] I better appreciate the power of art to inform science in three major ways: (1) by illustrating objects that exist in nature but are not visible to us in our daily lives; (2) by portraying objects that exist in nature but would never be so juxtaposed; (3) by fabricating objects that do not or cannot exist, but that provoke our thoughts about the regularities followed by nature in her actual constructions.[28]

Gould emphasized that Rockman, via his artwork, challenges human preferences for seeing a hierarchy of value in nature, which, for example, leads people to commonly see mammals as superior to other animals, vertebrates to invertebrates, and animals to plants. In related fashion, Rockman, like Gould, contests the view that history is a march of progress leading inevitably to human dominance. Rockman creates natural history murals that undermine the traditional form of the genre—which depict progress in life's history from left to right— by, for example, presenting "a zoo with movement in all directions, not a sequence toward progress."[29] Likewise, he portrays a variety of evolutionary trees that tweak the traditional presentation in various ways so as to lead the viewer to question whether the species at the top are more "advanced." Rockman also defies the boundaries between species by creating impossible hybrids, not to challenge the fact that typically "species are long separate evolutionary populations," but to use "artistic fabrication for provocative ends" and to question "species constancy by showing a range of mutant forms."[30] Thus Gould saw Rockman as an example of an artist who contributes to scientific discourse by forcing us to rethink the categories and boundaries we impose on nature. With enthusiasm, Gould pronounced:

> I do applaud the partnership [between art and nature] that allows art, for all its celebrated ambiguity and stress upon the arcane, to bring nature out of her hiding places, down from her mountaintops, and into our scrutiny—by asking more varied questions, rather than supplying fewer integrated answers.[31]

In the last few years of his life, Gould took a particular interest in the work of the famous artist Marcel Duchamp, which was part of his ongoing commitment to overcoming the gap between art and science as well as his effort to demonstrate how scientific insights were evident within art.[32] For Gould and Shearer, "Duchamp's art" illustrates "the fundamental compatibility between these two great domains of human creativity."[33] As a reflection of this, they made Duchamp's work a focus of research at the ASRL, and analyzed Duchamp's artistic and scientific contributions. Shearer and Gould proposed:

> Marcel Duchamp (1887–1968) may even surpass Picasso in his influence upon the history of 20th-century art—especially in his conventional image as the ultimate Dada jokester, the enfant terrible who festooned the Mona Lisa with a beard, a moustache and a salacious caption, and then called the product art under his own signature; the man who submitted an ordinary urinal as his own sculpture, entitled "Fountain," to a major art show. But Duchamp, as a disciple of [the great mathematician and

physicist] Henri Poincaré, also understood the mathematics of non-
Euclidean geometry and higher dimensionality in a far more serious and
technical way than any other artist of his time. He maintained a passion-
ate interest in science throughout his life, and he made several innovations, in optics, mathematics and perception.[34]

Duchamp frequently addressed scientific and mathematical
issues in his art, demonstrating a particular interest in issues relating
to dimensionality. For example, as part of the *White Box*—a 1967
publication in an edition of 150 copies of a box with facsimiles of 79
notes primarily devoted to scientific subjects relating to *The Large
Glass*, one of his most renowned works of art—he included an illusion hidden on an apparent postcard (of his own creation), with an
original painting on one side and handwritten text on the other dis-
cussing a metaphor about the fourth dimension.[35] Long assumed to
be simply part of his notes incidentally written on the back of an
ordinary postcard, Duchamp's artistic presentation of a scientific
insight was missed by art scholars. Gould and Shearer made an original discovery about this work. They revealed how rotating the
"postcard" 90 degrees leads to a shift from interpreting the picture
as one of boats in a three-dimensional representation to one of
deckchairs in a two-dimensional representation. Gould and Shearer
noted the brilliance of this construction in that the optical illusions
presented in this piece of work play with the issues of perception in
different dimensions. With this "postcard," Duchamp attempted to
assess what it would be like to see in four dimensions, since the two
different images in the artwork, the boats and the deckchairs, could
only be perceived simultaneously if hypothetically viewed in four
dimensions. Within this piece of artwork, Duchamp "provided a
remarkable insight into this perennially fascinating and frustrating
topic of higher dimensional worlds that we can conceptualize reasonably well, and characterize rigorously in mathematical terms—
but that we cannot possibly 'see' directly because we live in a universe where immediate perception only extends into three dimensions."[36] The structure of our three-dimensional world prevents the

simultaneous viewing of the two images Duchamp created. Thus a change of vantage point, a 90-degree rotation in the case of the "postcard," is necessary (which involves the passing of time) to perceive both images. Then the information must be integrated into a single presentation. Duchamp worked in his art to find a route for us to conceptualize a fourth dimension, addressing an issue that was of great interest in mathematics and physics, underscoring Gould's argument that art and science should not be seen as separated from one another by a gulf that cannot be spanned.

Beyond interrogating scientific understandings of nature and providing ways to conceptualize scientific and mathematical abstractions, Gould explained that some artistic works make actual direct scientific contributions, presenting original scientific discoveries or experiments. In this vein, Duchamp's Rotoreliefs provide a striking example of scientific research presented as art. The Rotoreliefs were discs (twelve in all) designed for spinning on a record turntable. When viewed face on, the spinning discs create an illusion of three-dimensional depth (the spinning discs can be viewed on the ASRL website).[37] What is remarkable about this illusion is that it allows for the perception of depth with one eye alone, thus not requiring stereoscopy. Shearer and Gould point out:

Although Italian scientists (unaware of Duchamp's work) found and named this particular form of illusion as "the stereo-kinetic effect" in 1924, Duchamp apparently discovered this perceptual phenomenon independently in the early 1920s, and completed the first set of discs in 1923. . . . Duchamp knew what he had done, and he explicitly regarded the Rotoreliefs as a contribution to science.[38]

In this case, what is often taken as simply a work of art (and, sadly, the discs have typically been displayed in art museums not in motion, but as static objects) is in fact the presentation of a scientific discovery. Shearer and Gould noted that there are many other examples of artists who made scientific discoveries, including the eighteenth-century Dutch intellectual Petrus Camper who "established rules for depicting characteristic differences in the physiognomies of human groups" and the twentieth-century American painter A. H. Thayer who "discovered the adaptive value of countershading."[39] It is only surprising that artists have made scientific discoveries because of our inappropriate tendency to see art and science as entirely separate pursuits. In contrast, it is wise to recognize that artists are in effect researchers who specialize in human perception. As a result, we should expect that they would have keen insights about form and optics.

THE COMMON TENT OF WISDOM

Gould took the subtle and nuanced view that the humanities, including art, and the sciences have legitimate and separate domains, while arguing that there are important connections between these fields of study and that the boundaries between the two should not be rigidly enforced. He loved "the sensitive and intelligent conjunction of art and nature—not the domination of one by the other."[40] He stressed that there are "deep similarities in intellectual procedure" between the two realms of inquiry.[41] In this, science and art are not alien to each other, since both require creativity and attention to detail and accuracy. Furthermore, science often makes artistic contributions, just as art can be scientific in nature and even occasionally presents genuine scientific discoveries. Gould insisted that truly appreciating the richness of life involves recognizing the diversity of the human struggle to understand nature and ourselves, which requires us to embrace both scientific and humanistic pursuits.

The need for a union between these two realms is not mere intellectual chatter. Gould felt that this dialogue and engagement were more important than ever:

> For never before have we been surrounded with such confusion, such a drive to narrow specialization, and such indifference to the striving for connection and integration that defines the best in the humanist tradition. Artists dare not hold science in contempt, and scientists will work

in a moral and aesthetic desert—a most dangerous place in our age of potentially instant destruction—without art.[42]

Gould advocated a "consilience of equal regard" whereby the knowledge from both the sciences and the humanities could contribute to human understanding, serving "as the two great poles of support to raise the common tent of wisdom."[43] He saw this as necessary for empowering people and improving the human condition.

Nonmoral Nature
and the Human Condition

In reflecting on the diverse subjects and arguments of his essays for *Natural History*, Stephen Jay Gould professed that "an overarching theme" that united this work was his attempt to formulate "a humanistic natural history." This statement embodied Gould's keen awareness of the social context of knowledge, whereby science is socially embedded, but attempts to understand the workings of nature in materialist terms. Gould pronounced: "I do love nature—as fiercely as anyone who has ever taken up a pen in her service. But I am even more fascinated by the complex level of analysis just above and beyond (and I do mean 'abstracted from,' not 'better than')—that is, the history of how humans have learned to study and understand nature. I am primarily a 'humanistic naturalist' in this crucial sense."[1]

Gould held that a "factual reality exists," filled with emergent order and unique patterns, as well as irreducible complexity and disorder.[2] The properties and organization of the natural world can be understood, even if they must be filtered through a scientific process forever tied to the idiosyncrasies and preferences of humans. In his work he presented "the interaction of this outside world [nature] with something unique in the history of life on Earth—the struggle of a conscious and questioning agent to understand the whys and wherefores, and to integrate this knowledge with the meaning of its own existence. That is, I am enthused by nature's constitution, but even more fascinated by trying to grasp how an odd and excessively fragile instrument—the human mind—comes to know this world outside, and how the contingent history of the human body, personality, and society impacts the pathways of this knowledge."[3] Not only is nature endlessly fascinating, but so is the human condition.

THE NATURE OF NATURE

Gould sought to further understanding of nature—its organization, its patterns, its history. As discussed in previous chapters, he challenged many of the assumptions of the modern synthesis, such as the assertion (also present in Darwin's presentation of evolution) that evolution was marked primarily by slow, gradual changes in the features of organisms, and the microevolutionary perspective that reduced all causal explanations for evolution to the level of the organism or, in some cases, the level of the gene. Gould put forward alternative arguments addressing the tempo of evolutionary change and the level of causation within evolutionary processes. He advocated a pluralistic theory of evolution. Based on evidence in the fossil record, he argued that evolutionary change is better conceptualized in terms of punctuated equilibrium, where change typically takes place in rapid bursts (in geological time) that are followed by long periods of stasis. Gould incorporated a dialectical understanding of evolution, noting that forces both external and internal to organisms shape the course of development and history. Natural selection acts on an organism that already has an existing structure, which constrains the types of form that may arise. The structure of an organism limits the types of phenotypic variation that are possible. An organism is an integrated whole, rather than simply being an assembly of various parts. Thus evolutionary changes in one characteristic of an organism often have a ripple effect, altering other features. Although change is channeled, its outcome is not predictable. Gould offered a macroevolutionary perspective of evolution, assessing large-scale patterns over geological time, rather than simply selection in ecological time. The non-linear and non-additive interactions that are part of complex structures create emergent properties and higher levels of organization that are distinct. Following this logic, Gould proposed a hierarchical theory of evolution to account for causal forces that act at the level of species (as well as other levels of aggregation). It is important to remember that Gould was not dismissing or rejecting the classical Darwinian theory of evolution (for which he had the utmost respect) or the insights of the neo-Darwinian modern synthesis. Instead, he was proposing expanding evolutionary theory to account for causal forces that act on various levels of aggregation, which had been neglected by the modern synthesis.

As part of Gould's project, he engaged in a critique of progress. Too often, he pointed out, humans impose their own preferences on the empirical world, seeking to find meaning and purpose in nature. As a result, evolution has been perceived as an inevitable march of progress, leading to ever "higher" and "better" life-forms, a process that was predestined to lead to the emergence of *Homo sapiens*. Such logic is evident in depictions of evolution as a ladder, whereby human beings are found at the top, where they are presumed to arrive after a long climb from "lower" forms. Gould fought against the smuggling of anthropocentric biases into the reading of the constitution of nature. He indicated that the assumption that progress characterized evolution was a reflection of human aspirations, and it hindered our capacity to understand the workings of nature.

Evolution is not a deterministic process. Instead it is an undirected wandering marked by emergent possibilities. Quirks particular to a given moment, chance events, unpredictable twists and turns, specific historical circumstances, inherited structural forms, and natural laws all shape evolutionary history. History does not unfold based on a grand design or with higher purpose or meaning. Given the emergent properties of complex systems in nature, contingency plays an important role in history. As an extreme example, the impact of an asteroid on Earth caused the End-Cretaceous extinction, fundamentally changing the course of evolutionary history. Gould's main point in regard to this subject is that the world we know today could have been different than it is. No species alive today could have been predicted to emerge and survive beforehand. Rather than viewing evolution as a ladder, Gould stressed the image of a bush. Such an image depicts the constant branching of life, where some twigs flourish and others die. There is no overall direction or ranking of one group as better or worse, higher or lower.

Evolution operates on its own terms without regard to the preferences of *Homo sapiens*. Nature is nonmoral. It holds no ethical message or grand plan. It is indifferent to our desires, aspirations, dreams, hopes, and existence. Gould indicated that it is pure human arrogance to believe that nature exists for any purpose or that humans are somehow central to it. Instead, "Nature simply is what she is; nature does not exist for our delectation, our moral instruction, and our pleasure. Therefore, nature will not always (or even preferentially) match our hopes."[4] We must understand that it is not possible to "go from the facts of nature to the oughts of action. They're just different things."[5]

Gould did not see the absence of meaning in nature as depressing. Instead it is liberating to recognize that meaning and morality are human projects. If this point is fully grasped, it allows humans to better understand the construction of nature, to appreciate its organization, its workings, and its history. Gould reflected:

> Aesthetic and moral truths, as *human* concepts, must be shaped in human terms, not "discovered" in nature. We must formulate these answers for ourselves and then approach nature as a partner who can answer other kinds of questions for us—questions about the factual state of the universe, not about the meaning of human life. If we grant nature the independence of her own domain—her answers unframed in human terms—then we can grasp her exquisite beauty in a free and

humble way. For then we become liberated to approach nature without the burden of an inappropriate and impossible quest for moral messages to assuage our hopes and fears. We can pay our proper respect to nature's independence and read her own ways as beauty or inspiration in our different terms.[6]

As a humanistic naturalist, Gould illuminated the richness of the natural world, celebrated science and its endeavors, and presented human struggles to comprehend the world in all of its complexities.

SCIENCE, THE GREAT ASYMMETRY, AND THE HUMAN CONDITION

Gould frequently emphasized that science is embedded within society. In other words, it is a social process conducted by men and women who possess various strengths, limitations, insights, and biases just like all people. It is also a social activity that is influenced by politics, economics, and culture. Social and political change potentially influences the type of questions and topics that scientists investigate. Nonetheless, Gould remained a strong proponent of science and its pursuits, indicating that its findings improve our understanding of history and the world.

An issue that concerned him was public perception and understanding of science. He noted that too often science is perceived in simplistic terms—such as either good or evil—about how science and technology are employed for particular ends, such as the development of medical devices or machines for warfare. Depictions of science as represented by the technological applications of a particular moment separate science from its social context, alienating humanity from a means to better comprehend society and nature. Part of Gould's concern was rooted in the recognition that if the public feared science, it led to a simple dismissal of its findings, often on issues where scientific insights were most needed—such as, for example, evolution and global climate change.

In the article "The Great Asymmetry" Gould sought to provide a sophisticated understanding of science and technology, which high-lighted human potential.[7] As part of this analysis, he needed to debunk the simplistic notions that science was either intrinsically good or inher-ently evil. The former position proposed that science progresses in a slow, steady manner, that improves the human condition. According to this position, irrationality is sometimes able to overwhelm science and its advances and, therefore, must be resisted. The latter position insists that the character of science inherently creates destruction and domina-tion. Such a conception often leads to an outright dismissal of science as a social project. Gould stressed that both of these simplistic positions distort our understanding of science. He pointed out, "Science cannot be separated from political change."[8] Furthermore, "science cannot be conflated with the uses of discovery." As Karl Marx explained, "The contemporary use of machines is one of the relations of our present eco-nomic system, but the way in which machinery is utilized is totally dis-tinct from the machinery itself. Powder is powder whether used to wound a man or to dress his wounds."[9] Along these lines, Gould asserted that with any scientific discovery there are a range of uses, "potential realizations," influenced by social choices.[10]

Despite the poor reasoning and false explanations of the two afore-mentioned positions, Gould indicated that within human history, "the worst destructions wrought by human hands have been potentiated by applied scientific knowledge, and could otherwise not have occurred at anything like their realized intensity."[11] To help understand science and its social context, Gould proposed that there is a great asymmetry that exists, where "the workings of nearly any complex system, may explain the disturbing correlation of applied scientific knowledge with the intensity of destructive events in human history." He explained that it takes millions of years for complex systems and organisms to develop. But, for example, the simple introduction of guns to New Zealand led to the moa being wiped out, following a pattern that has been realized with countless other animals around the world. Hence "destruction can occur in a minute fraction of the building time" that it took for a particular organism to evolve.[12] Gould stressed that

human beings are "not an evil or destructive species" that intentionally imposes such events on the world. Rather the asymmetry found
within "the architecture of structural complexity . . . permits moments
to undo what only centuries can build. The essential human tragedy,
and the true source of science's potential misuse for destruction, lies
in the ineluctable nature of this great asymmetry, not in the character
of knowledge itself."[13]

Gould often pointed out in his work that the emergence of consciousness was a contingent event in evolutionary history.
Furthermore, it is a spandrel tied to the development of the brain,
allowing humans to do wonderful and horrible things. Thus consciousness is a contingent outcome of history, making it possible for
humans to arrange social relations in various potential ways, with the
possibility of enhancing our collective quality of life. Gould remarked
that "intelligence has imposed a very different system of change"
since "anything you invent or learn or discover immediately accumulates and gets passed on—you have this powerful accumulative mechanism that doesn't exist in nature."[14] Technological and scientific
knowledge can be disseminated across social systems. As a result,
cultural development can take place in relatively brief moments of
time and specific applications of technology or actions can have long-
term consequences.

Human beings have the unique capability "of changing the earth's
surface, of intervening globally in its climate, of wiping others out."[15]
Although Gould did not examine the specific social drivers of environmental degradation, he did recognize the emerging planetary
emergency that confronted human beings. He commented: "No other
species has ever had the capacity to destroy itself and drag large parts
of the earth down with it." But, insightfully, he stressed, "These capacities for destruction are not explicitly built by natural selection, they're
side consequences of the complexity. You can't even say the potential
is built by natural selection, except in the most indirect way. Selection
builds the brain for a reason, and then by virtue of its structural complexity it can do many other things that fall outside the realm of evolutionary reasons for its construction in the first place."[16]

Consciousness provides a degree of power that is shaped by human history in all of its complexity.

To address the ecological crisis, the great asymmetry, and social problems is a human struggle. As Gould insisted:

> We have no choice, for humans must wonder, ask, and seek—and science must therefore break through the strictures of custom—to become either our greatest glory, and our most potent engine of benevolent change, or an accelerator of destruction on the wrong side of the great asymmetry. Human choice, not the intrinsic content of science, determines the outcome—and scientists, as human beings, therefore have a special responsibility to provide counsel rooted in expertise. The content of science can only enhance or potentiate choices rooted in our social and ethical values.[17]

Gould saw "the transformation of society by scientific progress" as "the greatest dialectic in human history."[18] It involves a world filled with constraints and possibilities. It creates contingent historical moments that force the confrontation between the power to change and the limits set by external structures. Lest we fool ourselves, this project is rooted in human meaning, as nature remains indifferent, even if its ecosystems are degraded. As Gould reflected, "Nature, in her geological majesty, will little note nor long remember our transient passage, but wouldn't we achieve a crowning glory for our unique intellect if we joined the power of science with our unrealized potential for decency to rein in the great asymmetry, and to build a just world."[19]

Gould fervently believed in advancing a more egalitarian world. He actively engaged in debates surrounding human equality. But he did not find it appropriate to impose his own preferences on nature. Thus his work on this front involved an examination of the scientific claims of sociobiologists and others who proposed that social inequalities were the product of biological inequalities. Gould highlighted the scientific flaws of these arguments. His own position on the relationship between nature and culture, biology and society is quite subtle and sophisticated. He indicated that human beings, like all organisms, are constrained by their biology, and that there is variation across the wide swath of humanity. But he pointed out that substantial differences across human groups had not been definitely established. Furthermore, social inequalities are not convincingly explained by biological differences. He did not suggest that any particular social system was more natural than any other. Instead, he indicated that nature did not preclude a social system based on equality and justice. It was the task of humanists to create a social order that enhanced human potential and justice. In this, Gould argued that the future is in humanity's collective hands. Social transformation is a matter of praxis in the realm of natural science, politics, economics, and culture.

Gould produced a rich and diverse body of work, traversing numerous subjects and arguments. He offered distinctive insights on evolutionary processes, the implications of evolution, the structure of nature, natural laws, the patterns of life, the human condition, the scientific process, knowledge, and various other vital issues. Gould's greatest achievement, perhaps, was the rich and distinctive worldview he consciously developed and that unified his diverse work. We anticipate that Gould's intellectual contributions will be assessed and debated for a long time to come.

Among his numerous achievements, Gould helped open up intellectual territory that had been closed off, given the rigid structure of the modern synthesis. He raised critical questions about how the world works. The theory of punctuated equilibrium that he proposed along with Niles Eldredge not only presented a challenge to gradualist approaches within evolutionary theory but also expanded the realm of questions that were possible for investigation. Furthermore, it forced a reconceptualization of what constitutes data, as long periods without change needed to be considered as important data, rather than ignored. Gould made a similar point in regard to studies that investigated differences across human groups, such as supposed differences in cognitive styles between men and women. "The great majority of studies report no difference, and these have dropped from sight," whereas any finding of a difference no matter how slight is taken as important, and all the findings of no difference are ignored.[20]

Such a tendency reveals social biases in favor of finding differences, rather than similarities, since the latter is often not seen as data.

Gould adhered to the notion that it was important to be bold in arguments and research in order to raise critical questions. He viewed this as a necessary part of the scientific process, as it helped stimulate research, clarify theories, and prod new discoveries. Errors were part of this process and could be evaluated in relation to the development of scientific knowledge. Gould tirelessly worked to expand evolutionary theory. His research on the role of development contributed to the rise of evolutionary developmental biology (evo-devo), which now plays an important role in evolutionary theory.[21] He helped make macroevolution an acceptable realm of study. Whether his conception of a hierarchical theory of evolution proves useful remains to be seen. But the logic of his argument does direct attention to how distinct causal forces operate at different levels of organization. This point remains an important consideration within much of the social sciences.

For Gould, science and humanism were bound to each other, as we strive to understand the world and our place in it. His efforts to forge a humanistic natural history included recognition that we are conscious, intelligent beings involved in a process where "round and round we go—into a whorl that may be endless and eternal, yet seems to feature some form of increasing understanding in all the gyrations that . . . provide some insight into the nature of our being."[22] This process—the dialectic between science and humanism—is part of grappling with the complexity of human experience, knowledge, and history; it helps us locate our position within natural history, but it also reveals the potential of humanity to make history and create a better world.

Notes

PREFACE
1.   Riley E. Dunlap and William R. Catton, Jr., "Struggling with Human Exemptionalism," *American Sociologist* 25/1 (1994): 5–30.
2.   Richard York and Brett Clark, "The Science and Humanism of Stephen Jay Gould," *Critical Sociology* 31/1–2 (2005): 281–95.
3.   Brett Clark and Richard York, "Dialectical Nature: Reflections in Honor of the Twentieth Anniversary of Levins and Lewontin's *The Dialectical Biologist*," *Monthly Review* 57/1 (2005): 13–22; Richard York and Brett Clark, "Natural History and the Nature of History," *Monthly Review* 57/7 (2005): 21–29.
4.   Richard York and Brett Clark, "Debunking as Positive Science: Reflections in Honor of the Twenty-Fifth Anniversary of Stephen Jay Gould's *The Mismeasure of Man*," *Monthly Review* 57/9 (2006): 3–15; Richard York, "*Homo Floresiensis* and Human Equality: Enduring Lessons from Stephen Jay Gould," *Monthly Review* 56/10 (2005): 14–19.

INTRODUCTION: STEPHEN JAY GOULD'S VIEW OF LIFE
1.   See Richard Levins and Richard Lewontin, *The Dialectical Biologist* (Cambridge, Mass.: Harvard University Press, 1985); see also, in particular, Stephen Jay Gould, *The Mismeasure of Man* (New York: W. W. Norton, 1981); Stephen Jay Gould, *An Urchin in the Storm* (New York: W. W. Norton, 1987); 107–54; Stephen Jay Gould, *The Mismeasure of Man*, rev. ed. (New York: W. W. Norton, 1996), 367–90.

2.   Richard Lewontin and Richard Levins, "Stephen Jay Gould—What Does
     It Mean to Be a Radical?" *Monthly Review* 54/6 (November 2002): 17–23.
3.   J. G. Crowther, *The Social Relations of Science* (London: Cresset Press,
     1967), 432; see also I. Bernard Cohen, "Introduction: The Impact of the
     Merton Thesis," in *Puritanism and the Rise of Modern Science*, ed. I.
     Bernard Cohen (New Brunswick: Rutgers University Press, 1990), 1–111,
     esp. 55–56.
4.   Boris Hessen, "The Social and Economic Roots of Newton's 'Principia,'"
     in *Science at the Cross Roads*, ed. N. I. Bukharin et al. (London: Frank Cass,
     1971), 147–212; see also Loren R. Graham, "The Socio-Political Roots of
     Boris Hessen: Soviet Marxism and the History of Science," *Social Studies
     of Science* 15/4 (1985): 703–22; David Joravsky, *Soviet Marxism and
     Nature Science 1917–1932* (New York: Columbia University Press, 1961);
     Neal Wood, *Communism and British Intellectuals* (Cambridge: Cambridge
     University Press. 1959), 145.
5.   John Bellamy Foster, *Marx's Ecology* (New York: Monthly Review Press,
     2000).
6.   Lancelot Hogben, *The Nature of Living Matter* (New York: Alfred A.
     Knopf, 1931), 224; Peder Anker, *Imperial Ecology: Environmental Order
     in the British Empire, 1895–1945* (Cambridge, Mass.: Harvard University
     Press, 2001); John Bellamy Foster and Brett Clark, "The Sociology of
     Ecology: Ecological Organicism versus Ecosystem Ecology in the Social
     Construction of Ecological Science, 1926–1935," *Organization &
     Environment* 21/3 (2008): 311–52.
7.   James Tabery, "R. A. Fisher, Lancelot Hogben, and the Origin(s) of
     Genotype-Environment Interaction," *Journal of the History of Biology* 41
     (2008): 717–61.
8.   Hyman Levy, *A Philosophy for a Modern Man* (New York: Alfred A. Knopf,
     1938), 91, 125–30, 199, 227; see also John Bellamy Foster, Brett Clark, and
     Richard York, *The Ecological Rift* (New York: Monthly Review, 2010),
     chap. 11.
9.   Foster, *Marx's Ecology*; Richard Levins and Richard Lewontin, *The Dialectical
     Biologist* (Cambridge, Mass: Harvard University Press, 1985), 277; J. D. Bernal,
     The Origins of Life (New York: World Publishing, 1967), 182.
10. Helena Sheehan, *Marxism and the Philosophy of Science* (Atlantic
     Highlands, N.J.: Humanities Press, 1985); Gary Werskey, *The Visible
     College* (New York: Holt, Rinehart, and Winston, 1978).
11. Lewontin and Levins, "Stephen Jay Gould," 20.
12. Stephen Jay Gould, *Dinosaur in a Haystack* (New York: Harmony Books,
     1995), xiv.
13. Stephen Jay Gould, *I Have Landed* (New York: Harmony Books, 2002),
     6–7.

14. Lewontin and Levins, "Stephen Jay Gould," 21–22; Warren D. Allmon, "The Structure of Gould," in *Stephen Jay Gould: Reflections on His View of Life*, ed. Warren D. Allmon, Patricia H. Kelley, and Robert M. Ross (New York: Oxford University Press, 2009), 42–46.

15. Stephen Jay Gould, *The Flamingo's Smile* (New York: W. W. Norton, 1985), 185.

16. Gould, *The Mismeasure of Man*, rev. ed., 50.

17. Gould, *I Have Landed*, 174.

18. Stephen Jay Gould, "Darwinism and the Expansion of Evolutionary Theory," *Science* 216 (1982): 380–87.

19. Elizabeth Pennisi, "Modernizing the Modern Synthesis," *Science* 321 (2008): 196–97; John Whitfield, "Postmodern Evolution?" *Nature* 455 (2008): 281–84.

20. Stephen Jay Gould, *The Structure of Evolutionary Theory* (Cambridge, Mass.: Harvard University Press, 2002).

21. Gould, *The Structure of Evolutionary Theory*; Richard Dawkins, *The Selfish Gene* (New York: Oxford University Press, 1976).

22. Sean B. Carroll, *Endless Forms Most Beautiful: The New Science of Evo Devo* (New York: Norton, 2005).

23. Niles Eldredge and Stephen Jay Gould, "Punctuated Equilibria: An Alternative to Phyletic Gradualism," in *Models of Paleobiology*, ed. Thomas J. M. Schopf (San Francisco: Freeman, Cooper, 1972), 82–115; Stephen Jay Gould and Niles Eldredge, "Punctuated Equilibria: The Tempo and Mode of Evolution Reconsidered," *Paleobiology* 3 (1977): 115–51.

24. Eldredge and Gould, "Punctuated Equilibria," 82–115.

25. Stephen Jay Gould, *Ever Since Darwin* (New York: W. W. Norton, 1977), 56–62.

26. Stephen Jay Gould, *Time's Arrow, Time's Cycle* (Cambridge, Mass.: Harvard University Press, 1987), 10–11.

27. Gould, *Mismeasure of Man*, rev. ed., 53–54.

28. Gould, *The Structure of Evolutionary Theory*.

29. Charles Darwin to Henry Fawcett, September 18, 1861, in Francis Darwin, ed., *More Letters of Charles Darwin*, vol. 1 (New York: D. Appleton, 1903), 194–96.

30. Gould, *Dinosaur in a Haystack*, 420.

31. Gould and Eldredge, "Punctuated Equilibria," 115–51.

32. Gould, *The Structure of Evolutionary Theory*, 1018.

33. Gould and Eldredge, "Punctuated Equilibria," 145–47.

CHAPTER 1: NATURAL HISTORY AND THE NATURE OF HISTORY

1. See George Gaylord Simpson, *Tempo and Mode in Evolution* (New York: Columbia University Press, 1944).

2. Stephen Jay Gould and Niles Eldredge, "Punctuated Equilibria: The Tempo and Mode of Evolution Reconsidered," *Paleobiology* 3/2 (1977): 115–51. Quotes in this and the subsequent paragraph are from p. 145.

3. Originally, the theory was named "punctuated equilibria," but subsequently became commonly referred to as "punctuated equilibrium," including by Gould. Thus we refer to the theory as punctuated equilibrium throughout this book.

4. Stephen Jay Gould, "Is Uniformitarianism Necessary?" *American Journal of Science* 263 (1965): 223–28.

5. Stephen Jay Gould, *Ever Since Darwin* (New York: W. W. Norton, 1977), 147–52. Subsequent quotes from p. 151. Charles Lyell, *Principles of Geology* (Chicago: University of Chicago Press, 1990). In addition to sources directly referenced in the text, our discussion of uniformitarianism draws upon Gould's essay "Lyell's Pillars of Wisdom" in his book *The Lying Stones of Marrakech* (New York: Harmony Books, 2000). For contemporary adherents to gradualism and the view that history unfolds in a slow and orderly manner, see Daniel Dennett, *Darwin's Dangerous Idea* (New York: Simon & Schuster, 1995); Richard Dawkins, *The Ancestor's Tale* (Boston: Houghton Mifflin, 2004); and Simon Conway Morris, *The Crucible of Creation* (New York: Oxford University Press, 1998) and *Life's Solution* (New York: Cambridge University Press, 2003). For an analysis of the causes of mass extinctions, including a presentation of the evidence indicating that the Cretaceous extinction was caused by the collision of a comet with Earth, see David M. Raup, *Extinction* (New York: W. W. Norton, 1991).

6. Janet Browne, *Charles Darwin: Voyaging* (Princeton: Princeton University Press, 1995); Adrian Desmond and James Moore, *Darwin* (New York: W. W. Norton, 1991).

7. The Cretaceous-Tertiary boundary is now often referred to as the Cretaceous-Paleogene boundary due to the division of the Tertiary Period into the Paleogene and the Neogene by the Internal Commission on Stratigraphy.

8. Gould, *Ever Since Darwin*; Gould, *The Lying Stones*; Raup, *Extinction*.

9. Karl Marx, *Grundrisse: Foundations of the Critique of Political Economy* (New York: Penguin Books, 1993); and *Economic and Philosophic Manuscripts of 1844* (New York: International Publishers, 1964).

10. Stephen Jay Gould, *The Panda's Thumb* (New York: W. W. Norton, 2000), 196–97.

11. See Niles Eldredge, "The Allopatric Model and Phylogeny in Paleozoic Invertebrates," *Evolution* 25/1 (1971): 156–67; Niles Eldredge and Stephen Jay Gould, "Punctuated Equilibria: An Alternative to Phyletic Gradualism," in *Models in Paleobiology*, ed. Thomas J. M. Schopf (San Francisco: Freeman, Cooper, 1972), 82–115; Gould and Eldredge, "Punctuated Equilibria."

12. Stephen Jay Gould, *The Structure of Evolutionary History* (Cambridge, Mass.: Belknap Press of Harvard University Press, 2002).

CHAPTER 2: THE STRUCTURE OF NATURE AND THE NATURE OF STRUCTURE

1.   Max Tegmark, "Parallel Universes," *Scientific American* (May 2003): 40–51.

2.   Ibid., 49.

3.   Stephen Jay Gould, "Darwinism and the Expansion of Evolutionary Theory," *Science* 216 (1982): 380–87.

4.   Morris Kline, *Mathematical Thought from Ancient to Modern Times*, vol. 1 (Oxford: Oxford University Press, 1972), 44.

5.   Ernst Mayr, *The Growth of Biological Thought: Diversity, Evolution, and Inheritance* (Cambridge, Mass.: Harvard University Press, 1982), 38.

6.   Kline, *Mathematical Thought*, 151.

7.   Ibid., 51.

8.   Ibid., 151.

9.   Mayr, *The Growth of Biological Thought*, 25.

10. Ibid., 152.

11. Here we refer to Aristotelian and Platonic paradigms in a specific sense pertaining to assumptions regarding the nature of reality and appropriate ways to classify and understand natural diversity, particularly based on mathematical methods. We recognize that Plato and Aristotle have large and diverse bodies of work and that the distinction we make here does not fully capture the differences (and similarities) in their perspectives. Both scholars, particularly Aristotle, are notoriously difficult to characterize, and interpretations of their different perspectives have varied considerably during the ages that separate them from us. Mayr notes that Aristotle's approach to biology (as well as his general philosophy) has been interpreted during some eras in a fashion that makes it contradictory to how it has been interpreted during other times. (See Mayr, *The Growth of Biological Thought*, 149–54.) For example, as part of his advocacy for an inductive scientific program, Francis Bacon in the *Novum Organum* infamously denigrated Aristotelian philosophy as overly deductive and disinterested in empirical evidence, in sharp contrast to Mayr's interpretation of Aristotle's biology. See Francis Bacon, *The New*

Organon (Cambridge: Cambridge University Press, 2000). We do not intend in this book to enter the debate about the "proper" interpretation of Aristotle's or Plato's respective philosophies, but rather to use the distinction outlined in the text and paradigms attributed to these philosophers as a heuristic device for understanding approaches to mathematical biology. When we refer to specific research traditions as Platonic or Aristotelian, we are doing so in this restricted sense. Furthermore, we are aware that sophisticated research traditions are typically quite complex, and may contain a variety of elements that could be characterized in a manner differently from the one we use here.

12.   See Frank J. Sulloway, "Darwin and His Finches: The Evolution of a Legend," *Journal of the History of Biology* 15/1 (1982): 1–53; Frank J. Sulloway, "Darwin's Conversion: The *Beagle* Voyage and Its Aftermath," *Journal of the History of Biology* 15/3 (1982): 325–96. It is important to note that debate still continues regarding when Darwin converted to an evolutionary perspective, with some scholars still supporting the view that the conversion occurred before the *Beagle*'s return to England. Niles Eldredge, Gould's close colleague, has recently come to support the argument that Darwin was at least partially converted to the evolutionary perspective while still on the *Beagle* voyage. See Niles Eldredge, *Darwin: Discovering the Tree of Life* (New York: W. W. Norton, 2005).

13.   Sulloway, "Darwin and His Finches," 18–19; Sulloway, "Darwin's Conversion," 387–88.

14.   Stephen Jay Gould, *The Flamingo's Smile* (New York: W. W. Norton, 1985), 353–55.

15.   Nora Barlow, "Darwin's Ornithological Notes," *Bulletin of the British Museum (Natural History), Historical Series* 2/7 (1963): 201–78; Charles Darwin, *The Voyage of the Beagle* (New York: P. F. Collier and Son, 1937), 376–405; Adrian Desmond and James Moore, *Darwin: The Life of a Tormented Evolutionist* (New York: W.W. Norton, 1994), 186.

16.   Charles Darwin, *Charles Darwin's Diary of the Voyage of H.M.S. "Beagle."* (Cambridge: Cambridge University Press, 1934), 383.

17.   Gould, "Darwinism and the Expansion of Evolutionary Theory," 380. This is not to say that the core of natural selection is not logically derived. If (1) the characteristics of organisms vary from one to another, (2) the source of these characteristics is at least in part heritable, and (3) these characteristics influence reproductive success, evolution by natural selection is a logical consequence. However, the logic of natural selection does not allow for a prediction of the course of evolutionary history nor the types of organisms and relationships among them that will emerge over time. Thus, unlike Newtonian celestial mechanics, given a starting point, Darwinian theory does not allow for the logical deduction of future states.

18. Stephen Jay Gould, *The Structure of Evolutionary Theory* (Cambridge, Mass.: Harvard University Press, 2002).

19. Ibid., 284.

20. Ibid.

21. Gould, "Darwinism and the Expansion of Evolutionary Theory."

22. Stuart Kauffman and Brian Goodwin are perhaps the most well-known contemporary proponents of deep mathematical structure in organisms and the evolutionary process. See Stuart A. Kauffman, *The Origins of Order: Self-Organization and Selection in Evolution* (Oxford: Oxford University Press, 1993); Brian Goodwin, *How the Leopard Changed Its Spots* (New York: Charles Scribner's Sons, 1994). Gould provides a history of this tradition, from its pre-Darwinian origins to the present. See Gould, *The Structure of Evolutionary Theory.*

23. See D'Arcy Wentworth Thompson, *On Growth and Form* (Cambridge: Cambridge University Press, 1917); D'Arcy Wentworth Thompson, *On Growth and Form: A New Edition* (Cambridge: Cambridge University Press, 1942).

24. It is perhaps ironic, given that we refer to Thompson's work in biology as an exemplar of the Platonic paradigm, that he was a renowned student of Aristotle and produced standard translations of two of Aristotle's biological treatises.

25. Ian Stewart, *Nature's Numbers* (New York: Basic Books, 1995), 135.

26. Thompson, *On Growth and Form: A New Edition*, 527.

27. Ibid., 748–911.

28. Gould, *The Structure of Evolutionary Theory*, 1181.

29. See Goodwin, *How the Leopard*, 124; Stewart, *Nature's Numbers*, 136; Thompson, *On Growth and Form: A New Edition*, 923. These types of spirals are also observed in pineapples and various types of pinecones.

30. The series is named for Leonardo of Pisa (c. 1170–1250), who was nicknamed Fi Bonacci, and who proposed a mathematical problem about the growth of a hypothetical rabbit population, which produces the Fibonacci series. See Stewart, *Nature's Numbers*, 136; Thompson, *On Growth and Form: A New Edition*, 923.

31. The property of the Golden Ratio (φ) that so appealed to the Greeks is that a rectangle with this ratio between its sides can be divided into a square and a smaller rectangle with the same ratio between its sides as the original rectangle. For discussions of the Fibonacci series and its relationship to the Golden Ratio (Divine Proportion, Golden Section, Golden Mean, Golden Number, Golden Angle), see Goodwin, *How the Leopard*, 121–33; H. E. Huntley, *The Divine Proportion: A Study in Mathematical Beauty* (New York: Dover, 1970); Stewart, *Nature's Numbers*, 135–43; Thompson, *On Growth and Form: A New Edition*, 923–33.

32. S. Douady and Y. Couder, "Phyllotaxis as a Physical Self-Organized Growth Process," *Physical Review Letters* 68/13 (1992): 2098–2101.

33. Gould, *The Structure of Evolutionary Theory*, 1192.

34. Kauffman, *The Origins of Order*.

35. Thompson, *On Growth and Form: A New Edition*, 1094; Kauffman, *The Origins of Order*.

36. Kauffman, *The Origins of Order*, 482.

37. See Goodwin, *How the Leopard*; Kauffman, *The Origins of Order*; Stewart, *Nature's Numbers*; Thompson, *On Growth and Form: A New Edition*.

38. However, Thompson and some other adherents to this perspective had as an explicit or implicit goal the marginalization of natural selection as an evolutionary force, and the totality of such an approach could be considered anti-Darwinian. Nonetheless, admitting the existence of structural explanations of some phenomena is not necessarily a challenge to the central importance of natural selection. Indeed, most contemporary evolutionary theorists acknowledge the validity of some of Thompson's arguments, while remaining deeply committed to the dominance of Darwinian forces in the evolutionary process.

39. Stephen Jay Gould, *Ontogeny and Phylogeny* (Cambridge, Mass.: Harvard University Press, 1977).

40. Gould, *The Structure of Evolutionary Theory*, 141–46.

41. Ibid., 1025–37.

42. Stephen Jay Gould and Richard Lewontin, "The Spandrels of San Marco and the Panglossian Paradigm: A Critique of the Adaptationist Program," *Proceedings of the Royal Society of London. Series B, Biological Sciences* 205/1161 (1979): 581–98.

43. Voltaire, *Candide* (London: Penguin, 1947), 20, 136.

44. Gould and Lewontin, "The Spandrels of San Marco," 585–86.

45. Stephen Jay Gould, "The Evolutionary Significance of 'Bizarre' Structures: Antler Size and Skull Size in the 'Irish Elk,' *Megaloceros giganteus*," *Evolution* 28 (1974): 191–220.

46. Stephen Jay Gould, *Ever Since Darwin* (New York: W. W. Norton, 1977), 79–90.

47. Gould, *Ever Since Darwin*, 85–87.

48. In dialectical fashion, Gould goes on to note that the reverse could also have been true: it was large antlers that were selected for and large body size was the side effect of no necessary adaptive importance.

49. Gould and Lewontin, "The Spandrels of San Marco," 147–48.

50. Gould, *The Structure of Evolutionary Theory*, 1259.

51. Ibid.

52. Ibid., 1260.

53. Gould and Lewontin, "The Spandrels of San Marco," 587.

54. Stephen Jay Gould and Elisabeth S. Vrba, "Exaptation—A Missing Term in the Science of Form," *Paleobiology* 8 (1982): 4–15.

55. Stephen Jay Gould, "Exaptation: A Crucial Tool for an Evolutionary Psychology," *Journal of Social Issues* 47/3 (1991): 43–65.

56. Ibid.; Gould and Vrba, "Exaptation," 4.

57. Gould, *The Structure of Evolutionary Theory*, 1259; Gould, "Exaptation," 47; Stephen Jay Gould, *Bully for Brontosaurus* (New York: W.W. Norton, 1991), 139–51.

58. Gould, *The Structure of Evolutionary Theory*; Steven Rose, *The Future of the Brain: The Promise and Perils of Tomorrow's Neuroscience* (Oxford: Oxford University Press, 2005); Ian Tattersall, *Becoming Human: Evolution and Human Uniqueness* (New York: Harcourt Brace, 1998).

59. Gould, "Exaptation," 58.

60. Elisabeth S. Vrba and Stephen Jay Gould, "The Hierarchical Expansion of Sorting and Selection: Sorting and Selection Cannot Be Equated," *Paleobiology* 12 (1986): 217–28.

61. Gould and Lewontin, "The Spandrels of San Marco," 594.

62. Stephen Jay Gould, *Hen's Teeth and Horse's Toes* (New York: W. W. Norton, 1983), 158–65.

63. Ibid., 160.

64. Ibid., 163.

65. Gould and Lewontin, "The Spandrels of San Marco," 585, 592–93.

66. Stephen Jay Gould, *Wonderful Life* (New York: W.W. Norton, 1989), 64.

67. Ernst Mayr, *Animal Species* (Cambridge, Mass: Belknap Press, 1963).

68. Stephen Jay Gould, *Leonardo's Mountain of Clams and the Diet of Worms* (New York: Three Rivers Press, 1988), 330–31.

69. Ibid., 333.

70. Ibid., 334; see also Gould, *The Structure of Evolutionary Theory*, 1117–22.

71. Stephen Jay Gould, *The Panda's Thumb* (New York: W. W. Norton, 1980), 20–26.

72. Gould, *The Structure of Evolutionary Theory*, 82.

73. Ibid., 1105; see also Robert L. Dorit, "Genetics and Development: Good as Gould," in *Stephen Jay Gould: Reflections on His View of Life*, ed. Warren D. Allmon, Patricia H. Kelley, Robert M. Ross (New York: Oxford University Press, 2009), 313–33.

74. Noam Chomsky, *Aspects of the Theory of Syntax* (Cambridge: M.I.T. Press, 1965). See also Dorit, "Genetics and Development: Good as Gould," 325.

75.   Gould, *Leonardo's Mountain*, 17–44.

76.   Ibid., 30–31.

77.   Ibid., 31.

78.   Frank Zöllner, *Leonardo da Vinci: The Complete Paintings* (Los Angeles: Taschen, 2004), 92.

79.   Ibid., 92.

CHAPTER 3: CONTINGENCY AND CONVERGENCE

1.   Michael B. Shermer, "This View of Science: Stephen Jay Gould as Historian of Science and Scientific Historian, Popular Scientist and Scientific Popularizer," *Social Studies of Science* 32/4 (2002): 489–524.

2.   David Sepkoski, "Stephen Jay Gould, Jack Sepkoski, and the 'Quantitative Revolution' in American Paleobiology," *Journal of the History of Biology* 38 (2005): 209–37; Stephen Jay Gould, "Dollo on Dollo's Law: Irreversibility and the Status of Evolutionary Laws," *Journal of the History of Biology* 3/2 (1970): 189–212.

3.   Gould, "Dollo on Dollo's Law," 209.

4.   Ernst Mayr, *Toward a New Philosophy of Biology: Observations of an Evolutionist* (Cambridge, Mass.: Harvard University Press, 1988), 19; See also Ernst Mayr, *The Growth of Biological Thought: Diversity, Evolution, and Inheritance* (Cambridge, Mass.: Harvard University Press, 1982); Ernst Mayr, *What Makes Biology Unique? Considerations on the Autonomy of a Scientific Discipline* (Cambridge: Cambridge University Press, 2005); Stephen Jay Gould, *Leonardo's Mountain of Clams and the Diet of Worms* (New York: Harmony Books, 1988).

5.   Stephen Jay Gould, *The Structure of Evolutionary Theory* (Cambridge, Mass.: Harvard University Press, 2002); Mayr, *The Growth of Biological Thought*.

6.   Stephen Jay Gould, *Eight Little Piggies* (New York: W. W. Norton, 1993), 302–3.

7.   Darwin quoted in ibid., 302; see also Charles Darwin, *On the Origin of Species* (Cambridge, Mass.: Harvard University Press, 1964), 67; Charles Darwin, *Charles Darwin's Notebooks, 1836–1844* (Ithaca, N.Y.: Cornell University Press, 1987), 375–76.

8.   Gould, *Eight Little Piggies*, 303.

9.   Charles Darwin, *The Origin of Species* (New York: Penguin Books, 1985), 336–37; Darwin quoted in Gould, *Eight Little Piggies*, 303.

10.   Quoted from a letter Gould wrote; see Warren D. Allmon, "The Structure of Gould," in *Stephen Jay Gould: Reflections on His View of Life*, ed. Warren D. Allmon, Patricia H. Kelley, and Robert M. Ross (New York: Oxford University Press, 2009), 55; and Richard K. Bambach, "Diversity

in the Fossil Record and Stephen Jay Gould's Evolving View of the History of Life," in *Stephen Jay Gould: Reflections on His View of Life*, 70.

11. Stephen Jay Gould, *The Flamingo's Smile* (New York: W. W. Norton, 1985), 448.

12. Stephen Jay Gould, "The Paradox of the First Tier: An Agenda for Paleobiology," *Paleobiology* 11/1 (1985): 2–12, quote on 2–3.

13. Ibid., 3.

14. Ibid., 10.

15. Stephen Jay Gould, *Wonderful Life* (New York: W. W. Norton, 1989).

16. Stephen Jay Gould, *The Flamingo's Smile* (New York: W. W. Norton, 1985), 281–90; Arthur Lovejoy, *The Great Chain of Being* (Cambridge, Mass.: Harvard University Press).

17. It should be noted that Darwin, despite struggling with this conclusion, understood that *Homo sapiens* were the product of contingent events of history and were therefore not foreordained to develop. See Darwin, *Origin of Species*; Charles Darwin, *The Descent of Man, and Selection in Relation to Sex* (Princeton, N.J.: Princeton University Press, 1981); John Bellamy Foster, *Marx's Ecology* (New York: Monthly Review Press, 2000).

18. As quoted by Stephen Jay Gould in an interview in Wim Kayzer, *A Glorious Accident: Understanding Our Place in the Cosmic Puzzle* (New York: W. H. Freeman, 1997), 84; see also Darwin Correspondence Project Database, http://www.darwinproject.ac.uk, letter no. 8658.

19. Gould, "The Paradox of the First Tier," 3.

20. For a discussion of the role of chance—"bad luck"—in extinction, see David Raup, *Extinction* (New York: W. W. Norton, 1991).

21. For an assessment of potential causes of the Permian extinction and a presentation of its consequences, see Douglas H. Erwin's *Extinction: How Life on Earth Nearly Ended 250 Million Years Ago* (Princeton, N.J.: Princeton University Press, 2006).

22. Stephen Jay Gould, "The Persistently Flat Earth: Irrationality and Dogmatism Are Foes of Both Science and Religion," *Natural History* 103/3 (1994): 12–19, quote on 19.

23. Gould, *Wonderful Life*, 45.

24. Mark Twain, *Letters from the Earth* (New York: Harper & Row, 1962), 222–23.

25. Ibid., 226.

26. Gould, *The Structure of Evolutionary Theory*; Stephen Jay Gould, "Is a New and General Theory of Evolution Emerging?" *Paleobiology* 6/1 (1980): 119–30.

27. Gould, "Is a New and General Theory of Evolution Emerging?" 129; Richard Lewontin, *The Triple Helix: Gene, Organism, and Environment* (Cambridge, Mass.: Harvard University Press, 2000).

28. Gould, *Eight Little Piggies*; Gould, "Is a New and General Theory of Evolution Emerging?" 129.

29. Gould, *The Structure of Evolutionary Theory*.

30. Ibid., 251-60.

31. Ibid., 351.

32. Stephen Jay Gould, *Full House* (New York: Harmony Books, 1996).

33. However, this diversification has been based on fewer themes, as there was greater *disparity* among organisms in the Cambrian, when more fundamental body plans existed, as Gould argues in *Wonderful Life*.

34. Gould, *Full House*.

35. Robert Wright, *Nonzero: The Logic of Human Destiny* (New York: Pantheon, 2000).

36. Ibid., 16-17.

37. Richard Dawkins, *The Ancestor's Tale: A Pilgrimage to the Dawn of Evolution* (New York: Houghton Mifflin, 2006), 597-605.

38. Daniel C. Dennett, *Darwin's Dangerous Idea: Evolution and the Meaning of Life* (New York: Simon & Schuster, 1995), 308.

39. Richard Dawkins, *Climbing Mount Improbable* (New York: W. W. Norton, 1996), 138-97.

40. Gould, *The Structure of Evolutionary Theory*, 1123-34.

41. Simon Conway Morris, *The Crucible of Creation: The Burgess Shale and the Rise of Animals* (Oxford: Oxford University Press, 1998); Simon Conway Morris, *Life's Solution: Inevitable Humans in a Lonely Universe* (Cambridge: Cambridge University Press, 2004).

42. Conway Morris, *Life's Solution*.

43. Simon Conway Morris, ed., *The Deep Structure of Biology: Is Convergence Sufficiently Ubiquitous to Give a Directional Signal?* (West Conshohocken, Penn.: Templeton Foundation Press, 2008).

44. Conway Morris, "Evolution and Convergence: Some Wider Considerations," in ibid., 60-62.

45. John F. Haught, "The Purpose in Nature: On the Possibility of a Theology of Evolution," in ibid., 230.

46. Dawkins, *The Ancestor's Tale*, 595-96.

47. Stephen Jay Gould, *The Flamingo's Smile* (New York: W. W. Norton, 1985), 393-95.

48. Ibid., 397.

49. Gould, interviewed in Kayzer, *A Glorious Accident*, 92-93.

CHAPTER 4: EMERGENCE, HIERARCHY, AND THE LIMITS OF REDUCTIONISM

1. For a discussion of the development and hardening of the modern synthesis, see Stephen Jay Gould, *The Structure of Evolutionary Theory* (Cambridge, Mass.: Harvard University Press, 2002), 503–84.

2. Karl Marx and Frederick Engels, *Collected Works* (New York: International Publishers, 1975), vol. 25, 22.

3. Richard Levins and Richard Lewontin, *The Dialectical Biologist* (Cambridge, Mass.: Harvard University Press, 1985), 135, 159, 269.

4. Ibid., 2.

5. Stephen Jay Gould, *The Hedgehog, The Fox, and the Magister's Pox* (New York: Harmony Books, 2003), 201–2.

6. Ibid., 138.

7. George Homans, *Social Behavior: Its Elementary Forms* (New York: Harcourt, Brace, Jovanovich, 1974); Jon Elster, *Nuts and Bolts for the Social Sciences* (Cambridge: Cambridge University Press, 1989); Gary S. Becker, *The Economic Approach to Human Behavior* (Chicago: Chicago University Press, 1976); Cristina Bicchieri, *Rationality and Coordination* (Cambridge: Cambridge University Press, 1993).

8. John Kenneth Galbraith, *The Economics of Peace and Laughter* (New York: New American Library, 1971), 67–74; John Kenneth Galbraith, *The Affluent Society* (New York: New American Library, 1984).

9. Michael Dawson, *The Consumer Trap* (Urbana: University of Illinois Press, 2003).

10. Dick Hebdige, *Hiding in the Light* (New York: Routledge, 1988); F. R. Ankersmit, "Historiography and Postmodernism," *History and Theory* 28/2 (1989): 137–53; Bryan Palmer, *Descent into Discourse* (Philadelphia: Temple University Press, 1990); Michel Foucault, *The Foucault Reader* (New York: Pantheon, 1984); Steve Woolgar, *Science: The Very Idea!* (London: Tavistock, 1988); Steven Yearly, *The Green Case* (New York: Harper and Row, 1991), 136–37.

11. On the role of the principle of historical specificity of historical materialism see Karl Korsch, *Karl Marx* (New York: Russell and Russell, 1938), 24–44. See also C. Wright Mills, *The Sociological Imagination* (New York: Oxford University Press, 1959), 143–64; Richard York and Brett Clark, "Marxism, Positivism, and Scientific Sociology: Social Gravity and Historicity," *Sociological Quarterly* 47 (2006): 425–50.

12. Raymond Williams, *The Country and the City* (New York: Oxford University Press, 1975); Raymond Williams, *Marx and Literature* (Oxford: Oxford University Press, 1977); Raymond Williams, *Problems in Materialism and Culture* (London: Verso, 1980); Ellen Meiksins Wood, "What Is the 'Postmodern' Agenda?" in *In Defense of History: Marxism*

and the Postmodern Agenda, ed. Ellen Meiksins Wood and John Bellamy Foster (New York: Monthly Review Press, 1997), 1-16; John Bellamy Foster, "In Defense of History," in *In Defense of History*, 184-194.

13. Lee Ross, "The Intuitive Psychologist and His Shortcomings: Distortions in the Attribution Process," in *Advances in Experimental Social Psychology*, ed. L. Berkowitz (New York: Academic Press, 1977), vol. 10, 173-220; Edward E. Jones and Victor Harris, "The Attribution of Attitudes," *Journal of Experimental Social Psychology* 3 (1967): 1-24.

14. Gould, *The Hedgehog, The Fox, and the Magister's Pox*, 221.

15. Ibid., 223; Levins and Lewontin, *The Dialectical Biologist*, 3.

16. Richard Dawkins, *The Selfish Gene* (New York: Oxford University Press, 1976); Daniel Dennet, *Darwin's Dangerous Idea* (London: Simon & Schuster, 1995).

17. Warren D. Allmon, "The Structure of Gould," in *Stephen Jay Gould: Reflections on His View of Life*, ed. Warren D. Allmon, Patricia H. Kelley, and Robert M. Ross (New York: Oxford University Press, 2009), 51.

18. Elizabeth Pennisi, "Modernizing the Modern Synthesis," *Science* 321 (2008): 196-97; John Whitfield, "Postmodern Evolution?" *Nature* 455 (2008): 281-84; P. M. Binder, "The Edge of Reductionism," *Nature* 459 (2009): 332-34.

19. Stephen Jay Gould, *The Structure of Evolutionary Theory* (Cambridge, Mass.: Harvard University Press, 2002), 598.

20. Stephen Jay Gould and Elisabeth A. Lloyd, "Individuality and Adaptation Across Levels of Selection: How Shall We Name and Generalize the Unit of Darwinism?" *Proceedings of the National Academy of Sciences of the United States of America* 96 (1999): 11904-9; Elisabeth A. Lloyd and Stephen Jay Gould, "Species Selection on Variability," *Proceedings of the National Academy of Sciences of the United States of America* 90 (1993): 595-99; Elisabeth S. Vrba and Stephen Jay Gould, "The Hierarchical Expansion of Sorting and Selection: Sorting and Selection Cannot Be Equated," *Paleobiology* 12 (1986): 217-28; Gould, *The Structure of Evolutionary Theory*.

21. Gould, *The Structure of Evolutionary Theory*, 599.

22. Ibid., 602.

23. Ibid., 608.

24. There is an important debate regarding whether species-level selection operates on the "emergent characters" or "emergent fitness" of species. The emergent character approach "requires that a trait functioning in species selection be emergent at the species level—basically defined as origin by non-additive interaction among lower-level constituents" (Gould, *The Structure of Evolutionary Theory*, 657). The emergent fitness approach is broader, encompassing emergent characters as best cases, but also including "features that seem to 'belong' to [species] as an entity, but

that arise additively as 'aggregate' or 'sum-of-the-parts' characters," such as variability (658). Gould originally allied himself with the emergent character approach, but came to support the emergent fitness approach. See his discussion in *The Structure of Evolutionary Theory*, 656–66. We do not focus on the distinction between the emergent character and the emergent fitness approaches here, since it is somewhat beyond our more general interest in emergence, reductionism, and hierarchy.

25. Ibid., 707–9.

26. Ibid., 657.

27. Lloyd and Gould, "Species Selection on Variability." Variability is, of course, not simply related to population size. A large population could have low variability if its members are homogeneous. However, a very small population cannot have a great deal of *absolute* diversity, though a large population has at least the capacity to have many different types of individual organisms in it.

28. Stephen Jay Gould, "The Meaning of Punctuated Equilibrium and Its Role in Validating a Hierarchical Approach to Macroevolution," in *Perspectives on Evolution*, ed. Roger Milkman (Sunderland, Mass.: Sinauer Associates, 1982), 83–104; see also Richard K. Bambach, "Diversity in the Fossil Record and Stephen Jay Gould's Evolving View of the History of Life," in *Stephen Jay Gould: Reflections on His View of Life*, 69–126.

29. Stephen Jay Gould and C. Bradford Calloway, "Clams and Brachiopods— Ships that Pass in the Night," *Paleobiology* 6/4 (1980): 383–96.

30. Gould, *The Structure of Evolutionary Theory*, 646–52.

31. Many examples of altruistic behavior can be explained in terms of kin selection, where the acts of an individual organism may reduce its own reproductive success but may enhance the success of its kin, which share its genes, and thus the "altruistic" behavior serves to increase the success of its genes. Kin selection has often been used to explain cases of apparent interdemic selection away and is clearly highly important in evolution. However, there remain compelling theoretical defenses of multilevel selection and its importance to the emergence of altruism. See Elliot Sober and David Sloan Wilson, *Unto Others* (Harvard University Press, 1998).

32. Gould, *The Structure of Evolutionary Theory*, 613, 632–37.

33. George C. Williams, *Adaptation and Natural Selection* (Oxford: Oxford University Press, 1966).

34. David L. Hull, "Individuality and Selection," *Annual Review of Ecology and Systematics* 11 (1980): 311–32.

35. As Gould recognized, there is also selection at the level of the gene, where genes are genuine interactors, but the gene is only one level in the hierarchy of interactors.

36. Gould, *The Structure of Evolutionary Theory*, 632.

CHAPTER 5: DEBUNKING AS POSITIVE SCIENCE

1. The Sokal affair, including the original article and many of the subsequent comments on it by a variety of scholars, is recounted in *The Sokal Hoax: The Sham that Shook the Academy* (Lincoln: University of Nebraska Press, 2000), edited by the editors of *Lingua Franca*, the publication in which the hoax was first revealed. Sokal and Jean Bricmont published *Fashionable Nonsense: Postmodern Intellectuals' Abuse of Science* (New York: Picador, 1998), which serves to debunk some of the poorly reasoned work that counts as scholarship in some sectors of the academy. In *The Hedgehog, the Fox, and the Magister's Pox* (New York: Harmony Books, 2003) Stephen Jay Gould expressed mixed feelings about the hoax (100), since, although he found it amusing and that it made a point, he also found the implication that science studies in general are nonsense disquieting, since many critiques of science by social scientists raise important and valid points. Paul Gross and Norman Levitt's book *Higher Superstition: The Academic Left and Its Quarrels with Science* (Baltimore: Johns Hopkins University Press, 1994), in part inspired Sokal to perform his hoax. It is worth noting that Gross and Levitt, while criticizing elements on the left, fail to seriously acknowledge the strong anti-science tendencies of the right and the long tradition on the left of commitment to reason. They also cast an overly wide net, criticizing some scholars who provide reasoned critiques of particular scientific practices and/or scientific institutions but who do not deny the intellectual value of rationalism and empiricism that form the foundation of science. Gould suggests in *The Hedgehog, the Fox, and the Magister's Pox* that Gross and Levitt caricature the position they criticize and that their argument is largely unconstructive (99).

2. John Bellamy Foster, Brett Clark, and Richard York, *The Critique of Intelligent Design: Materialism versus Creationism from Antiquity to the Present* (New York: Monthly Review Press, 2008).

3. It is worth noting that Gould recognized the potentially sexist nature of using the term "man" to refer to all people. He explains, "My title parodies Protagoras's famous aphorism about all people, and also notes the reality of a truly sexist past that regarded males as standards for humanity and therefore tended to mismeasure men, while ignoring women." See Stephen Jay Gould, *The Mismeasure of Man*, rev. ed. (New York: W. W. Norton, 1996), 20.

4. Ibid., 20, 40.

5. Mark Bowen, *Censoring Science: Inside the Attack on Dr. James Hansen and the Truth of Global Warming* (New York: E. P. Dutton, 2008); Chris Mooney, *The Republican War on Science* (New York: Basic Books, 2005).

6. Arthur Jensen, "How Much Can We Boost IQ and Scholastic Achievement?" *Harvard Education Review* 39 (1969): 1–123, 449–83;

Leon Kamin, *The Science and Politics of IQ* (Potomac, Md.: Lawrence Erlbaum Associates, 1974); Oliver Gillie, *Who Do You Think You Are?: Man or Superman—The Genetic Controversy* (New York: Saturday Review Press, 1976).

7. Stephen Jay Gould, *The Mismeasure of Man*, original edition (New York: W. W. Norton, 1981), 54.

8. Ibid., 68.

9. Ibid.

10. Ibid., 69.

11. Ibid., 79.

12. Gould, *Mismeasure*, rev. ed., 23.

13. R. S. Nickerson, "Confirmation Bias: A Ubiquitous Phenomenon in Many Guises," *Review of General Psychology* 2/2 (1998): 175–220.

14. Gould, *Mismeasure*, rev. ed., 114–26.

15. This interpretation is now considered to have much merit by evolutionary theorists. Gould wrote an interesting essay on the topic in his first book, *Ever Since Darwin* (New York: W. W. Norton, 1977).

16. Gould, *Mismeasure*, orig. ed., 121.

17. Gould, *Mismeasure*, rev. ed., 26–27.

18. Ibid., 28.

19. Ibid., 367–90.

CHAPTER 6: THE CRITIQUE OF BIOLOGICAL DETERMINISM

1. Richard Lewontin, *The Triple Helix* (Cambridge, Mass.: Harvard University Press, 2000), 3–5.

2. Hilary Rose and Steven Rose, "Darwin and After," *New Left Review* 63 (2010): 91–113, see p. 106.

3. See ibid.; Daniel Dennet, *Darwin's Dangerous Idea* (London: Simon & Schuster, 1996).

4. Richard Lewontin and Richard Levins, *Biology Under the Influence* (New York: Monthly Review Press, 2007), 59–60.

5. Edward O. Wilson, "Human Decency Is Animal," *The New York Times Magazine* (October 12, 1975): 48–50.

6. Stephen Jay Gould, *The Mismeasure of Man*, rev. ed. (New York: W. W. Norton, 1996), 27.

7. Ibid., 28.

8. For a historical discussion of the sociobiology conflict, see Ullica Segerstråle, *Defenders of the Truth* (Oxford: Oxford University Press, 2001).

9. See John Bellamy Foster, Brett Clark, and Richard York, *Critique of Intelligent Design* (New York: Monthly Review Press, 2008).

10.   Edward O. Wilson, *Sociobiology: The New Synthesis*, twenty-fifth anniversary ed. (Cambridge, Mass.: Harvard University Press, 2000), 3–5.

11.   Ibid., 575.

12.   Edward O. Wilson, *Consilience: The Unity of Knowledge* (New York: Knopf, 1998).

13.   See Wilson, *Sociobiology*.

14.   See Charles J. Lumsden and Edward O. Wilson, *Promethean Fire: Reflections on the Origin of Mind* (Cambridge, Mass.: Harvard University Press, 1981); Wilson, *Sociobiology*; Edward O. Wilson, *On Human Nature* (Cambridge, Mass.: Harvard University Press, 1978).

15.   Richard J. Herrnstein and Charles Murray, *The Bell Curve: Intelligence and Class Structure in American Life* (New York: Free Press, 1994).

16.   Timothy J. Biblarz and Adrian E. Raftery, "Family Structure, Educational Attainment, and Socioeconomic Success: Rethinking the 'Pathology of Matriarchy,'" *American Journal of Sociology* 105/2 (1999): 321–65; David M. Buss, *Evolutionary Psychology: The New Science of the Mind* (Boston: Allyn & Bacon, 1999); Jeremy Freese and Brian Powell, "Sociobiology, Status, and Parental Investment in Sons and Daughters: Testing the Trivers-Willard Hypothesis," *American Journal of Sociology* 106/6 (1999): 1704–43; Christine Horne, "Values and Evolutionary Psychology," *Sociological Theory* 22/3 (2004): 477–503; Satoshi Kanazawa, "De Gustibus *Est* Disputandum," *Social Forces* 79/3 (2001): 1131–63; Satoshi Kanazawa, "Can Evolutionary Psychology Explain Reproductive Behavior in the Contemporary United States?" *The Sociological Quarterly* 44/2 (2003): 291–302; Satoshi Kanazawa and Greit Vandermassen, "Engineers Have More Sons, Nurses Have More Daughters: An Evolutionary Psychological Extension of Baron-Cohen's Extreme Male Brain Theory of Autism," *Journal of Theoretical Biology* 233 (2005): 589–99; J. Philippe Rushton, *Altruism, Socialization, and Society* (Englewood Cliffs, N.J.: Prentice-Hall, 1980); Joanne Savage and Satoshi Kanazawa, "Social Capital and the Human Psyche: Why Is Social Life 'Capital,'" *Sociological Theory* 22/3 (2004): 504–24; Randy Thornhill and Craig Palmer, *A Natural History of Rape: Biological Bases of Sexual Coercion* (Cambridge, Mass.: Harvard University Press, 2000); John Tooby and Leda Cosmides, "Friendship and Banker's Paradox: Other Pathways to the Evolution of Adaptations for Altruism," *Proceedings of the British Academy* 88 (1996): 119–43; Robert L. Trivers and Dan E. Willard, "Natural Selection of the Parental Ability to Vary the Sex Ratio of Offspring," *Science* 179 (1975): 90–91; Edward O. Wilson, "Kin Selection as the Key to Altruism: Its Rise and Fall," *Social Research* 72/1 (2005): 159–66.

17.   Savage and Kanazawa, "Social Capital and the Human Psyche," 506.

18. David M. Buss and D. T. Kenrick, "Evolutionary Social Psychology," in *The Handbook of Social Psychology*, ed. D. T. Gilbert, S. T. Fiske, and G. Lindzey, 4th ed. (New York: McGraw Hill, 1998), vol. 2, 982–1026; Horne, "Values and Evolutionary Psychology," 478.

19. Savage and Kanazawa, "Social Capital and the Human Psyche," 506.

20. See Jeremy Freese, Jui-Chung Allen Li, and Lisa D. Wade, "The Potential Relevances of Biology to Social Inquiry," *Annual Review of Sociology* 29 (2003): 233–56.

21. Savage and Kanazawa, "Social Capital and the Human Psyche," 506–8.

22. Leda Cosmides and John Tooby, "Beyond Intuition and Instinct Blindness: Toward an Evolutionary Rigorous Cognitive Science," in *Cognition on Cognition*, ed. Jacques Mehler and Susana Franck (Cambridge, Mass.: MIT Press, 1995).

23. Savage and Kanazawa, "Social Capital and the Human Psyche," 505–7.

24. Gerd Gigerenzer, *Adaptive Thinking: Rationality in the Real World* (Oxford: Oxford University Press, 2000).

25. Stephen Jay Gould, *An Urchin in the Storm* (New York: W. W. Norton, 1987), 113.

26. Richard C. Lewontin, Steven Rose, and Leon J. Kamin, *Not in Our Genes: Biology, Ideology, and Human Nature* (New York: Pantheon Books, 1984), 10.

27. Richard Machalek and Michael W. Martin, "Sociology and the Second Darwinian Revolution: A Metatheoretical Analysis," *Sociological Theory* 22/3 (2004): 455–76.

28. Ernst Mayr, *The Growth of Biological Thought: Diversity, Evolution, and Inheritance* (Cambridge, Mass.: Harvard University Press, 1982), 63.

29. Ibid.,; Ernst Mayr, *What Makes Biology Unique? Considerations on the Autonomy of a Scientific Discipline* (Cambridge: Cambridge University Press, 2005).

30. Richard Levins and Richard C. Lewontin, *The Dialectical Biologist* (Cambridge, Mass.: Harvard University Press, 1985), 135–36; Gould, *An Urchin in the Storm*, 217–24.

31. Stephan Jay Gould, *The Hedgehog, the Fox, and the Magister's Pox: Mending the Gap between Science and the Humanities* (New York: Harmony Books, 2003), 221.

32. Steven Rose, *The Making of Memory: From Molecules to Mind* (New York: Anchor Books, 1992), 328.

33. Gould referred to this process as disciplinary imperialism, where the social sciences are pushed into a position of subservience to biology, just as the biological sciences are treated as subservient to chemistry and physics. See Stephen Jay Gould, "Exaptation: A Crucial Tool for an Evolutionary Psychology," *Journal of Social Issues* 47/3 (1991): 43–65.

34. Employing the "norm of reaction," if properly assessed, does not strengthen the position of sociobiologists. Instead, it reveals the limitations of their position.

35. Machalek and Martin, "Sociology and the Second Darwinian Revolution," 460; see also Richard Dawkins, *The Selfish Gene* (New York: Oxford University Press, 1976).

36. Wilson, *Consilience*, 151; Robert Plomin and Kathryn Asbury, "Nature *And* Nurture: Genetic and Environmental Influences on Behavior," *Annals of the American Academy* 600 (2005): 86–98.

37. Gould, *The Mismeasure of Man*, rev. ed., 34.

38. Ibid.

39. Levins and Lewontin, *The Dialectical Biologist*, 279.

40. Wilson, *Consilience*.

41. Levins and Lewontin, *The Dialectical Biologist*, 258.

42. Richard Lewontin, *Biology as Ideology: The Doctrine of DNA* (New York: Harper Perennial, 1991), 107.

43. Ibid., 92–93.

44. Lewontin and Levins, *Biology Under the Influence*.

45. Barry Commoner, "Unraveling the DNA Myth: The Spurious Foundation of Genetic Engineering," *Harper's Magazine* 304/1821 (2002): 39–47.

46. Richard Lewontin, *It Ain't Necessarily So*, 2nd ed. (New York: New York Review of Books, 2001), 139.

47. Ibid.

48. Commoner, "Unraveling the DNA Myth," 47.

49. Lewontin, *Biology as Ideology*, 48.

50. Ibid., 141–43.

51. Lewontin, *The Triple Helix*, 17.

52. Lewontin, *Biology as Ideology*, 64.

53. Gould, *An Urchin in the Storm*, 159.

54. Lewontin, *Biology as Ideology*, 48.

55. Ibid., 63.

56. Interview with Stephen Jay Gould in Wim Kayzer, *A Glorious Accident: Understanding Our Place in the Cosmic Puzzle* (New York: W. H. Freeman, 1997), 91–92.

57. Richard Lewontin, "Not So Natural Selection," *New York Review of Books* (May 27, 2010), 34–36.

58. Gould, *An Urchin in the Storm*, 31.

59. Stephen Jay Gould, *I Have Landed* (New York: Harmony Books, 2002), 227.

60. Lewontin, *Biology as Ideology*, 64.

61. Levins and Lewontin, *The Dialectical Biologist*, 89.

62. Ibid., 89–106; Lewontin, *Biology As Ideology*, 109–19.

63. John Odling-Smee, Kevin N. Laland, and Marcus W. Feldman, *Niche Construction* (Princeton, N.J.: Princeton University Press, 2003).

64. Lewontin, *The Triple Helix*, 44–48, 82; Lewontin and Levins, *Biology Under the Influence*.

65. Gould, *The Hedgehog, the Fox, and the Magister's Pox*, 231. Gould indicates that it was from the social sciences that he came to learn the importance of contingency.

66. Richard Lewontin, "Sleight of Hand," *The Sciences* July/August (1981): 23–26.

67. Herman Daly, *Steady-State Economics* (San Francisco: W. H. Freeman, 1977), 23.

68. Lewontin and Levins, *Biology Under the Influence*, 46.

69. Gould, *The Hedgehog, the Fox, and the Magister's Pox*, 223.

70. Simon Baron-Cohen, *The Essential Difference* (London: Penguin, 2003).

71. Kanazawa, "De Gustibus *Est* Disputandum."

72. Robert Wright, *The Moral Animal* (New York: Random House, 1994).

73. Ian Tattersall, *Becoming Human: Evolution and Human Uniqueness* (New York: Harcourt Brace, 1998).

74. Rose and Rose, "Darwin and After."

75. Stephen Jay Gould, *The Structure of Evolutionary Theory* (Cambridge, Mass.: Harvard University Press, 2002), 1264–65; see also Stephen Jay Gould, "More Things in Heaven and Earth," in *Alas, Poor Darwin*, ed. Hilary Rose and Steven Rose (New York: Harmony Books, 2000), 101–25.

76. Stephen Jay Gould and Richard C. Lewontin, "The Spandrels of San Marco and the Panglossian Paradigm: A Critique of the Adaptationist Programme," *Proceedings of the Royal Society of London B* 205 (1979): 581–98.

77. Stephen Jay Gould, "More Things in Heaven and Earth," 123.

78. Stephen Jay Gould and Elisabeth S. Vrba, "Exaptation—A Missing Term in the Science of Form," *Paleobiology* 8 (1982): 4–15.

79. Gould, *An Urchin in the Storm*, 30.

80. Gould, "Exaptation," 51.

81. Gould, *An Urchin in the Storm*, 120–22; Steven Rose, *The 21st-Century Brain: Explaining, Mending and Manipulating the Mind* (London: Jonathan Cape, 2005); Gould, "Exaptation."

82. Gould, "Exaptation"; Gould, *An Urchin in the Storm*.

83. Gould and Lewontin, "The Spandrels of San Marco and the Panglossian Paradigm," 597.

84. Charles Darwin, *The Voyage of the Beagle* (New York: P. F. Collier, 1937), 503.

CHAPTER 7: *HOMO FLORESIENSIS* AND HUMAN EQUALITY

1.   Until recently, it was typical to use the term "hominid" to refer to humans and their ancestors. However, over the past two decades it has become well established that humans are much more closely related to bonobos, chimpanzees, and gorillas than previously thought. This has led to a restructuring of the taxonomic system to recognize the close relationship between humans and the African apes so that the category of "hominid" now includes chimpanzees and gorillas. In this new system, "hominin" refers exclusively to humans and their ancestors. See also The News Staff, "Breakthrough of the Year: The Runners-Up," *Science* 306 (2004): 2013-17; Richard A. Kerr, "Breakthrough of the Year: The Winner," *Science* 306 (2004): 2010-12.

2.   P. Brown et al., "A New Small-Bodied Hominin from the Late Pleistocene of Flores, Indonesia," *Nature* 431 (2004): 1055-61.

3.   The discovery of *Homo floresiensis* has led to a great deal of controversy, with some scholars asserting that it is a distinct species and others arguing that the skeletal remains attributed to *Homo floresiensis* are merely those of an abnormal modern human. We will not review this extensive literature here, but it seems fair to say at this time that the weight of scholarly opinion favors recognizing *Homo floresiensis* as a distinct new species. M. W. Tocheri et al., "The Primitive Wrist of *Homo floresiensis* and Its Implications for Human Evolution," *Science* 317 (2007): 1743-45; D. Falk et al., "Brain Shape in Human Microcephalics and *Homo floresiensis*," *Proceedings of the National Academy of Science of the USA* 104/7 (2007): 2513-18; D. E. Lieberman, "*Homo floresiensis* from Head to Toe," *Nature* 459 (2009): 41-42; W. L. Jungers et al., "The Foot of *Homo floresiensis*," *Nature* 459 (2009): 81-84; E. M. Weston and A. M. Lister, "Insular Dwarfism in Hippos and a Model Brain Size Reduction in *Homo floresiensis*," *Nature* 459 (2009): 85-88; and the 2009 special issue of *Journal of Human Evolution* 57/5, examining the finds Liang Bua on Flores.

4.   M. J. Morwood et al., "Archaeology and Age of a New Hominin from Flores in Eastern Indonesia," *Nature* 431 (2004): 1087-91.

5.   M. W. Moore et al., "Continuities in Stone Flaking Technology in Liang Bua, Flores, Indonesia," *Journal of Human Evolution* 57 (2009): 503-26.

6.   Michael Balter, "Skeptics Question Whether Flores Hominid Is a New Species," *Science* 306 (2004): 1116; Ann Gibbons, "New Species of Small Human Found in Indonesia," *Science* 306 (2004): 789; T. Jacob et al., "Pygmoid Australomelanesian *Homo sapiens* Skeletal Remains from Liang Bua, Flores," *Proceedings of the National Academy of Sciences of the USA* 103/36 (2006): 13421-26. See sources in note 3 above for subsequent research refuting the claim that the skeleton attributed to *Homo floresiensis* is a deformed modern human and supporting the claim that *Homo floresiensis* is a distinct hominin species.

7. See in particular, Stephen Jay Gould, *Wonderful Life* (New York: W. W. Norton, 1989).

8. Stephen Jay Gould, *Full House* (New York: W. W. Norton, 1996).

9. See the chapter "Bushes and Ladders in Human Evolution" in Stephen Jay Gould, *Ever Since Darwin* (New York: W. W. Norton, 1977), 56–62.

10. C. C. Swisher et al., "Latest *Homo Erectus* of Java: Potential Contemporaneity with *Homo Sapiens* in Southeast Asia," *Science* 274 (1996): 1870–74.

11. See the chapter "Our Unusual Unity" in Stephen Jay Gould, *Leonardo's Mountain of Clams and the Diet of Worms* (New York: Harmony Books, 1998), 197–212.

12. Jared Diamond, "The Astonishing Micropygmies," *Science* 306 (2004): 2047–48.

13. Christopher Stringer and Robin McKie, *African Exodus: The Origins of Modern Humanity* (New York: Owl Books, 1998). The shrinking of our brains was likely due to climatic changes—the size of other species of animals was likewise affected—and probably does not reflect a decline in intellectual ability. However, this point also shows, in much the same way as the dwarfism generated by isolation on an island, that humans are not exempt from the forces that affect other animals.

14. Milford Wolpoff and Rachel Caspari, *Race and Human Evolution: A Fatal Attraction* (New York: Simon & Schuster, 1997).

15. For a discussion of polygenism, see Stephen Jay Gould, *The Mismeasure of Man* (New York: W. W. Norton, 1981); and Adrian Desmond and James Moore, *Darwin's Sacred Cause* (Boston: Houghton Mifflin Harcourt, 2009).

16. Wolpoff and Caspari, *Race and Human Evolution*.

17. Stringer and McKie, *African Exodus*.

18. Marta Mirazón Lahr and Robert Foley, "Human Evolution Writ Small," *Nature* 431 (2004): 1043–44.

19. Gould, *Full House*, 42. For a discussion of the continuity between human beings and other animals, see Charles Darwin, *The Descent of Man, and Selection in Relation to Sex* (Princeton, N.J.: Princeton University Press, 1981); Charles Darwin, *The Expression of the Emotions in Man and Animals* (Oxford: Oxford University Press, 1998).

20. See the chapter "Human Equality Is a Contingent Fact of History" in Stephen Jay Gould, *The Flamingo's Smile* (New York: W. W. Norton, 1985), 185–98.

21. Gould, *Leonardo's Mountain*, 212.

CHAPTER 8: ART, SCIENCE, AND HUMANISM

1. This lecture became the basis for the subsequent book, C. P. Snow, *The Two Cultures and the Scientific Revolution* (Cambridge: Cambridge University Press, 1960).

2. Stephen Jay Gould, *The Hedgehog, the Fox, and the Magister's Pox: Mending the Gap between Science and the Humanities* (New York: Harmony Books, 2003).

3. Edward O. Wilson, *Consilience: The Unity of Knowledge* (New York: Random House, 1998), 266.

4. Ibid., 267.

5. Gould, *The Hedgehog, the Fox, and the Magister's Pox*, 192–93.

6. See Stephen Jay Gould, *The Structure of Evolutionary Theory* (Cambridge, Mass.: Harvard University Press, 2002), 108–11.

7. Gould, *The Hedgehog, the Fox, and the Magister's Pox*, 194–220.

8. Wilson, *Consilience*, 245–46, 260, 273.

9. Gould, *The Hedgehog, the Fox, and the Magister's Pox*, 201.

10. Ibid., 202–3.

11. Ibid., 242–43.

12. Ibid., 251.

13. Ibid., 259.

14. Ibid., 87, 245.

15. See the ASRL website at http://www.artscienceresearchlab.org/.

16. Stephen Jay Gould, "No Science Without Fancy, No Art without Facts: The Lepidoptery of Vladimir Nabokov," in *I Have Landed* (New York: Harmony Books, 2002), 52.

17. Stephen Jay Gould, "Art Meets Science in *The Heart of the Andes*," in *I Have Landed*, 91.

18. Ibid., 99–100.

19. Ibid., 108.

20. Gould, *The Hedgehog, the Fox, and the Magister's Pox*, 157–63.

21. This quote is Gould's translation of Haeckel's German. See ibid., 159.

22. Stephen Jay Gould and Rosamond Wolff Purcell, *Crossing Over: Where Art and Science Meet* (New York: Three Rivers Press, 2000); Rosamond Wolff Purcell and Stephen Jay Gould, *Illuminations: A Bestiary* (New York: W. W. Norton, 1986); Rosamond Wolff Purcell and Stephen Jay Gould, *Finders, Keepers: Eight Collectors* (New York: W. W. Norton, 1992).

23. Purcell and Gould, *Illuminations*, 11.

24. Ibid., 10.

25. Purcell and Gould, *Finders, Keepers*, 94.

26. Purcell and Gould, *Crossing Over*, 79.

27. Stephen Jay Gould, "Boundaries and Categories," in Alexis Rockman, *Alexis Rockman* (New York: Monacelli Press, 2003), 14.

28. Ibid., 15.

29. Ibid., 16.

30. Ibid.

31. Ibid., 17.

32. See also Stephen Jay Gould, "The Substantial Ghost: Towards a General Exegesis of Duchamp's Artful Wordplays," *Tout-Fait: The Marcel Duchamp Studies Online Journal*, 1/2 (2000), available at http://www.tout-fait.com/; Rhonda Roland Shearer and Stephen Jay Gould, "The *Green Box* Stripped Bare: Marcel Duchamp's 1934 'Facsimiles' Yield Surprises," *Tout-Fait: The Marcel Duchamp Studies Online Journal* 1/1 (2000); Rhonda Roland Shearer and Stephen Jay Gould, "Hidden in Plain Sight: Duchamp's *3 Standard Stoppages*, More Truly a 'Stoppage' (An Invisible Mending) than We Ever Realized," *Tout-Fait: The Marcel Duchamp Studies Online Journal* 1/1 (1999).

33. The following essay was simultaneously published in two publications. See Stephen Jay Gould and Rhonda Roland Shearer, "Boats and Deckchairs," *Natural History Magazine* 10/10 (1999): 32–44, and *Tout-Fait: The Marcel Duchamp Studies Online Journal*, 1/1 (1999).

34. Rhonda Roland Shearer and Stephen Jay Gould, "Of Two Minds and One Nature," *Science* 286 (1999): 1093–1094, quote on 1094.

35. Gould and Shearer, "Boats and Deckchairs."

36. Ibid.

37. See the ASRL website at http://www.artscienceresearchlab.org/.

38. Shearer and Gould, "Of Two Minds and One Nature," 1094.

39. Ibid. See also Gould, *The Hedgehog, the Fox, and the Magister's Pox*, 168–79.

40. Stephen Jay Gould, *Leonardo's Mountain of Clams and the Diet of Worms* (New York: Harmony Books, 1988), 2.

41. Gould, *I Have Landed*, 51.

42. Ibid., 108.

43. Gould, *The Hedgehog, the Fox, and the Magister's Pox*, 259.

CONCLUSION: NONMORAL NATURE AND THE HUMAN CONDITION

1. Stephen Jay Gould, *Leonardo's Mountain of Clams and the Diet of Worms* (New York: Harmony Books, 1988), 4–5.

2. Stephen Jay Gould, *Mismeasure of Man* (New York: W. W. Norton, 1996), 53–54.

3. Gould, *Leonardo's Mountain of Clams*, 5.

4. Stephen Jay Gould, *I Have Landed* (New York: Harmony Books, 2002), 108.

5.   Interview with Stephen Jay Gould in Wim Kayzer, *A Glorious Accident: Understanding Our Place in the Cosmic Puzzle* (New York: W. H. Freeman, 1997), 93.

6.   Gould, *I Have Landed*, 109.

7.   Stephen Jay Gould, "The Great Asymmetry," *Science* 279 (1998): 812–13.

8.   Ibid.

9.   Karl Marx and Frederick Engels, *Selected Correspondence* (Moscow: Progress, 1975), 33.

10. Gould, "The Great Asymmetry," 812–13.

11. Ibid.

12. Ibid.

13. Ibid.

14. Gould in Kayzer, *A Glorious Accident*, 92–95.

15. Ibid., 94.

16. Ibid., 99–100.

17. Gould, "The Great Asymmetry," 812–13.

18. Stephen Jay Gould, *The Lying Stones of Marrakech* (London: Random House, 2000), 31.

19. Gould, "The Great Asymmetry," 812–13.

20. Stephen Jay Gould, *An Urchin in the Storm* (New York: W. W. Norton, 1987), 38.

21. Sean B. Carroll, *Endless Forms Most Beautiful: The New Science of Evo Devo* (New York: W. W. Norton, 2005).

22. Gould, *Leonardo's Mountain of Clams*, 13.

Index

adaptations and adaptationism, 54; alternatives to, 58–59; functionalism and, 147–51; progress in, 75; in sociobiology, 132, 136

Agassiz, Louis, 49

agency, 19, 23

allometry, 57

altruistic behavior, 105, 203*n*31

anthropic principle, 89

anti-science attitudes, 112

antlers, 57

Aristotle and Aristotelianism, 43–45, 65–66, 193–94*n*11; in biology, 45–47

art, Gould on connections between science and, 166–75

Arthropoda, 62–64

Art Science Research Laboratory (ASRL), 165

Augustine (saint), 49

Australia, Darwin in, 48

Bacon, Francis, 162, 193–94*n*11

Baconian Marxists, 14–16

bacteria, flagella of, 61–62

Baron-Cohen, Simon, 147

Beagle (ship), 38, 47, 194*n*12

Bean, Robert Bennett, 117–18

The Bell Curve (Herrnstein and Murray), 112, 113, 122–24, 132

Bernal, J. D., 14–15

biases, 115

biological determinism, 25, 119–20, 123, 128–29; genetic determinism, 140–41; Gould on, 129–30; *Mismeasure of Man* on, 113; sociobiology as, 127

biology: in explanations of inequality, 128–29; generalization in, 69; as historical science, 90; Platonic and Aristotelian approaches to, 45–47; reductionism in, 137–38

Bolk, Louis, 121–22

brains: of hominin species, 156; of
   Homo floresiensis, 153; *see also*
   human brain
Bretz, J Harlen, 40
Broca, Paul, 120
Burgess Shale, 62
Burt, Sir Cyril, 114–15, 118
Bush, George W., 114

Calloway, C. Bradford, 104
Cambrian explosion, 62
Camper, Petrus, 173–74
catastrophism, 37–40
chimpanzees, 158
Chomsky, Noam, 64, 82
Chordata, 62–64
chordates, 73
Church, Frederic Edwin, 166–67
climate change, 114
complexity, in evolution, 82–84
consilience, 163–64
Consilience (Wilson), 163–64
consumer sovereignty, 97
contingency: Gould on, 90,
   96–97; in history, 67–69,
   75–76, 78
contingent convergence, 81–82,
   86–87
convergence, 78–79, 87–88; contingent convergence, 86–87;
   meta-convergence, 79, 84, 85
Conway Morris, Simon, 84, 87–90
Cope, E. D., 121
Cosmides, Leda, 133
craniometry, 115–18
creationism: Gould's testimony in
   Arkansas trial of, 17; Platonism
   in, 47, 49
Cretaceous extinction, 39, 76, 180

Cretaceous-Tertiary boundary, 39
culture: Snow on, 161; sociobiology on, 139, 140, 146

Darwin, Charles: on contingency
   in evolution of humans,
   199n17; conversion to natural
   selection by, 47–48, 194n12;
   Gould's admiration of, 18–19;
   gradualism of, 34, 35, 38; on
   multiple causes of evolution,
   94; Platonism of, 50; on
   progress in evolution, 70–71,
   75; on social context of observations, 27–28; on social
   inequality, 152
Darwinism: gradualism in, 34;
   Platonism and, 47–50; ultra-
   Darwinians, 55–56
Dawkins, Richard, 84–90, 139; on
   convergence, 86–88; on evolution at genetic level, 19; on
   progress in evolution, 85, 90;
   reductionism of, 23, 139, 142;
   selfish gene theory of, 105
debunking, 124
demes, 104–5
Dennett, Daniel, 84–86, 105
Derrida, Jacques, 97
Descartes, René, 128
development, evolutionary, 20, 21
dialectical approach, 139, 140,
   143–44, 151–52
Diamond, Jared, 156
dinosaurs, Cretaceous extinction
   of, 76
DNA, 140–43
Duchamp, Marcel, 171–73
Dyson, Freeman, 89

ecological time (first tier), 71–73
efficacy, 19–20
Eldredge, Niles, 102; on Darwin's
    conversion to natural selection,
    194n12; punctuated equilibri-
    um theory of Gould's and, 21,
    33–35, 40–41, 185
emergence, 96, 106–7
emergent characters approach,
    202–3n24
emergent fitness approach,
    202–3n24
Engels, Frederick, 94–95
environment: dialectical approach
    to, 144; human-caused changes
    in, 146, 183; interaction
    between genes and, 143; organ-
    isms interacting with, 144–45;
    in sociobiology, 139, 208n34
environment of evolutionary
    adaptedness (EEA), 148–49
epigenesis, 139
equality: Gould on, 17, 159;
    Mismeasure of Man on,
    112–13; *see also* inequality
eugenics movement, 15
evolution: complexity in, 82–84;
    convergence in, 78–79; Gould's
    testimony in Arkansas trial of,
    17; hierarchy in, 104–5; as
    metaphor used outside of biol-
    ogy, 128; progress in, 68,
    70–71, 74–75, 84, 90, 179–80;
    punctuated equilibrium theory
    of, 21, 40–41, 102; recapitula-
    tionist theory of, 121; Twain
    on, 76–78
evolutionary development, 20,
    186

evolutionary psychology, 130,
    132–34, 136; Gould on, 149;
    on human brain, 148
exaptation, 58–60
extinctions: population size and,
    103–4; *see also* mass extinctions
eyes, evolution of, 86

factor analysis, 118–19
facts, cultural context of, 27
Farrington, Benjamin, 14–15
fertility, of humans, 151
Fibronacci series, 52, 195n30
flagella, 61–62
Flores (Indonesia), 153
formalism (biological), 21–22
fossil record, Burgess Shale in, 62
Full House (Gould), 82
functionalism: adaptation and,
    147–51; structuralism versus,
    44, 81
fundamental attribution error, 98

Galápagos Islands, Darwin in,
    47–48
Galbraith, John Kenneth, 97
Galton, Francis, 80–81
gender: brain size and, 116,
    117–18; differences in human
    brain by, 147–48; division of
    labor by, 129; evolutionary psy-
    chology on, 133
genes: culture versus, 146; evolu-
    tion at level of, 105–6; *Hox*
    genes, 64; Lewontin on, 141;
    norm of reaction in expression
    of, 139, 140, 208n34; structur-
    al effects of, 55; transposition
    of, 141–42; Wilson on, 131

genetic determinism, 140–43
genetics: in modern synthesis, 18;
    sociobiology on, 139–40
geological timescale, 72
geology, uniformitarianism and
    catastrophism in, 35–40
God, at top of great chain of
    being, 74
Goethe, Johann Wolfgang von, 49,
    81
Golden Ratio, 52, 195–96n31
Goodwin, Brian, 195n22
Gould, Stephen Jay: on adapta-
    tionism, 147, 149–50; on bio-
    logical determinism, 129–30;
    on complexity in evolution,
    82–84; on connections between
    art and science, 166–75; on
    contingency and determinism,
    67–69; on convergence, 78–79;
    Darwin admired by, 18–19;
    dialectical approach of,
    151–52; on distinction between
    sciences and humanities,
    164–65; on functionalism and
    structuralism, 44; on gap
    between sciences and humani-
    ties, 162–63; on genes as level
    of evolution, 105–6; on genetic
    determinism, 142–43; on hier-
    archy, 101–2, 104; on his essays
    in Natural History, 16; on
    human equality, 159; intellectu-
    al influences on, 13; on intelli-
    gence testing, 114–15, 118–19;
    Mismeasure of Man by, 112–14,
    122–24; on modern synthesis,
    93–94; philosophy of science
    of, 26–29; political activities of,

17; on progress in evolution,
    75; on progress versus histori-
    cal contingency, 22–23; punc-
    tuated equilibrium theory of
    Eldredge's and, 21, 34–35,
    40–42; on racial theories of
    development, 121–22; on
    reductionism, 95–96, 99, 138,
    145; on size of human brain,
    115–18; on sociobiology, 127,
    134–36; structuralism of,
    54–64; on timescales, 72–74;
    on transposition of genes,
    141–42; on Wallace, 89–90; on
    Wilson's Consilience, 163–64
gradualism, 34–39; in geology,
    39–40
great chain of being, 74
Gross, Paul, 204n1

Haeckel, Ernst, 121, 167–68
Haldane, J. B. S., 13–16
Haught, John F., 88
The Hedgehog, the Fox, and the
    Magister's Pox (Gould), 162, 163
Herrnstein, Richard, 112, 123
Hessen, Boris, 14–16
hierarchy: in evolution, 95, 104–5;
    Gould on, 101–2
historical contingency, progress
    versus, 22–23
history: contingency and deter-
    minism in, 67–69, 75–76;
    progress in, 90, 179–80
history of science: Gould on, 26;
    Hessen on, 14–15
Hogben, Lancelot, 14–15
hominins, 153, 154–55, 159, 210n1
Homo (genus), 154–56

Homo erectus, 153, 155; modern humans descended from, 157; modern humans living contemporaneously with, 158

Homo floresiensis, 153–58

Homo neanderthalensis, 155, 156; modern humans living contemporaneously with, 158

Homo sapiens, see humans

Hox genes, 64, 82, 87

Hull, David, 105

human brain, 60; Broca's study of, 120; evolutionary psychology on, 133–34, 148; flexibility of, 150; gender differences between, 147; intelligence and, 122; shrinking of, 211*n*13; studies of size of, 115–18

human condition, 24–26

human exemptionalism, 8

humanities, 26; Gould on gap between sciences and, 162–63; sciences distinguished from, 164–65; Snow on gap between sciences and, 161

human nature, evolutionary psychology on, 148

humans: changes in environment caused by, 146, 183; coexisting with other hominid species, 155, 158; Darwin on contingency in evolution of, 199*n*17; descended from *Homo erectus,* 157; environment of evolutionary adaptedness for, 148–49; equality among, 159; in evolutionary psychology, 132–33; fertility of, 151; in great chain of being, 74; *Homo floresiensis*

and, 154, 156; inevitability of, 87–88; intelligence of, 113, 118–19; languages of, 64; size of brain of, 115–18, 120; sociobiology on, 134–37; theories of development of, 121–22; Twain on history of, 76–78; *see also* human brain

Humboldt, Alexander von, 166–67

Hume, David, 164

Huxley, Julian, 57

Hyatt, Alpheus, 75

hyper-reductionism, 105

inequality: biological explanations of, 128–30, 132; Darwin on, 152; Gould on, 185; polygenism theory on, 157

intelligence: brain size and, 117–18, 122; Burt's fraudulent work on, 114–15; *Mismeasure of Man* on, 113; testing of, 118–20

intelligent design, 87, 112

interdemic selection, 104–5

International Congress of the History of Science and Technology (London, 1931), 14–15

IQ tests, 118–19, 122, 123

iridium, 39

Irish Elk, 57

Jensen, Arthur, 115

Kamin, Leon, 115, 135–36

Kanazawa, Satoshi, 134

Kauffman, Stuart, 53, 195*n*22

kin selection, 203*n*31

Kline, Morris, 45–46

Lake Missoula (Montana), 40
Lamarck, Jean-Baptiste, 81
languages, 64, 150
Leibniz, Gottfried, 56
Leonardo da Vinci, 65–66
Leonardo of Pisa (Fi Bonacci),
    195n30
Levins, Richard, 13, 16, 128–29,
    139
Levitt, Norman, 204n1
Levy, Hyman, 14–15
Lewontin, Richard, 13, 60; on
    adaptationist program, 149; on
    biological determinism,
    128–29; on culture, 145–46; on
    dialectical approach, 139, 140,
    143–44; on DNA, 140–42; on
    Gould's radicalism, 16; on
    Panglossian Paradigm, 55–58;
    on sociobiology, 135–36; on
    twin research, 122; on use of
    metaphors, 127–28
life, Baconian Marxists on origin
    of, 15
Linnaeus, Carolus, 38
Lloyd, Elisabeth A., 101
Lovejoy, Arthur, 74
Lumsden, Charles J., 134–35
Lyell, Charles, 35–40

Machalek, Richard, 136
macroevolution, 93–94, 100, 104,
    186
Mall, Franklin P., 117–18
Martin, Michael W., 136
Marx, Karl, 25–26, 34, 39, 94,
    125, 182

Marxism, 13; of Baconian
    Marxists, 14–16
mass extinctions: causes of, 147;
    Cretaceous, 39, 76, 180;
    Darwin on, 38; paradox of
    progress and, 73; Permian, 76,
    199n21; timescale for, 72
materialism: anti-science attitudes
    and, 112; in uniformitarianism
    versus catastrophism debate,
    37–38
mathematics: in Darwinism, 49; in
    natural structures, 51–53; in
    Platonism and Aristotelianism,
    45–46
Mayr, Ernst, 45–47, 69; on
    Aristotle, 193–94n11; on
    reductionism, 137
meta-convergence, 79, 84, 85, 87
metaphors, 128
metazoans, 82
methodological individualism, 97
microevolution, 93, 100, 104
The Mismeasure of Man (Gould),
    112–14, 122–23, 127
modern synthesis, 18–19; func-
    tionalism of, 44; Gould on,
    93–94; progress central to, 75;
    reductionism in, 23–24;
    timescale in, 71; unit of evolu-
    tion in, 99–100
Morton, Samuel George, 115–17
multiregionalism, 157–58
Murray, Charles, 112, 123

Nabokov, Vladimir, 166
Natural History (magazine),
    Gould on his essays in, 16
natural selection, 48; adaptation-

ism in, 147; convergence in,
    78–79; Darwin's conversion to,
    47–48, 194n12; on genetic
    level, 142; Gould's critique of,
    54–55; prediction in, 194n17;
    Thompson on, 196n38
nature, nonmoral nature of, 180
Needham, Joseph, 14–16
neo-Darwinism, Gould on,
    18–19
neotony, 121–22
Newton, Isaac, 14

objectivity, 124
ontogeny, 55, 79–80; recapitula-
    tionist theory on, 121
Ontogeny and Phylogeny (Gould),
    21–22, 54
Oparin, Alexander I., 15
organisms: in evolutionary theory,
    152; interacting with environ-
    ment, 144–45

pandas, 63–64
The Panda's Thumb (Gould),
    39–40, 63
Panglossian Paradigm, 55–56
parasites, 83
Pax genes, 86
Permian extinction, 76, 199n21
philosophy: Platonic and
    Aristotelian, 43–44; of science,
    Gould's, 26–29
phylogeny, 51; recapitulationist
    theory on, 121
physics, 44, 47
Pikaia, 73–74
Plato and Platonism, 43–44,
    65–66, 193–94n11; in biology,

45–47; Darwinism and, 47–50;
    persistence of, 50–54
Poincare, Henri, 172
polygenism, 157
populations, extinction and size
    of, 103–4
postmodernism, 27, 97–98, 124;
    Social Text hoax and, 111
Principles of Geology (Lyell), 35,
    38
progress: in ecological time (first
    tier), 73; in evolution, 70–71,
    74–77, 82–84, 89, 179–80; his-
    torical contingency versus,
    22–23; in history, 68, 90; reca-
    pitulationist theory of evolution
    on, 121
punctuated equilibrium, 21, 28,
    40–42, 102, 185; timescale for,
    72
Purcell, Rosamond Wolff, 168–69

race: developmental theories on,
    121–22; in great chain of being,
    74; polygenism theory of ori-
    gins of, 157; studies of brain
    size and, 115–18
Raphael, 43, 65
recapitulationist theory, 121–22
reductionism, 94–99; in biology,
    137–38; consilience and, 164;
    in genetic determinism,
    142–43; Gould on, 145; in
    sociobiology, 136, 139–40,
    142, 147; Wilson on, 163
reification, 118
religion, in uniformitarianism
    versus catastrophism debate,
    37–38

Rockman, Alexis, 169–71
Rose, Hilary, 128, 148
Rose, Steven, 128, 135–36, 138, 148

Saint-Hilaire, Étienne Geoffroy, 49, 63, 81
Savage, Joanne, 134
science: connections between humanities and, 26; debunking as, 124; Gould on connections between art and, 166–75; Gould on gap between humanities and, 162–63; human condition and, 24–26; humanities distinguished from, 164–65; postmodernist and other critiques of, 204n1; public perception of, 181; Snow on gap between humanities and, 161; social context of, 182
Science for the People, 17
scientists, 162; Gould on social obligation of, 17
scope, evolutionary, 20
The Selfish Gene (Dawkins), 105
sex, see gender
Shearer, Rhonda Roland, 165, 171–72
Simpson, George Gaylord, 33
Snow, C. P., 161
social behavior, sociobiology on, 139
social sciences, reductionism in, 98–99
Social Text (journal), 111
sociobiology, 129–32, 134–37; adaptationism in, 147; culture in, 146; Gould on, 127, 150; reductionism in, 139–40, 147

sociology, 138; sociobiology and, 136
Sokal, Alan, 111–12, 124, 204n1
South Africa, 15
spandrels, 58–60, 149–50, 183
speciation, in punctuated equilibrium, 41
species, 101; as individuals, 102–3; Platonic view of, 47–49; progress in evolution of, 68; selection on level of, 202–3n24
Stewart, Ian, 50–51
structuralism (biological), 21–22; functionalism versus, 44, 81; Gould's, 54–64; ontogeny in, 79–80
The Structure of Evolutionary Theory (Gould), 19, 27; on development of human traits, 149; on hierarchy, 101; on nonadaptive structural elements, 58; punctuated equilibrium in, 41–42; wedge metaphor in, 70–71
survival of the fittest, 75,

Tattersall, Ian, 148
Tegmark, Max, 44
Thayer, A. H., 174
theories, cultural context of, 27
Thompson, D'Arcy Wentworth, 50–52, 61, 195n24, 196n38
Thurstone, L. L., 119
time, 23; three tiers of, 71–73
Time's Arrow, Time's Cycle (Gould), 23
Tooby, John, 133
trilobites, 76
Twain, Mark, 76–78, 87

twin research, 122

uniformitarianism, 20, 35–39

variability, within species, 103,
    203n27
variation, 54–55
Victorian era, 70, 75
Vitruvius, 65
Voltaire, 55–56
Vrba, Elisabeth S., 58, 60, 149–50

Wallace, Alfred Russel, 89

wedge metaphor, 70–71
wheels, 61
Whewell, William, 163
Williams, George, 105
Wilson, Edward O., 129, 131;
    Consilience by, 163–64; disci-
    plinary imperialism of, 139;
    Gould on, 134–35, 150
women, in gender-based division
    of labor, 129
Wonderful Life (Gould), 62, 74
Wright, Robert, 84, 148